FIGHT BACK AND WIN

FIGHT BACK AND WIN

**MY THIRTY-YEAR FIGHT AGAINST INJUSTICE—
AND HOW YOU CAN WIN YOUR OWN BATTLES**

GLORIA ALLRED

WITH DEBORAH CAULFIELD RYBAK

ReganBooks
An Imprint of HarperCollinsPublishers

Insert Photograph Credits: page 1: author's collection; page 2: author's collection (top), courtesy of Dean Musgrove (bottom); page 3: AP Wide World (top), *Daily News*/Herb Carlton (bottom); page 4: Berliner Studios/BEI Images (top), AP Wide World (bottom); page 5: AP Wide World (top), Rafael Maldonado/reprinted with permission from the *Santa Barbara News-Press* (bottom); page 6: Copyright 1986 *Los Angeles Times*/reprinted with permission (top photos), AP Wide World (bottom left), *New York Post*/Mary McLaughlin (bottom right); page 7: AP Wide World (top), Barry E. Levine (bottom); page 8: AP Wide World (top), ©David Paul Morris/Pool/Reuters/Corbis (bottom); page 9: AP Wide World (top and bottom); page 10 (clockwise from top): AP Wide World, *San Gabriel Valley Tribune*/James Ku, *San Gabriel Valley Tribune*/Staff File Photo; page 11: *Daily Breeze* (top photos), courtesy of Milton and Betty Dykstra (bottom right), courtesy of Art Harris (bottom left); page 12: Anda Chu/*Oakland Tribune* (top), AP Wide World (bottom); page 13: AP Wide World (top and bottom); page 14: Marilynn Young (top), Ken Kwok (bottom); page 15: AP Wide World (top and bottom); page 16: author's collection

HarperCollins books may be purchased for educational, business, or sales promotional use. For information please write: Special Markets Department, HarperCollins Publishers Inc., 10 East 53rd Street, New York, NY 10022.

FIRST EDITION

Designed by Publications Development Company of Texas

Printed on acid-free paper

Library of Congress Cataloging-in-Publication Data has been applied for.

ISBN 10: 0-06-073928-2
ISBN 13: 978-0-06-073928-7

06   07   08   09   10   PDC/RRD   10   9   8   7   6   5   4   3   2   1

To my law partners Nathan and Michael,
without whom my battle against injustice
would not have been possible.

You must be the change you wish to see in the world.

—Mahatma Gandhi

Contents

Foreword

Lisa Bloom

All my life, through every stage—from my childhood, when she was a union organizer and teacher, during my high school years, when she started taking on high-profile cases, to my adulthood, when she has become one of the best-known lawyers in America—friends, colleagues, and strangers on the street have asked me the same question: "What's it like to grow up with Gloria Allred as your mother?"

Let me use this opportunity to answer this question once and for all. I am, after all, the only person on earth who can answer it.

In a word, an old-fashioned feminist word: *empowering*.

When I was in the fourth grade, my public elementary school allowed girls to wear pants to school for the first time. One day, attired in my new snappy orange knit flare-leg pantsuit (it was the seventies, okay?), I was told that I would not be permitted to square dance, my favorite school activity, because I was not wearing a skirt. This was one of those exceptions to the new rule—apparently made up by the teacher on the spot.

During dinner that evening, when my mom asked, "What did you do in school today?" I told her that I sat at my desk and cried because I didn't get to square dance.

Some mothers would have baked me cupcakes to help me get over it.

My mother marched into school with me the next day and explained to the principal that this was sex discrimination because only girls were denied access to this school activity based on their clothing. He looked at her as though she'd sprouted a giant green head, but by the end of her argument he announced that, henceforth, no girl would be forced to sit out the *do-si-do* for wearing slacks. I kicked up my heels in glee for the rest of the term.

In sixth grade, the annual Faculty/Student Softball Game rolled around. Some of my athletic girlfriends wanted to play and questioned the long-entrenched tradition that the game was only for boys. Weren't the girls students, too? Small for my age and terrified of balls being thrown anywhere near me, I supported them in spirit but didn't see this as my battle.

Some mothers would have said, "Stay out of it."

My mother said that powerless people must always organize for the greater good. She suggested that I get as many girls as possible to band together, and each could contribute in her own way. Some, like me, could organize and make placards. Others could write letters and lead a rally. So we picketed and chanted slogans and—guess what? We won. My girlfriends got to play ball with the teachers that year and every year after. And we learned the most valuable lesson of our sixth grade year: "Don't agonize, organize!"

Those were heady days. The barriers to females' full participation in American life were toppling due to the hard work, sacrifice, and creativity of women like my mother.

Some mothers want their daughters to collect tea sets. With my mom's support, I collected feminist buttons and bumper stickers:

A Woman Without a Man Is Like a Fish Without a Bicycle.

A Man of Quality Is Not Threatened by a Woman of Equality.

Everything a Woman Does She Must Do Twice as Well as Men to Be Thought Half as Good . . . Luckily This Is Not Difficult.

Question Authority.

And my favorite:

Women Who Seek to Be Equal to Men Lack Ambition.

On Back-to-School Night, when all the parents were politely schmoozing with the teachers, my mother would riffle through the history textbooks and ask pointedly why we weren't being taught anything about the history of women and minorities in America. In my junior high school English class, she wanted to know why we were only reading books by white males. In physical education, she'd inquire about gender parity in the funding of sports programs. (In those days, girls' sports got about as much budget attention as the leaky water fountain in study hall.)

I was a little embarrassed because that's how teenagers feel; but I had to admit, the woman had a point.

Every kid asks his or her parents at some point, "Why is there a Mother's Day and a Father's Day, but no Children's Day?" Most get the pablum answer: "Because, honey, *every day* is Children's Day." Not my mom. When I came to her with that question, she said, "Lisa, because children do not have the right to vote. As a disenfranchised minority, they don't have the political power as a voting bloc to get Congress to pass the necessary law to give them a Children's Day."

Oh.

She is relentless. When I was in college, my debate team won the national championship. The local paper ran an article on me, complete with my smiling picture and caption, "Top Female Debater." I was thrilled, but my mother pointed out that "female" had nothing to do with it. Why not simply "Top Debater"?

Oh, right.

My mother encouraged me to go to law school. As many unfortunate defendants have learned in the years since, when Gloria Allred "encourages" you to do something, your options are (a) do it now; or (b) years later, look back and wish you had chosen option (a).

She has a sign in her office that reads, "Be Reasonable. Do It My Way."

I went to Yale Law School and loved every minute of it. . . . Except the fact that I was three thousand miles away from my mother. But we kept up in weekly phone chats. In one memorable call, my mom asked me how I was doing in school, how I was handling the cold New England weather, the usual chitchat. When I finally asked her how she was doing, she said, "Oh, I'm fine. But I am locked in at the District Attorney's office. They've padlocked the doors for the night with me inside because I made it clear I was not leaving until the DA meets with me to explain why we have one of the worst child support enforcement programs in the state."

I said, "You let me go on and on before you told me that!" She laughed and told me she could see the news articles hitting the wire machines through the window in the pressroom door. She slept on the floor of the hallway that night, but the media went wild and the DA wisely met with her later and started taking child support enforcement seriously.

Thus did my mother teach by example two key Gloria Allred principles:

1. When you want something, and someone in power says no, that's just the beginning of the conversation.
2. When you want to go where you are not invited, dress well, hold your head high, act like you belong, and just march right in.

Crack open any chapter of this book and you'll learn surprising factoids about my mother. You may think you know her from her many television appearances, but did you know she was a high school cheerleader? Well, she was—at an all girls' high school (see Chapter 1). And she's been a cheerleader for girls and women ever since, without apology. Why should she apologize for doing the right thing? As my mother often reminds me, females apologize much too much. We should be less sorry and more uppity.

You may know that she's an aggressive combatant in the court-room, but did you know she has an outrageous sense of humor? To protest the exclusion of women from a private club, would *your* mother jump into a steam room with a bunch of naked men, armed only with a tape measure while singing Peggy Lee's "Is That All There Is?" (see Chapter 6).

My mother is truly one of a kind, but her story is in many ways an everywoman story. As a single mother, a victim of sexual vio-lence, a professional who's been paid less than men in the same job, a woman who has had bad luck with husbands . . . her story is our story, and she tells it bravely and honestly here.

Unlike nearly every other attorney in this country, my mother is not a hired gun. She only takes cases she truly believes in. And as you'll learn in this book, woe unto those who try to fight her, once she's decided to act. She will fight for years, decades in some cases, to right an injustice, even on behalf of a chimp (see Chapter 13). She has a long memory, a stubborn streak, and endless stores of energy.

She exhausts her teenaged grandchildren.

She's never cared how I decorated my apartment, whether my nails were manicured, or if I could cook. She cares a great deal about how I am being treated in the workplace and in my relation-ships—and, now most of all, how her grandkids are doing. (Very well, thanks.)

She taught me not to care a whit about what people think, to live life by my own values. If I want to climb Kilimanjaro, go climb it. (I did.) If I want to beat the boys in college debate, beat them. (I did.) If I want to have martial arts sparring matches with men . . . well, that one she wasn't crazy about, but she closed her eyes tightly and told me to go for it. (I did.) She also taught me to stand up against sexual harassment, to fight for the best for my children, and to insist on being treated right by the men in my life. (I did, did, did.)

Every woman in my generation owes a tremendous debt of gratitude to the feminists who came before us and fought like hell for each little scrap of human rights for us. Those rights rarely came easily. Doors were unlocked, pried or kicked open for us by women who would not sleep until equal rights were ours.

Chief among this fearless group of women is my mother. She has spent a lifetime sacrificing, strategizing, organizing, filing lawsuits, protesting politicians, changing laws, upending sexist traditions, all to insist on what she knows is right not only for me, her daughter, but for all daughters—and, for that matter, all disenfranchised people.

It's long overdue, but let me say it here.

Thanks, Mom.

Lisa Bloom is an attorney, columnist, Court TV anchor, CourtTV.com columnist, ABC News Legal Contributor, and Gloria's daughter.

Introduction

P eople often tell me how much they admire my fighting spirit. They want to know where I find the courage to stand up against the rich, the powerful, and a justice system that is often anything but just. They ask how I have won so many victories for my clients, and they want to know more about the many high-profile and extraordinary cases I have handled.

Those questions inspired me to write this book.

I am a civil rights lawyer and a feminist. My firm, Allred, Maroko & Goldberg, handles cases involving employment discrimination based on race, gender, sexual orientation, disability, age, religion, AIDS, and national origin. We also handle wrongful discharge in violation of public policy and whistle-blower cases. We are well known for our representation of clients in sexual harassment cases, complicated family law, and victims' rights cases. I've repeatedly been honored by my peers as one of the "Best Lawyers in America."

I am not a philosopher—for that I suggest you turn to great thinkers such as Mahatma Gandhi and Gloria Steinem. I am a warrior and a passionate advocate for the people I represent. For the past thirty years, I have been fighting on the front lines for victims' rights. My battles have taken me from the courthouse to the White House, fighting for women, minorities, and other individuals in need of justice. I have sat in and been thrown out. I have filed lawsuits, marched, fasted, litigated, and argued multimillion dollar cases. I have faced off against nearly every type of opponent—from presidents to prizefighters, from corporations to celebrities, from priests to murderers.

It hasn't been easy, but few battles worth winning ever are, and I've learned a few things along the way. Through my many legal cases, I hope to show you the possibilities and potential for combating injustice in your own life. I want you to recognize that you have options, that you have access to the justice system, and that you have more strength and courage within you to help you fight back and win than you ever realized.

To help you find that strength, even when it seems impossible to win and hopeless to try, I will share the stories of people just like you who were once victims, but became survivors, and then fighters, and ultimately won change for themselves, their families, their coworkers, and our society. I have been proud to represent these people. They have demonstrated tremendous courage in stepping into the public arena to fight for the issues in which they believe. Many of them have won battles that they never imagined they could win.

Most of these cases take place in California, which is where I'm licensed to practice law, but in many instances their outcomes have set precedents felt around the country and, in one case, the world. The cases range widely in terms of circumstance, issues, and even outcome—but they are all important. For instance, in one case, a customer challenges a department store policy on clothing alterations that cost women more money than men. In another case, a mother must struggle for decades to find the father of her child among the seven Catholic priests who sexually abused her. Other cases involve some well-known names, including O. J. Simpson, Michael Jackson, and Amber Frey.

I will also tell you how I have fought back in my own life—how I overcame divorce, the inability to collect child support, rape, abortion, and political opposition. I can say from experience that fighting for your civil rights is difficult. It takes hard work, stamina, courage, resources, and a plan to win. That's why, at the end of each case, I have included what I call an "Empowerment Lesson." Each lesson includes practical suggestions that I've extracted from each case to help inform and inspire you in your own fight for justice.

FIGHT BACK AND WIN, the message of this book, presents a powerful challenge to you. While you can't expect to win every battle, you can be sure that you'll never win if you don't fight. Some victories come quickly; some take considerably longer. That's the way it is with civil rights, but unless somebody takes that first step on the moon, there will never be others who can begin to build a space station. So begins the journey toward justice, and a great adventure.

CHAPTER 1

To Conquer, You Must First Conquer Yourself

My Life Lessons

My address is like my shoes. It travels with me. I abide where there is a fight against wrong.

—Mary Harris "Mother" Jones

I was born Gloria Rachel Bloom on July 3, 1941—an only child in a working-class home in southwest Philadelphia. My dad, Morris, was a door-to-door salesman with an eighth-grade education. Selling Fuller brushes and photo enlargements, he worked twelve hours a day, six days a week, and rarely had time to spend with me, except on Sundays. We never had a car. We lived modestly in a row house with a view of a stone wall. I always wanted to get beyond the stone wall in my life.

My mother, Stella, was originally from Manchester, England. She didn't work outside the home, but devoted her life to me and was adamant that I get a good education. She had been forced to leave school in the eighth grade to support her family. Even though she was lighthearted and easy going, my mother never seemed content about being a stay-at-home mom. All her life, she looked back with regret and imagined what she could have achieved if she had been able to get the education and enjoy the opportunities that her intelligence warranted. My mother insisted that I grow up to have the opportunities she missed.

"Don't grow up to be like me," she would tell me.

My father was very strong; some called him stubborn. He was like a rock, which was good because you could lean on him, but bad because he was hard to move. He made up his mind fairly quickly. He seldom talked, except to tell jokes. In order to challenge him, I had to be really strong and use my wits. My father agreed with my mother that I should have a career if I wanted it. He always told me I would be going to college. I wasn't supposed to worry about it—the money would be there.

Even though they were poor, my parents tried to give me the best of everything. If we could afford only one ticket to a movie, my father would pay my way and wait for me in the park. I earned extra money by selling potholders that I made myself. I also sold new and used comic books and, of course, the old standby— lemonade. I was fairly successful at sales. Every birthday I would ask my parents to put some money away for me, in case I ever needed it for a rainy day.

I didn't have much in the way of toys. I had Scrabble, Monopoly, a checkers game, and a couple of dolls. I loved to read, and my father regularly took me to the library. I enjoyed books by Charles Dickens and Somerset Maugham. *Little Women* by Louisa May Alcott was one of my favorites.

I was fortunate to be accepted into an all-academic, all-girls public high school, the Philadelphia High School for Girls (aka Girls' High). It was like a private school. Many people believed that girls could receive a better education there than at the public coed high schools in Philadelphia, where more attention was paid to boys. To attend Girls' High, a girl either had to have a high IQ or be at the top of her class. No one ever told me which category I'd qualified under, but I was excited to be admitted. I met my best friend, Fern Brown Caplan, during my first week at school and she remains my best friend to this day.

The faculty of the school consisted mainly of women who emphasized the academy's motto: *Vincit Qui Se Vincit* ("She conquers, who conquers herself"). The vice-principal once told us, "Girls, your husbands or your boyfriends will probably say to you, 'Send me to medical school or law school, or graduate school.' You just look them in the eye and say, 'No. You send me.'"

It was a truly rebellious statement for that time. I remember all of us looking at each other as though somebody might burst through the door at any minute and arrest the vice-principal for saying something that radical. I think, for many of my classmates, she was their first exposure to a feminist.

It wasn't mine. My father's cousin, Rachel Ash, was—as far as we know—the first female cardiologist at the Children's Heart Hospital in Philadelphia. I considered her a revolutionary. She never married and never had any children. In addition, she was the only woman I ever knew who didn't cook. We would see her about once a year, and during those visits she would have food delivered to the house (remember, there were very few take-out places in those days) then serve it right out of the take-out containers. She didn't cook and she didn't care. That was extraordinary to me. Aunt Rachel, as I called her, wasn't particularly interested in my mother and father (they seemed to be a bit of an annoyance to her) but she took an interest in me. She sent me to a special science seminar in Philadelphia one summer, and stayed in contact with me over the years.

At Girls' High, we were encouraged to aspire to fulfillment through careers and community leadership, in addition to marriage. The classes were hard. I remember thinking at one point, "This is too much for me. I'm going to drop out." I was also feeling insecure because my parents only had eighth-grade educations, and the parents of many of my classmates were lawyers, bankers, and other leaders in Philadelphia. I felt that they had an edge over me.

I went to the counselor and asked to return to "regular" high school. "I'm not smart enough for this school," I told her.

"Gloria, who do you think the smartest person in this school is?" she asked me.

"Sandra Walkowitz," I replied.

She took out a file, opened it up, and looked at me. "Okay, I'm looking at Sandra Walkowitz's IQ and I have your IQ here. Did you know that her IQ is only five points higher than yours? That's not even statistically significant. I can't let you drop out. You belong here."

I didn't realize until many, many years later that she never had Sandra Walkowitz's IQ in that file. Nor did I realize that I could have dropped out without the counselor's permission. I'm so grateful to her for giving me that confidence.

Students at Girls' High School were taught to have confidence. There was no room for further insecurity on my part. I realized that just because my parents might not have had certain advantages, I could still measure up to girls from more privileged homes. All Girls' High students were expected to compete and to succeed. I dated a few boys in high school, but at Girls' High we didn't spend a lot of time worrying about what boys would think about us. We had so many women teachers—strong women—who inspired us to learn to make our own internal assessments about ourselves.

I became a class officer and a cheerleader for our all-girls' basketball team. I remember a boy I knew saying that he couldn't understand how I could be a cheerleader for girls: "What's there to cheer about?" He thought that it was only worthwhile to cheer for boys because girls were of no value or importance. In many ways, I still am a cheerleader for girls, and now for women, too.

Throughout high school I studied hard. I think I got a better education there than I would have received at a coed high school. During those days, girls at traditional coed high schools often weren't treated with as much respect as boys were. The thinking was that women were just going to get married anyway. Some even argued that it wasn't important to educate young women because "they would only be raising children"—but isn't that the most important job of all?

After high school graduation, I received a partial scholarship to the University of Pennsylvania and qualified for the Honors-in-English program. I couldn't be a cheerleader at Penn—I was told that only boys could be cheerleaders for boys. At a mixer during my first week of college, I met Peyton Bray, a tall, handsome, blond, blue-blooded boy who swept me off my feet. He was brilliant and had a great sense of humor. We decided to get married my sophomore year. My parents, who pretty much supported whatever I did, accepted this decision.

Peyton and I didn't have much money. Despite his pedigree, he was expected to find a job after he graduated. We lived in a very small, one-bedroom, one-bath apartment, and we ate off the coffee table in the living room.

I got pregnant when I was only nineteen, which was really too young. It was a lot for me to handle, especially since my marriage was not going very well. Peyton had serious mental health issues that prevented him from being able to enjoy a close relationship, with himself or anybody else. He had entered the military for a while, but wound up in the hospital. When I went to visit him there, I thought maybe he was just faking a nervous breakdown to get out of the service. Peyton had always been a rebel and loved to play practical jokes, but—in fact—he had suffered some kind of mental breakdown, and it was no joke.

When I was about to give birth during my junior year, we couldn't afford to go to the hospital. That's when the rainy day fund I'd asked my parents to set up for me came in handy. I used up all of my birthday money from all those years to pay the doctors and the hospital for the best birthday gift of all: my beautiful baby girl, Lisa.

Peyton took me to the hospital, but instead of staying to help me through the labor, he went out for a beer. Afterward, when I confronted him about this and told him that I couldn't believe he'd left the hospital when I was screaming from the pain of labor, he told me the nurse had said he could leave because it would be a while before the baby came. It never occurred to Peyton or the nurse that I might want to hold my husband's hand while I was going through hours of labor before finally delivering my baby.

My dream marriage was turning into a nightmare. When I wasn't caring for Lisa, I was cooking, cleaning, studying, or sleeping, in that order. Occasionally, I would sneak a peek at the television while ironing my husband's shirts or stirring a pot on the stove top. Only two things on the television could capture my attention—an episode of I Love Lucy or an appearance by President John F. Kennedy.

JFK's inaugural call to "ask not what your country can do for you; ask what you can do for your country" and to serve a cause higher than oneself inspired me from the moment he uttered it. But back in those days, I couldn't foresee how I might ever be able to do good for anyone. My life wasn't much larger than the set of I Love Lucy. I had a small apartment, the Penn campus, and a trolley car ride between the two.

I loved Lucy because she never stopped trying to step out from her husband's shadow. Sometimes she got into trouble, particularly while trying to start a show business career of her own, but she could always climb her way out of a fix. At the start of every episode, she seemed to be a happy homemaker, but by the show's end, she'd become uncorked. She loved her husband and baby, but could never stop herself from wanting more. I wanted more, too.

My relationship with my husband continued to deteriorate. He became emotionally abusive and began to throw things. I started to worry that this might not be a good environment for Lisa. I began to think about leaving, although I didn't know anyone at the time who was divorced. My parents had been married their whole adult lives. I remember my next door neighbor's mother suggesting, "Gloria, why don't you give it another try?'"

I thought about it a long time, but in the end, although I loved him, I just couldn't stay. There was no counseling, treatment, or medication that could help him and, regardless of the stigma of divorce at the time, I knew I had to leave for my daughter's sake. Years later, Peyton lost his fight with bipolar disorder and used a gun to commit suicide.

I recall that when we divorced during my senior year, my lawyer said to me, "You know, you're divorced now; you're a single mother. Don't you think it's time to get rid of the knee socks?" I guess he was saying, "Grow up." He was right, because now I was a single mother and had responsibilities.

I moved back home with my parents and worked on completing my last year of college. I guess my future as a fighter was apparent even then. During my senior year at Penn, I had to do a dissertation as part of my Honors-in-English program. I told my faculty adviser that I wanted to do mine on black novelists.

He said, "Why do you want to do that?"

"Because I know nothing about them," I replied.

"But they haven't written anything worth reading," he told me.

"How can I know that if I don't read them?" I persisted. He said if I proceeded with this idea, I might not be graduated with an Honors-in-English designation on my diploma. I decided I would take the risk.

I went ahead and immersed myself in the writings of Ralph Ellison, Alex Haley, and James Baldwin. I turned in my dissertation and waited. All my classmates got their dissertations back and passed. I heard nothing.

Then, *Time* magazine came out with James Baldwin on the cover. After that, I was graduated with Honors in English.

Still, it wasn't the graduation I'd envisioned. When I was a girl, I dreamed of white dresses, black caps and gowns, bouquets of

flowers, boyfriends, and beaming parents. On my actual graduation day, although I had my diploma in hand, I also had a baby on
my hip. I was flat broke, recently divorced, and undecided about
how to make my way in life. However, feeling sorry for myself was
not a luxury I could afford.

Experience was teaching me that fairy tales don't come true. I
settled back into my old room at my parents' house, where I had
once fantasized about knights in shining armor. I decided to look
for a job because I realized that no such knight was going to rescue
me. This was the beginning of my survival story. It was 1963.

I applied for a job as an assistant to an executive at Scott
Paper in Philadelphia. The interviewer asked me, "Is this what
you want to be?" I said, "Yes, for now, but some day I want to be
an executive."

"Oh no, we don't want someone who ever wants to be anything
else," he said. So that was the end of that.

I also applied for a job at an advertising agency. The interviewers asked me if I could type and I said no. They found that incredible—a Penn girl who couldn't type? They wouldn't hire me. I
think if I had typed, I might still be typing and would never have
become a lawyer.

There was a bright spot to that interview, however. I met a
woman in the waiting room who also had been rejected for the job
because she couldn't type. We became friends and would later be
roommates when we both made big changes in our lives.

I found a job as an assistant buyer at Gimbel Brothers Department Store. I was earning $75 a week, while a man in the same
position was earning $90. When I inquired why there was a differ-
ence in pay, someone in management told me that he had a family
to support. In truth, he was a bachelor with no family. I was a single parent supporting a baby and helping out my parents. I was
learning that discrimination was everywhere, but I didn't realize
there was anything I could do about it. To me it was a fact of life.

Not only was Gimbel's pay low, the hours were very long. I noticed that one of my bosses was constantly taking Gelusil for ulcers. I wondered, *Is this where I want to be in ten years?* What I wanted was to spend more time with my daughter and earn a better living.

I decided to try my hand at teaching while commuting by train to New York City twice a week to pursue a master's degree at New York University. I took the teaching test required to teach in Philadelphia and did well. At the time, a court case had recently found that many of the most disadvantaged schools in Philadelphia had teachers with the lowest scores on their teaching tests. The court had determined to reverse that situation by having the highest-scoring teachers assigned to those schools instead.

I was sent to Benjamin Franklin High School, one of the most difficult schools in Philadelphia. Almost the entire student body was composed of African American boys and there were very few women teachers. I was told, "You will teach here, or your name will go to the bottom of the list and you may not get a job this year."

I paid a visit to the school. What I found were kids from the same poor background as mine. I thought, *Why shouldn't they get a well-qualified teacher?* They wanted to learn just as badly as I did when I went to high school. This proved to be one of my most valuable experiences because it exposed me to the problems of minorities.

Prejudice never existed in my family. My parents had raised me to be color-blind. My father would sell anywhere to make a living. One day he got beaten up and robbed in a very tough African American neighborhood. He appeared at the door of our house covered in blood, with a serious gash in his head. Even then, he only said, "Gloria, I had some bad luck." He never mentioned race.

When I told my students at Benjamin Franklin about what happened to my dad, they were very upset. They cared about me, perhaps because they knew I respected them and wanted them to succeed through hard work. Sometimes they would warn me, "Mrs. Bray, don't go down into the subway today; there's going to be a fight." We got along extremely well.

The Vietnam War was heating up while I was teaching at Ben Franklin High and I was upset that so many soldiers were coming home wounded, maimed, and disfigured. I organized my students to put on a talent show for wounded veterans in a nearby hospital. I called it "Operation Handshake." I knew nothing about political action in those days, but I wanted to do something to thank our men and women for their service to our country.

I also organized a "Pen Is Mightier Than the Sword" campaign. Many of my students didn't want to bring their own pens to school—I guess they thought it would make them look uncool with their friends. They were always asking me for pens. I told them, "You know, kids in Vietnam, they don't have anything, not even a pen or a pencil. They don't even have teachers who can give them a pen." I suggested that we have a drive to see how many pens we could get donated to send to those Vietnamese kids. The students brought in thousands, which we sent overseas. After that, many of my students began to bring pens to class because they realized how lucky they were to have the tools to learn.

That was about the extent of my political activism at that time.

One of my professors at New York University once asked me, "You teach in an all-black high school, so you obviously care about their rights. Have you ever thought about your own rights?" I asked him what he meant and he said, "You know, women's rights."

"What rights don't women have?" I asked. He told me that I'd have to find the answer to that question myself. This was disturbing to me. I just didn't know what he was talking about. But I would learn later, the hard way.

In those days, I was more worried about surviving. I was working a job, going to school, and raising a daughter without the benefit of child support. My ex-husband's child support payments were sporadic at best, and I finally decided to do something about it. I got an attorney who contacted the district attorney and eventually Peyton was arrested. My mother-in-law, with whom I had a very good relationship, called and said, "No one in our family has ever been arrested before." I told her that in my family parents supported their children and that I didn't want to go on welfare. I added that I hadn't known that he would be arrested, but that he did owe me child support. I didn't want help from her. It was her son's obligation, and he was avoiding it. After that, I realized I'd have to provide for Lisa myself. I'd never be able to depend on anyone else.

I dated a law student for a while and developed an interest in what he was studying. Law seemed like a good way to fight injustice. I began to think about becoming a lawyer, but when I went to the University of Pennsylvania Law School to pick up an application, I thought, *There's no way I can do this*. It was expensive, I couldn't afford it, and I doubted that I'd ever be able to get a scholarship, so I crumpled up the application and forgot about it—for a while.

I wanted a better life for my daughter. I wanted her to grow up in the sunshine and I figured, if I was going to be poor, then I'd be poor where it was warm. Philadelphia's winters were getting to me. In 1966, a year after the Watts rebellion tore apart Los Angeles, recruiters from the Los Angeles School District came to Philadelphia looking for teachers. I jumped at the opportunity.

My decision was a traumatic one for my mother. She said, "Gloria, how can you pack up your life in a suitcase and move across the country with only a hundred dollars, a five-year-old child, and a lot of dreams? You don't know where you are going to go when you get off the plane!"

I reminded her, "That's what you did, and you took a risk that was even greater than the one I'm taking."

When my mother was in her early twenties, she bravely embarked on a sea voyage from England to the United States. She traveled solo and didn't know where she would go when she got off the boat, but she hoped for a better life, and this had been in the 1920s, when it was much harder for a woman to make her way alone in the world. Her example inspired me to find my own way, and to take an educated risk to better my life and the life of my daughter.

My friend from the unsuccessful advertising agency interview moved to Los Angeles, too, and we found a house together on Mariposa Street, near the Hollywood Freeway. She had three children and I had one. I went to work at Jordan High School in Watts and again taught at an almost all African American school.

I wasn't trying to be a do-gooder. I simply understood these kids; I'd grown up the same way. Just because we didn't have much economically didn't mean we couldn't strive for and get a good education. I had students who were in the eleventh grade who couldn't read, and I wanted to teach them. They were good kids, and even the tough ones didn't give me problems.

My next job was with the Los Angeles Teachers Association, where I became its first full-time female staff member—a labor organizer assigned to schools in East Los Angeles. I wanted to improve conditions in the schools. That was the year Mexican American students and their parents staged walkouts to protest the substandard education they were receiving. I organized a teach-in for teachers, students, and parents to talk about it at the school. Those were some turbulent times, but it was a good experience for me. I learned how effective community protest could be in helping to improve education specifically and the system in general.

After that, I returned to teaching in Watts, this time at Fremont High School, where I worked with many African American and Latino students. I had to fight to get that job. At first, the school district told me there were no openings, which didn't make sense to me, so I went down to the school and talked to the principal. He told me there were indeed vacancies for someone with my qualifications.

I went back to the hiring office and relayed that conversation. I was told that I couldn't just go down and talk to the principal directly. It became clear that they were often putting substandard substitute teachers in that school instead of qualified ones. I said I wanted to teach there and was qualified to do so. I was an Ivy League college graduate with honors in English and a master's degree. I gave them a hard time. It worked. I got the job, and I loved the students. They really wanted to learn, and I really wanted to teach.

In all, I worked as a teacher in Los Angeles for four years, and earned my credentials as a high school principal, although I never actually became one. The school district had adopted a practice of hiring only African American principals for African American schools, which is where I wanted to be. I understood the reasons behind this practice and decided it was time to leave teaching to go to law school. I had always wanted to go to law school, but there had always been some reason—usually financial—why I couldn't.

In 1966, I had a life-changing experience that would ultimately solidify my decision to become a lawyer and fight for women's rights. I was raped at gunpoint.

I was on vacation in Acapulco when I met a local physician. He invited me out to dinner, but said he had to make some house calls first. The last stop was a motel, where he said he had to see a sick patient. We went to the room but, when we entered, no one was there. He pulled a gun and raped me. I didn't tell the authorities at the time because I didn't think they'd believe an American girl against a well-known and respected Mexican doctor.

After I got home from Mexico, I discovered I was pregnant. I was divorced and a single parent. I believed that an abortion was necessary for me to be able to survive and build a future for my daughter. I could barely support her, let alone another child as well. But this was in the days before Roe v. Wade, when it was illegal in many states for a doctor to perform abortions. In 1966, Section 274 of the California Penal Code read:

> Every person who provides, supplies, or administers to any woman, or procures any woman to take any medicine, drug, or substance, or uses or employs any instrument or other means whatever, with intent thereby to procure miscarriage of such woman, unless the same is necessary to preserve her life, is punishable by imprisonment in the State prison not less than two nor more than five years.
> *Cal. Penal Code 274*

I was forced to undergo an illegal abortion. The man I found told me very little, except to show up for the appointment alone. Afterward, I began to hemorrhage heavily. I called the man who performed the abortion, but all he told me was, "We did what you paid for and we're not responsible for what happens to you afterward."

I was afraid to seek medical aid because I knew abortion was against the law. I developed a fever of 106 degrees from the infection that resulted. I almost bled to death. Finally, like other young women in my situation, I was taken to the hospital to a special ward where women who were dying from abortions were treated. I was packed in ice, placed in intensive care, and given antibiotics and an I.V. Fortunately I lived. Others in my situation did not.

I remember one nurse coming around to me and saying, "This will teach you a lesson."

No woman wants an illegal abortion as part of her life history. However, because of that experience, I am committed to assuring that abortion is safe, legal, and available. I don't want anyone else to have to suffer what I had to endure, not knowing whether I would live or die from an unsafe and illegal abortion.

Shortly after I married my second husband in 1968 (we divorced in the 1980s), I decided to pursue my earlier dream of becoming a lawyer. With my experience in labor relations and education, I thought a law degree would help me get a position to improve conditions in public schools or work with the National Labor Relations Board in collective bargaining. When I was thirty, I enrolled in Southwestern University School of Law and later transferred to Loyola University School of Law in Los Angeles.

I became friendly with two fellow students, Michael Maroko and Nathan Goldberg. The three of us were in the district attorney's clinical training program at Loyola. They were at the top of our class. We talked about forming our own law firm when we graduated. I knew they would be outstanding lawyers, not only because they were smart, but because they were *mensches*—really good-hearted people—who even in difficult circumstances would do the right thing.

They were also sensible and asked me the requisite questions: "Why should we go into practice with you? We've got offers from the best firms in towns. That will mean really good money and great opportunity. Who do you know?"

"I don't know anybody and nobody knows me," I told them.

"Well, where are the clients going to come from?" they asked.

I said, "We're going to do good things for people and good is going to come back to us."

They thought it was a risk. I asked them, "Do you ever want to have your own firm?"

They said yes.

"Well, in ten years, you'll have marriages and kids and expenses. The risk will be much greater. You might not want to take a risk then. Why not take it now when there's nothing to lose?"

I guess I was pretty persuasive. We graduated and the law practice of Allred, Maroko & Goldberg was born in January 1976. We've been partners for thirty years.

At first I wasn't sure what kind of law I'd practice. I thought maybe something related to women, but I wasn't really focused yet. All I knew for sure was that I'd been very fortunate to be able to go to law school and I wanted to give something back.

Our first office was in Hollywood. We started off doing some criminal defense work to generate a regular income. I also taught two courses at the University of Southern California: Management Policy in Labor Relations and the Legal Environment of Business.

After a few years, Michael and Nathan said that we needed to focus our practice in a specific civil area and stop doing criminal defense. I hated to give it up, but they were right. We needed to develop expertise in the civil area. They also said we should all stop teaching. I hated to give that up, too, but we needed to focus on our law practice. We started taking on some sex discrimination, sexual harassment, and race discrimination employment cases—which we all liked. We also developed expertise in family law.

My partners and I describe ourselves as feminists, defined as people who believe in social, political, economic, and legal equality for women. Many people have a negative perception of what a feminist is, but once I give the definition, they often say, "Oh, then I must be a feminist, too."

I started volunteering some time with the Los Angeles chapter of the National Organization for Women (NOW). I was asked to do some cases—ones that no one else wanted to do. I did my very first news conference when the National Women's Political Caucus asked me to hold one to point out that then-Governor Jerry Brown wasn't appointing enough women judges. I had no idea what a news conference was. I didn't know anybody and no one knew me. Why would anybody come? The Caucus leaders said, "Don't worry, just show up. We're going to give you a piece of paper to read and that's it."

I asked again, "But why me?"

They said, "If you want to help the cause of getting more women judges, just do it."

So I did. We had a pretty good turnout, and in the next few weeks Governor Brown did appoint more women judges. The Caucus decided that its strategy had worked. They asked me to do another news conference a few months later. Again we received good news coverage and again Governor Brown appointed more women judges.

Years later, I figured out the "Why me?" part. Everyone else in the room had political aspirations and couldn't afford to antagonize the governor. They wanted to be appointed to a board, a commission, an agency, or a judgeship. I didn't, but I was too naïve to realize that's why I was chosen. I was the only one who didn't understand how the system worked! In retrospect, using me was a smart choice because I have never had a desire to be a political appointee.

I ran into Governor Brown some time later and he asked me why I always gave him a hard time for not appointing more women judges. He went on to name several women he had appointed. I told him that I doubted he could list by name all the men he had appointed.

"When you can't remember all the names of the women you've appointed, then you'll know you've appointed enough, and I'll stop criticizing you," I told him.

He asked me what I wanted. Did I want to be appointed to something? I said no, I just wanted good government and fairness for women.

What I learned most from those first news conferences is that they worked! A woman from NOW who worked in public relations felt that we should do more of them. She taught me how to plan them, think out the material, write it ahead of time, and contact the press. News conferences may seem spontaneous, but they never are. I thoroughly think through every single aspect of a news conference before I do one, and I will never hold one unless I think it will help my client. Not all clients will benefit from press coverage, and in most cases I think it is better to keep the matter confidential.

As I got involved in more women's rights cases, I saw many parallels with my own life. I became aware of the millions of mothers who couldn't collect their child support, and I realized that we had a system where deadbeat dads were getting away with not paying support.

I also started seeing rape survivors. These women told me that they didn't want to report the crime because they were afraid they wouldn't be believed. I realized that I had been afraid to report my own rape for the same reason. The system was letting men get away with raping women. Why weren't rape victims being believed? Why would judges and juries be more inclined to believe the denials of the rapists than the truthful allegations of the victims?

People also came to me with sex discrimination claims, which reminded me of the time I'd earned less than a man at Gimbel Brothers Department Store. There was clearly a pattern. I felt that something had to be done to make the wrongdoers more accountable, and that perhaps I could help.

Also at that time I met Midge McKenzie, who wrote *Shoulder to Shoulder*, a book on how women won the right to vote in England. She said to me, "Gloria, you have to do the same thing here." She urged me to help give women in this country a voice by holding news conferences with my clients whose rights had been violated. Victims of injustice needed to speak out in order to right the wrongs and empower women, not suffer in silence. They needed to know that they were not alone and that they still had to fight for their rights. She told me that I should speak out publicly to inspire other women to do the same. I have followed her advice ever since. I testified before the California State Legislature. I lobbied, picketed, demonstrated, and filed cases. I became an outspoken advocate and activist.

Some lawyers were critical of my activities outside the courtroom, but I didn't care what they thought. I've always tried to give a voice to the powerless. Lawyers are privileged people. I wanted to help those who weren't. Just sitting there in white gloves at luncheons talking about academic issues or going to lawyers' conventions didn't do it for me. I wanted to make a significant difference in people's lives.

After serving as president of the Los Angeles Chapter of NOW, I formed my own organization, the Women's Equal Rights Legal Defense and Education Fund. Its mission is to help educate women about their rights and to assist them in vindicating those rights by providing access to the courts.

I never would have thought that thirty years later I would still be fighting for women's rights. I guess I thought that, by now, the world would have changed significantly. We have made progress, but there is still a long way to go.

In college I was taught that if you have the ability to help others, and the opportunity and desire to act, then helping is the only moral choice to make. That is why I do what I do. And I plan to continue to help victims as long as God gives me the gift of life.

CHAPTER 2

Don't Be Victimized Twice

Amber Frey's Fight for Justice

On a warm spring day in 2003, I slipped through the back door of the North Park Community Church in Fresno, California. Waiting inside was a young woman who would soon become like a daughter to me. Her name was Amber Frey.

In late December 2002, the disappearance of pregnant homemaker Laci Peterson of Modesto, California, generated national media attention as details unfolded in a case that came to implicate her husband Scott Peterson. Peterson said he had been fishing when his twenty-seven-year-old wife disappeared from the couple's home on Christmas Eve.

Among those interested in the news of Laci's disappearance was another twenty-seven-year-old—Amber Frey, a massage therapist in Fresno who had been dating Scott. Amber was horrified to discover that Scott Peterson was married, had a missing, pregnant wife and was a suspect in that disappearance. He'd told her that he was single.

She immediately contacted the Modesto police because she recognized that she had information that might be relevant to a criminal investigation. When the police suggested that she could help by taping her telephone calls with Scott, Amber quickly agreed. She did this for one reason and one reason only—to help find a missing, pregnant woman.

As news leaked out about her relationship with Scott Peterson, Amber found herself the victim of unwanted media attention. She was hounded with telephone calls and offered money for her story. Her private life vanished in the white-hot glare of what would become one of the biggest murder stories since O. J. Simpson. The kind of attention that was focused on Amber might have been extremely difficult for anyone, but it was particularly hard on Amber, who so values her privacy. It only got worse in April 2003, after the bodies of Laci and her fetus, Connor, washed ashore in San Francisco Bay.

Many people ask how I came to represent Amber Frey. It was in the same way that I've come to represent hundreds of people over the years. She called me. Amber found herself in the middle of the highest profile criminal double-murder case in the country. She had been a victim of Scott Peterson's deception. Now she was under attack by the media, despite the fact that she had done the right thing by contacting law enforcement and agreeing to assist them in the criminal investigation.

Stereotypes about her were circulating, inaccurate statements were being made, and unwarranted stories were being published that had no basis in reality. Someone was attempting to exploit her by publishing on the Internet and placing for sale seminude photos of her. *Hustler* magazine was said to be interested in purchasing them. Amber had never given permission to have these outdated modeling pictures sold, published, or given to anyone, and she was distressed that someone would attempt to sell or show them.

Amber felt that she couldn't speak out because she needed to protect the integrity of her testimony. She wanted a jury to be the first to hear what she had to say. She didn't want to be defending herself in the media spotlight.

Amber's privacy had been invaded and her life had been severely disrupted. Certain friends of hers turned out not to be friends at all. They were selling stories and pictures of her to the tabloids. Amber Frey was under siege. She really needed some legal guidance and support through this crisis. I was honored that she called me and felt that it was my duty to support her. Amber was doing the right thing. I wanted to do the right thing as well by anchoring her through this legal tsunami that was engulfing her.

As a key prosecution witness in the case, she would need that support. In a criminal case, the prosecutor does not represent witnesses; he or she represents the state. Therefore, anything that Amber discussed with prosecutors would not be protected or confidential because they weren't her lawyers.

As her private attorney, however, I would keep anything that Amber said to me confidential. She could feel free to discuss everything and know that she could trust me never to disclose it unless she gave permission. Even then, unless I felt it was in her best interest, I would not disclose it.

I flew to Fresno to meet her in person so that we could both decide if we wanted to work together. We met at her church in a private room. There was so much media coverage of this case that I didn't want anyone to know I was going to meet Amber Frey. I wanted her to be able to decide, without media interference, whether or not she wanted me to represent her. I never want coverage of my meetings with persons who come to see me to determine if they will retain me. Over the years, I have gone to great lengths with some very high-profile people to make sure that no one knew we were meeting, in order to protect their privacy.

We talked in the church for many hours. I listened to her; she listened to me. I was in awe of this young woman, who had such tremendous courage to do what she was doing, despite the potential risk of harm to herself. Amber was very clear-thinking and very committed to doing the right thing. She had an enormous amount of common sense. We found that we could relate to each other on a personal as well as professional level. After the meeting, Amber decided that she'd like me to represent her.

Before leaving town, I stopped at her dad's house to meet him. Then I went to the airport and was about to board the plane when I heard that there were some media vans outside and television reporters saying things like, "Gloria Allred just left and we missed her." Rumors began to fly that I had been in town, although nobody really knew what was happening.

Up until then, I had been commenting on the case on Greta Van Susteren's Fox News Channel show, *On the Record*. I had seen interviews with Scott Peterson and I hadn't believed a word he'd said, for a number of reasons. For one thing, his body language appeared to be inconsistent with his words. For another, it appeared more likely than not that Laci was dead and I knew that the leading cause of death among pregnant women was murder by their husbands or significant others. I hadn't yet met Amber, but I had seen her news conference at the police station where she stated that she'd had a relationship with Scott Peterson, not knowing that he was married.

When I saw that press conference, I wasn't yet aware that she was assisting the police by taping her calls with Scott. However, I had strong feelings about this case because of my involvement in the O. J. Simpson murder case where the prosecution had alleged that another young mother—Nicole Brown Simpson—had been killed by her ex-husband. I thought that Amber could be an important witness in a possible murder case.

After our meeting in Fresno, Amber and I spent a lot of time together. In fact, I may have spent more time with Amber than I have with any other client. I came to feel like her honorary mom. For Amber, the months and years to come felt like an endless ride on an emotional roller coaster. The airwaves filled with nightly speculation about every aspect of the case. Amber tried to keep as much normalcy in her life as possible, but nothing in her life could have prepared her for this sort of thing.

To stop the media feeding frenzy, we held a press conference in my office on May 19, 2003. I announced to the reporters that I was now representing Amber.

"I anticipate attacks on her by the defense and I will respond to those attacks," I told them. "I would hope that press reports about her will be accurate, but if they are not, I will correct the record to protect Amber's reputation."

I made it clear that all future press inquiries about her should come to me and that they should not contact Amber. I acknowledged that she'd been offered money for interviews, which she refused and would continue to refuse. Her only interest was in doing her duty as a citizen by cooperating with the authorities and providing truthful information that might be relevant to the case.

I've dealt with the media for many years and they know when I am serious. I was very serious that day. They knew that there would be consequences if they didn't do what I suggested—I have a long memory. Many of the reporters would want interviews later on, so I made it clear that if they harassed Amber during that time, they wouldn't ever get those subsequent interviews. I don't make threats; I just ask people to please do what makes sense for everybody, especially my clients. Generally, they do.

After the press conference, my first task was to tackle the issue of the semi-nude photos of Amber that were on the Internet. Amber hadn't authorized anyone to sell or give away photographs of herself. She was stunned that someone was trying to profit from those pictures; she was in tears over it. I did two things: First, I contacted a law firm that had a great deal of expertise in First Amendment issues and the right to privacy, which could apply to the unauthorized sale and publication of these photos. I asked the attorneys to seek a federal injunction against the person who was attempting to publish the photos.

My second task involved a visit to someone few people would associate me with—*Hustler* magazine publisher Larry Flynt. I've known Larry for many years. I once represented his late wife, Althea, and his office is right down the street from mine. I went over to see him for a little heart-to-heart discussion about whether publishing photos of Amber in *Hustler* was really in his best interest as a businessman. As I walked through the *Hustler* office, I could feel the secretaries' eyes on me. I could only imagine what they were thinking, seeing me there. Larry and I had a good meeting and a number of subsequent phone conversations. As a result, he decided not to purchase or publish those photos. I commended Larry on his wise decision. He understood Amber's importance to the case and we contended that the person trying to sell the photos didn't have the legal right to sell them. Ultimately the federal court did grant an injunction against the person trying to sell those photos—just what I told Larry would happen.

As the case began to move through court, Stanislaus County Superior Court Judge Al Girolami issued a gag order preventing the prosecution and defense attorneys involved in the case from discussing the case in the media. The protective order also applied to their staff, court officials, potential witnesses, and law enforcement officials. Although it was well known that I was representing Amber, the gag order did not apply to me.

This gag order provoked the first of many instances where I butted heads with Scott Peterson's defense attorney, Mark Geragos. Some media people referred to Geragos and me as "the odd couple." There was a constant struggle and tug-of-war between us. We had never dealt directly with each other on a case before, but we had gone head-to-head on television on the Peterson case, prior to either of us becoming formally involved.

After the gag order was issued and the case was moved to Judge Alfred A. Delucchi's courtroom in Redwood City, I continued to discuss the case in the media—although I never discussed

Amber's potential testimony—while Mark Geragos could not. I continued to defend Amber publicly and, apparently, this rankled him. Geragos filed a motion for a court hearing to hold me in contempt for violation of the gag order. It was nonsense. I had never been covered by the gag order, and Mark Geragos should have known that. There was no need for me to be subjected to it, because I had never said that Scott Peterson was guilty. I always said that it was a matter for the jury to decide. I never discussed Amber's potential testimony or evidence, despite being asked about it repeatedly. Geragos's motion was an attempt to silence me when I had First Amendment rights to free speech.

I filed a response to his motion explaining that I could not be held in contempt of an order that never covered me in the first place. For a time, it became a huge issue. Geraldo Rivera had a whole show with lawyers debating whether or not Gloria Allred should be held in contempt of court. By the end, Geraldo decided that there wasn't enough evidence to justify such a ruling.

A hearing on whether or not to grant Geragos's motion was held, and my partner, John West, came to Redwood City to represent me. In the end, Judge Delucchi found in my favor. He indicated that the gag order was never intended to cover me, and there would be no subsequent hearing on whether or not to hold me in contempt.

Mark Geragos's strategy—to try to deflect attention away from his client who was charged with a double homicide and put others on trial instead—wasn't working. Strike one, Mark.

He didn't stop there. At another point in the case, he actually made a motion to exclude me from the courtroom. When I was called, I stepped up and made an argument opposing it. Again, the judge denied the motion. Strike two, Mark.

When it became clear that Amber would be called as a witness, my partner Nathan Goldberg and I began to prepare her for her courtroom appearance. I became concerned about possible attempts by the defense to invade her privacy while she was on the stand. I didn't want Amber asked embarrassing, humiliating questions about her personal life outside of her involvement with Scott. They would not be relevant to the criminal case and bringing them up could confuse or distract the jury.

My partners and I sent a letter to the prosecutors laying out our concerns and asked them to do everything within their power to protect her constitutional right to privacy. We asked the prosecutors to file a motion in advance of Amber's testimony asking the court to hold an "in camera" hearing (outside the presence of the public and the jury) to resolve privacy issues about her relationships with anyone other than Scott Peterson. We also asked them to object to any irrelevant questions that might be asked by the defense during the trial, if such questions invaded her privacy and were not directly related to the case. (Sometimes lawyers like to ask loaded questions—such as the classic example: "When did you stop beating your wife?"—that can do damage, even if the witness doesn't answer them.)

My associate, Maria Diaz, and I also wrote an article for the Southern California legal newspaper, the *Daily Journal*, entitled, "Does a Witness in a Criminal Case Have a Right to Privacy?" This was in the wake of the Kobe Bryant rape case, which provided a telling example of what could happen when a witness was not provided with the appropriate safeguards involving privacy rights. In that case, a young Vail, Colorado, woman had accused Bryant of raping her. Despite the existence of a "Rape Shield" law in the state, the young woman's alleged personal sexual history was exposed even before the trial began. Kobe's defense attorney asked a witness whether the nineteen-year-old victim's injuries were consistent with a "woman who had sex with three different men in three different days."

Amber had the right to proceed to the courthouse and engage in an important civic obligation without fear that her privacy would be invaded on the witness stand with irrelevant questions about her sexual history with anyone other than Scott Peterson. In our article and letter to the prosecutors, we discussed how Amber's pending testimony raised important questions about what type of privacy rights she would be afforded when she took the witness stand, and what she might have to reveal or should not be forced to reveal. We cited the cases that served as precedents. In this way, we provided all the ammunition the prosecutors would need, in case Amber's right to privacy became an issue.

In April 2004, Amber gave birth to a son, Justin Dean. The tabloids had reported that, because of the baby, she wouldn't be appearing as a witness. That was ridiculous, and I said so: "Amber Frey will testify if she is subpoenaed to testify."

The trial began on June 1, 2004, and became a nightly topic on numerous news shows. Amber's testimony was highly anticipated, although it would be months until she took the stand. Since no murder weapon had ever been found, the prosecution had a tough hill to climb with its evidence, and the media was highly critical of the way it was handling the case.

That opinion changed on August 10, 2004, when Amber took the stand, bringing with her appearance the introduction into evidence of hours of taped telephone conversations she'd had with Scott Peterson.

On the first day of her testimony, the press wanted me to bring her in the front of the courthouse so they could all see her, but Amber wasn't seeking to be a celebrity; she was a witness in a criminal trial. I didn't want her to have the extra stress of having cameras and microphones shoved in her face as she walked into the courthouse. I felt it would be best to arrive in a police vehicle at the back entrance.

Unfortunately, no one told me that the press had access to cars entering that area. As a result, they got pictures of us driving in—there's even a picture of me holding up my briefcase to shield her from the photographers. At the end of each day, she came down the escalator. I agreed that the media could photograph her on the escalator, because every other witness took the same route to get out of the building. However, I certainly didn't allow any questions to be put to her during that time.

During Amber's court appearance, every seat in the courtroom was taken. Media people flew in from all over the country to hear her testimony. A major magazine wanted to have her pose for its cover, but we said no. I didn't want her doing anything that could be used against her by the defense or that could possibly portray her as a celebrity wannabe, which she was not.

The tapes of Amber's conversations with Scott Peterson had a major impact on the trial. When Amber recorded the conversations with Scott, she never thought that these tapes would be played in a court of law. She certainly never thought they would be broadcast to millions of people on television and radio. In a way, that was probably a good thing. Had Amber known that the public would hear her exchanges with Scott, her conversations might not have been as natural. They probably wouldn't be the same tapes at all because Amber might have felt too self-conscious to say to him the things she said. A lot of the conversations were embarrassing and even humiliating to Amber, but as I told her, if anyone should be ashamed by what was being said on these tapes, it was Scott Peterson, not her.

The entire course of the trial would have been altered if those tapes hadn't existed. If Amber had only recounted the conversations—such as the time Peterson called on his cell phone to tell her he was at the Eiffel Tower in Paris, when, in truth, he was calling from a vigil for his missing wife—she might not have been believed. The whole thing would have sounded preposterous.

Amber's tapes were even more important because Peterson elected not to testify. He invoked his Fifth Amendment privilege against self-incrimination, so we never heard from him in the courtroom, except on those tapes. I thought they were very enlightening, especially because they revealed him to be a chronic liar. Most shocking was Peterson's acknowledgment, on tape, that he had told Amber before his wife went missing, "I've lost my wife and these will be my first holidays without her." To me, that was strong evidence of premeditation. I also found it interesting that Scott claimed during one taped conversation that he thought the best movie ever made was *The Shining*. That, of course, is the Jack Nicholson movie about a mentally deranged man who attempts to murder his wife and son.

I remember one day when a particularly emotional tape was being played in the courtroom. On it, Amber was crying as she confronted Scott about how he had deceived her, even after she had told him how important truthfulness was to her. As the tapes were played, Judge Delucchi allowed her to come down from the witness stand and sit next to me in the courtroom. I put my arm around her as she listened to the tape and quietly sobbed. Scott knew she had been hurt in the past, but still, on the tapes, he lied and lied and lied. It was heartbreaking.

At the end of days like that, I was concerned about her emotional state. Testifying in one of the nation's biggest trials is incredibly stressful, and Amber had a baby who needed to be nursed frequently. I don't think Amber got a full night's sleep the whole time she was testifying. Most people would have been totally exhausted from the stress and the tension of it. Amber, however, is a woman of incredible stamina, strength, and courage. Her two children remained her priority throughout the ordeal. And fortunately, Judge Delucchi was very kind to Amber. He understood that she was nursing her baby during breaks in her testimony, and knew that babies need to be fed on their own schedules—not just during midmorning court breaks or lunch. He gave her longer breaks when needed and was very generous in accommodating her.

In the evenings, Amber, my partner Nathan, and I would get together at the hotel and prepare for the next day. Those were long days, and they were important ones. Of course, in addition to the courtroom, we were also dealing with the court of public opinion. I would go out at least once a day and comment on what was going on in court. Some commentators who sided with the defense were trying to spin and undercut Amber's testimony, but their comments didn't matter. Her testimony changed the climate in the courtroom and helped turn the case around. Early in the case, although the prosecution was doing a fine job, it felt to me that—like the *Titanic*—the case was sinking. I was often the only one outside defending the prosecution in front of the cameras, but after Amber testified, there was a shift. It was as though the ship suddenly righted itself and began to head toward port.

Some attorneys came up to me and said, "Oh my God, we didn't realize what was going on. We'd heard and read a little about these tapes, but we didn't really get it until now." I felt very good about that, and I was proud of Amber. I think that the trial commentators were unanimous that Amber did a great job on the stand.

Still, there were those who claimed that all her testimony proved was that Scott Peterson was a "cad." A cad. I get this image of a guy in a smoking jacket with a martini, very 1950s—not Scott Peterson, a guy who drove a pickup truck. I believe this term was chosen by the defense to try to trivialize what Peterson had done to Amber—to diminish its importance to the case. Their suggestion was that just because he was an adulterer, it didn't mean that he was a murderer. Well, while that's true in many cases, in this case he was both!

Scott Peterson had a relationship with someone other than his wife and continued that relationship after his wife went missing. He spent an incredible number of hours on the phone with Amber, begging her to see him. He even left birthday gifts for her under a bush at Children's Hospital on her birthday—the day that Laci was supposed to deliver.

This made it clear to me that Scott Peterson was *not* a grieving husband. Moreover, it made a strong argument that he wanted his freedom from Laci.

There was quite a bit of discussion in the media as to whether Mark Geragos should even cross-examine Amber. Many people were saying he should just let her go. They felt that she had been a sympathetic witness; that she had been lied to by Scott Peterson, and was really an innocent victim in all of this. She had done the right thing by calling the police. For Geragos to attack her on cross-examination could boomerang strategically—not just on the attorney, but also on his client.

After the prosecution finished with Amber, Geragos got up and said, "No questions." The courtroom was silent as he sat down. Then he stood up again and said, "Just kidding!" A few people in the gallery laughed, but I didn't think it was funny or appropriate. I imagine Laci Peterson's family didn't appreciate it either.

Mark Geragos proceeded with his cross-examination, and it went poorly for him. Amber was ready for whatever he would ask her. We had spent days preparing her and she was a dream client because she was very cooperative. Part of the pleasure of working with Amber is that she has an excellent memory and is extremely truthful. These qualities made her an ideal witness—at least for the prosecution.

Geragos seemed to realize pretty quickly, after just a few questions, that he was outmaneuvered. He couldn't really do anything but shadow-box—Amber knew how to answer any question that came. For example, when he asked her if Scott had ever said that he loved her, she said, "not in those words," and that was true—not in those words. It didn't mean he didn't love her—maybe he did, maybe he didn't—but those aren't the words he said to her.

He also asked her about a suggestion that someone in the police department had once stated in a report that Amber had been involved with Laci's disappearance. Her response was that

Mr. Geragos would have to ask the police; she had never seen the report. That was true and exactly the right thing to say. It had become clear to police very early on that Amber had nothing to do with the crime. She had taken a polygraph and passed it. She had come to the police and volunteered her help.

The bottom line was that Mark Geragos simply couldn't make any inroads against Amber at all—not after those tapes had been played. They made it clear exactly who Scott Peterson was, a chronic liar. As Amber said on the tapes, he even lied about lying. I think they also showed how hurt she was. My sense was that Mark Geragos finally had to give up on the cross-examination—there was just nowhere for the defense to go with it.

I was a little bit frustrated, as I know Amber was, that there were some things Geragos asked her on the stand that she never got a chance to fully address. That is the nature of being on the witness stand. You have to answer the questions that are asked and you can't explain everything you'd like to in detail. For example, Geragos made a big point out of Amber's admission on the stand that she had called Scott Peterson fourteen times in one day. This left the impression that she might have been obsessed with him or stalking him—neither of which was true. That particular day she was calling to thank him for her Christmas gift. Those cell phone attempts did not go through. In fact, she didn't reach him at all that day.

Like many lawyers, I'm a big believer in the value of mind games. Lawyers often play them against each other. I felt that the defense was playing them, so I came up with a few myself. During Mark Geragos's cross-examination, I had been commenting in the media that what the defense was trying to do to Amber was just a lot of garbage. At the end of the defense's examination of Amber, we stopped at the store and got a garbage bag.

That day, I told the media gathered outside the courthouse, "The defense has said that this is all about sex." Then I wrote "all about sex" on a legal pad, ripped off the sheet and crumpled it up. "That is so much garbage—Scott never so much as mentioned sex on those tapes—and this is what should be done with garbage." I stuffed the crumpled wad of paper in the garbage bag. I called a few other of Geragos's suggestions "garbage," wrote them down, and did the same thing. The press laughed. Then I dumped the whole bag in the trash can and walked away.

That night on television some pundits, mostly supporters of the defense, debated my garbage bag tactic. They were taking sides—should she or should she not have used that garbage bag? I think somebody even took a vote. Some loved it and thought it was brilliant; others thought it inappropriate and beneath me. Whatever they thought, I had conveyed the message I wanted—that the defense's theory of the case was just garbage.

Representing Amber Frey wasn't my only involvement in the Laci Peterson case. During the trial, I was contacted by Anne Bird, Scott Peterson's half-sister. *Oh my God,* I thought. *What can this be about?* I met with Anne at my office. She was in a unique and terribly difficult situation. Anne had been placed for adoption at birth by her biological mother, Jackie, who later married and gave birth to Scott. Anne had been reunited with the Petersons shortly before Scott and Laci were married. She grew very close to Scott and came to think of Laci as a friend and sister. After Laci went missing, Scott lived on and off with Anne and her family until his arrest. Obviously, Scott trusted her.

Although Anne steadfastly believed at first in her half-brother's innocence, she had become increasingly disturbed by many things that Scott had said and done in the months after the bodies of Laci and Connor were found in San Francisco Bay. His actions forced her to a conclusion she was reluctant to make—that he was guilty. Anne was torn. She knew that if she went to the police and testified for the prosecution, that would be the end of her relationship with her newly discovered biological family. If she didn't, she would betray her own conscience. She also felt a duty to Laci, whom she loved dearly.

I was very impressed with Anne. She struck me as very credible and I understood that she had a terrible dilemma on her hands. After the meeting in my office, we met secretly a few times in Redwood City. No one in the press found out that I was representing her, which was how we wanted it. I didn't want to take her to the police until I knew that Anne was certain about her decision to assist the prosecution. I knew that once that bell was rung, it could never be unrung.

Eventually, we decided together that she should talk to the police and to the prosecution. Her potential value was as a rebuttal witness. After speaking to her, law enforcement and the prosecution appeared to regard her highly and felt that she did have something important to contribute. They also appeared to be sensitive to what might happen if she ended up having to testify in front of her biological mother. It would have forever shattered that relationship. The prosecutors had interviewed her fully and knew what she had to say. They were ready to call her as a rebuttal witness if they went in that direction.

Surprisingly, they did not. No rebuttal witnesses were called at all. They never said why, but I think they made the right decision. The defense case seemed to be so weak that there really wasn't anything to rebut.

Their decision to rest their case turned out to be the right one. On Friday, November 12, 2004, after seven days of deliberation, the jury returned with a verdict of guilty. Scott Peterson was convicted of one count of first-degree murder for his wife and one count of second-degree murder for his son, Connor. A month later, on December 13, the jury recommended that he be sentenced to death.

For two years, Amber had maintained her silence voluntarily. She had done so even before the judge imposed a gag order on all parties and witnesses, and even for several months before she re-tained me. During that time, she had endured a number of attacks on her character and her personal life. With the conviction of Scott Peterson, and the restrictions lifted, I felt it was time for her to speak out. Aside from her testimony, she'd had no opportunity to tell her own story. We began to talk about a book—something we'd never discussed at the time she was testifying. Amber decided to do it, and my partner Nathan Goldberg and I negotiated the book deal. After the publisher, ReganBooks, announced it, Amber was attacked by some trial commentators—defense attorneys mainly—for considering such a project.

I said to some of them, "I think Amber has something very valuable to say in her book. If you ever have anything valuable to say, maybe you can have a book, too, but you don't."

Later, it occurred to me that Anne Bird, who had not talked to the media or been called to testify, had an equally compelling story to tell. I thought people would be very interested to hear from Scott's half-sister, whom he had lived with on and off during the investigation. Again, I contacted ReganBooks and, before we knew it, Anne had a book deal as well.

It all seemed to happen at the speed of light. When the two books were published early in 2005, both hit number one on the *New York Times* nonfiction bestseller list. Anne and Amber each appeared on *Today, Dateline, Oprah,* and other major shows. I thought both of them conducted themselves with great courage and dignity. It's a very scary experience to be interviewed on na-tional television when you've never been interviewed before. Some interviewers were friendly, some less so, and some were actually antagonistic. Amber and Anne both did very well and I was very proud of both of them.

Mark Geragos, however, wanted one more time at bat to try to take a legal swing at me. On March 16, 2005, the day Scott Peter-son was to be formally sentenced by Judge Delucchi, the first order of court business involved a subpoena that Mark Geragos served upon me. He wanted to examine me as a witness regarding Amber Frey and Anne Bird. What a waste of time. In a million years, I would never disclose any confidential attorney/client information. That is my legal and ethical duty. The day he tried to have me served at my office, I wasn't even there. My office informed me and we decided that we would accept service and that I would appear. However, we would file objections to his demand that I testify.

Geragos also wanted me to accept service of subpoenas for Amber and Anne, which I refused to do. There was no way I was going to assist Mark Geragos in putting these two women on the witness stand. Amber had been through enough. Anne had never even testified in the case. I thought it was just a last-ditch grandstanding attempt to get in evidence information that was not relevant to the sentencing of Scott Peterson. I was not going to take the risk of their being present to be subpoenaed. Neither Amber nor Anne was interested in attending the sentencing anyway.

However, I was there when the courtroom was startled to learn that the Court's first order of business that day was a subpoena served on Gloria Allred. With me was one of my partners, Nathan Goldberg, who was prepared to argue my position if the judge wanted to hear it. If compelled to testify, I was prepared to refuse and go to jail if necessary. As it turned out, Judge Delucchi couldn't have been less interested in Mark Geragos's motion. As soon as the attorney got up and stated that he had proof of service on me, the judge said, "I see here that she's filed written objections and a motion to quash, and I'll quash this subpoena. Now let's get on with the sentencing."

Strike three, Mark. You're out.

Judge Delucchi was outstanding on this case, and I say so not just because he made rulings that were favorable to me. He was a calm, thoughtful, well-prepared jurist who was not going to tolerate games in a double-murder case. He allowed the fullest of rights for the defendant—to which Scott Peterson was entitled—but he also provided the people of California, through the prosecution, their rights as well.

The people were fortunate to be represented by Rick Distaso, Birgit Fladager, and Dave Harris, who were outstanding prosecutors. Amber was equally fortunate to have had Detective Jon Buehler of the Modesto Police Department assigned to her during the case. He is a consummate law enforcement professional and a caring human being. This was a team of which any city or county could be proud.

Empowerment Lesson

Do the right thing. If you have information relevant to a criminal case, contact law enforcement and provide that information.

Protect the integrity of your testimony by not talking to the press about your expected testimony. Do not accept money for an interview before you testify.

Seek the advice of a private attorney if possible, in order to obtain guidance and support throughout the case.

Always remember what is at stake. Conduct yourself in the way you would want a witness to act if you were a victim of a crime or a defendant. Remember that you are not an advocate. You are a neutral witness.

Form a support team of people you can trust to assist you through the crisis, but make clear to your family and friends that you cannot discuss your testimony with them.

Remember that if you are committed to telling the truth, you can have confidence when it is time to testify.

Have courage under fire.

CHAPTER 3

You Can Fight the Power

Politicians and Other Good Ol' Boys

THE SCHMITZ SMEAR

Early in my career, I decided that if I intended to be a strong advocate for women I couldn't be deterred by my critics. Besides, most of the verbal assaults I weathered were nothing but attempts to intimidate me into silence and scare me away from asserting my client's rights. I vowed not to let that tactic work, and instead to be strong for my clients and the causes in which I believed. However, when criticism sinks to the level of libel or slander, it may be time to stand and fight. That is how the case of Allred v. Schmitz came to be.

In 1981, California State Senator John Schmitz led a radical effort to outlaw abortion. The ultraconservative senator got his start in politics by saving a woman from assault. Ironically, his political career began its descent over his verbal assault of another woman—me.

John Schmitz and I were hardly strangers. For almost seven years, his wife Mary and I appeared regularly together on a local KNBC-TV show, *Free-4-All*. John and Mary had attended a surprise birthday party for me at my home, and I attended the wedding of one of their children.

At the same time, we were anything but friends. Schmitz was one of California's most extreme right-wing politicians. At one point, he served as the national director of the ultraconservative John Birch Society. His views were hardly mainstream. He once supported a three-tiered school system—one for blacks, one for whites, and one for those "who want to mix." Another time he called the Rev. Martin Luther King Jr. "a notorious liar." His comments that "Jews are like everybody else, only more so" and "I may not be Hispanic, but I'm close—I'm Catholic with a mustache" finally even cost him the support of the John Birch Society, which abandoned him.

In December 1981, Schmitz, who was then a California state senator, was holding public hearings up and down the state as part of his legislative proposal to ban abortion and limit other birth control options. I publicly challenged his position during a hearing in Los Angeles. First, I outlined all the legal reasons why his proposed bill was unconstitutional. Then I disclosed that I had had an abortion when it was illegal for a doctor to perform it (although not for a woman to have it) and that I had almost died. I emphasized that this was a major reason I wanted abortion to be safe and legal. I then approached the stage where the senator was seated. In front of all the reporters covering the hearings, I took out a chastity belt and handed it to him to demonstrate that, under his proposed law, such a device would be the only acceptable means of birth control.

"We think you are trying to force the chastity belt on us, so we'd like you to take this home to your wife, Mary, and ask her how she likes this as the only form of birth control," I told him, adding, "We're not going back to the Middle Ages."

His eyes bugged out in shock and his open-mouthed reaction ran on all the TV newscasts that night. Rather than appearing to be a courageous crusader, he looked like a fool. When I saw Mary Schmitz several days after the press conference, she told me that her husband had "loved" the publicity.

Yet, weeks later, Schmitz's office issued a press release with the headline "Senator Schmitz and his Committee Survive Attack of the Bulldykes." In a statement his office widely disseminated, he described his impression of some of the women who attended the hearings that he held on abortion: "With the exception of the Calexico hearings—which were held in Catholic, and therefore somewhat civilized territory—the Committee was greeted (at Fresno and San Diego) by pre-organized infestations of imported lesbians from anti-male and pro-abortion queer groups in San Francisco and other centers of decadence." In Los Angeles, he continued, the front rows were filled "with a sea of hard, Jewish, and (arguably) female faces whose general countenance reassured those of us on the Committee dais that had we somehow fallen from the stage we would have been devoured as so many carcasses thrown to the piranha."

Then the topic turned to me: "In Los Angeles, the Chairman was molested by a slick butch lawyeress, Gloria Allred, who threw a chastity belt at me in a crude propadentic [sic] to the mass abortions which continue in California at a cost to the state's taxpayers of over $100,000 a day."

He ended the release by congratulating his staff, who had been "fraught upon [sic] by the lesbians and the murderous marauders of the pro-abortion encampment."

The day this statement was released, I was in court in Santa Monica. When I called my office for messages, there were several from reporters who wanted my comment on the statement. It was only when I called back the Los Angeles Times that I learned of its content. It was one of the most disgusting press releases I've ever read—particularly from an elected public official. I was shocked that Senator Schmitz would say such things about me in light of our previously cordial relationship. More disturbing to me was the message it sent: If you exercise your constitutional right to testify at public hearings on issues you believe in, you'll be personally attacked.

His statement attacked Jewish women, lesbians, pro-choice groups, Protestants, and the people of San Francisco. Some groups wanted to sue but they had no legal standing because they had not been specifically named. However, I had been named, and I felt it was my duty to stand up and fight back. In January 1982, I filed a lawsuit against Schmitz for libel. I wanted him to apologize for his defamatory statements and to reiterate publicly the right of citizens to speak at public hearings without being subjected to personal attacks by an elected official.

I am not a lesbian and I don't think there is anything wrong with being one. I wasn't sure whether to sue on that basis, but my lesbian friends found the term "slick butch lawyeress" to be pejorative and urged me to do so.

Schmitz knew I wasn't a lesbian; he had visited my home and met my family. Still, he fought the lawsuit for six years. Then on August 21, 1986, the day my case was going to trial, Schmitz finally settled the lawsuit. As a condition of the settlement, he issued a statement that became part of the official public record. In it, he apologized to me and "to all others who may have been wrongfully characterized, hurt, or harmed in any way." He acknowledged that, "based upon my past relationships with Gloria Allred, her husband and her family, I have never considered her to be and recognize that she is not a 'slick butch lawyeress.'" Finally, he acknowledged that "any citizen has a right to be heard in any public hearing on those issues involving diverse public issues, particularly human rights, without being subjected to personal attacks."

During this time, he lost the support of his colleagues. I went to the state legislature and urged it to reprimand him and not pay either for his legal fees or for the cost of the settlement, as Schmitz had requested. I told legislators that elected officials should not be economically insulated from the cost of their wrongful acts. Ordering taxpayers to pay his fees would only encourage other elected officials in the future to defame other members of the public who testified at public hearings.

The State Senate heard me and voted to formally reprimand Schmitz for his statements and refused to pay his legal fees. Schmitz made a payment to me of $20,000, which I donated to pro-choice groups and others affected by his vile comments.

It wasn't the only time that Senator Schmitz and I became involved in an adversarial relationship. I learned that he planned to hold a press conference to discuss his recent meeting with Palestinian leader Yassar Arafat. Schmitz, had scheduled the conference on one of the Jewish High Holidays, which I felt was insulting to Jewish people.

One of my clients, a Holocaust survivor, told me that in the death camps, the Nazis would murder even more Jews on a High Holiday, just to show their total disrespect for Jewish people and their religion. For this reason, I found Schmitz's choice of a High Holiday for his news conference about Arafat to be very disturbing and probably not a coincidence. In the Bible, plagues were sent on the Egyptians when they held Jews as slaves. My partners and I decided that I should send a plague of frogs on Schmitz. I bought a "frogarium" at a local pet store, went to the Los Angeles Press Club, and released the frogs on the patio during Schmitz's press conference. Frogs were jumping everywhere and Schmitz was once again a laughingstock. (Please note that no frogs were hurt in the process, only Schmitz's credibility.)

Schmitz's political career continued its steep slide downhill when it was revealed that the married, family-values spouting conservative had—outside of his marriage—fathered two children with one of his former students at Santa Ana College where he was a lecturer for many years. The story became public when allegations of child abuse were raised after Schmitz's young son from the affair was found to have a hair wound so tightly around his penis that it had to be removed by a doctor.

All hell broke loose after that. When the press asked for my re-action, I said, "I guess I'm just waiting for John Schmitz to blame this one on me, too." Sure enough, Schmitz tried to blame the hair-wrapped penis on a babysitter named Gloria. I told reporters that I wasn't babysitting in my spare time.

The whole episode revealed the hypocrisy implicit in John Schmitz's right-wing philosophy. I did feel very sad that this had happened to his family. I'm sure it was a shock to his wife, al-though I don't recall Mary ever saying a public word about it.

Schmitz faded into obscurity, but his family did not. In 1997, his thirty-five-year-old daughter, Mary Kay Letourneau, was sen-tenced to prison for having sex with a student she taught in the sixth grade. Was she following in her father's footsteps? He had had sex with a student as well albeit a college student.

When John Schmitz died in 2001, he had fallen so far that his passing barely merited a paragraph in most newspapers. His last job reportedly was selling political memorabilia at Union Station in Washington DC. It was a short distance physically, but light years professionally, from his former prestigious position in the U.S. Congress.

Empowerment Lesson

Never be intimidated by an antagonist's tactics, or position of power. Despicable words can lead to even more dangerous actions. Speak up early and forcefully against hate speech and bigotry. Take a stand.

ILENE HILL AND THE GRANDSTANDING DEPUTY DISTRICT ATTORNEY

When government lawyers forget their roles as public servants and begin to trample the rights of individuals in pursuit of a personal or political agenda, it really makes me angry.

In 2005, I went head-to-head with a deputy district attorney in Yolo County, California, located near Sacramento. I believed that he had abused the rights of a battered woman and endangered the life of her child in order to get more money from the governor for child abduction programs.

Ilene Hill wanted a safe home for her daughter, Anna, when she agreed in March 2005 to place her child for adoption with an Alabama couple, Dawn and Brian Barlow. The Barlows had already adopted Ilene's other daughter.

Ilene asserted that she had gone through years of hell because of Jesse William Baldizan, her one-time boyfriend and Anna's father. In 2002, Baldizan had been charged by the Yolo County district attorney with a misdemeanor of battery on Ilene. In 2003, he had been prosecuted for felonies in which she was alleged to be the victim. He'd also been charged with a misdemeanor of abusing or endangering the health of a child. Photos of Ilene's injuries from her court records showed her with two swollen eyes, a cut above her left eyebrow, and bruising on the center of her throat and on her right arm. A police report noted that Ilene had older injuries as well, including a cut on her leg.

No trial was ever held, and Baldizan pled guilty only to violating a protective order—the least serious of the charges. According to Ilene, Baldizan paid little or no child support for Anna, and she alleged that the child's needs were not being adequately met.

Ilene's dire circumstances led to her decision to place her daughter for adoption. Far from trying to avoid the legal system or hide the adoption, she acted properly through an adoption agency and was represented by an attorney (not me). She filled out papers listing the telephone number and address of the father and paternal grandmother.

On her application she wrote, "I am placing my child for adoption because I believe I am unable to adequately provide for the needs of my child." She added that she wanted a better life for

Anna than what she could offer and, this way, "she gets to grow up with her sister."

Satisfied that she'd done the right thing for her daughters, Ilene Hill joined the army in order to start a new life and to make her children proud of her by serving her country.

Yolo County Deputy District Attorney Frank McGuire didn't share Ilene's dreams. After Ilene placed Anna for adoption with the Barlows, McGuire issued a press release in which he charged Ilene with "taking, enticing away, keeping, withholding, or concealing her child and maliciously depriving her child's father of his right to custody or right to visitation." If convicted, the release stated, she could be sentenced to "three years in state prison, and receive a fine of $10,000. Bail on warrant is set at $500,000."

Ilene Hill was arrested in boot camp in May 2005 and held in a jail in South Carolina, where her army unit was stationed. When Ilene's mother, Teresa, contacted me for help, I could barely believe the story she told me. The same DA's office that had, just years earlier, charged Jesse Baldizan with battery and various felonies (which they alleged that Baldizan had inflicted on Ilene Hill) was now prosecuting Hill and was, in effect, siding with Baldizan.

It didn't make sense until I read further in McGuire's press statement, where he referenced California Governor Arnold Schwarzenegger's decision to cut funds for the district attorneys' child abduction programs around the state. "Without state funding," McGuire's release read, "the counties will not be able to maintain their respective Child Abduction Units. Parents, like Jesse Baldizan, will then have nowhere to seek help when their children are abducted." In my opinion, McGuire was using Ilene Hill as a political pawn to obtain more money for his child abduction program.

Well, as far as I was concerned, he had picked the wrong case, at the wrong time, for the wrong reasons. What about money for programs aiding women who have been battered? What about women who cannot support their children because fathers do not pay child support? Where was McGuire's support for that?

This was not a case of child abduction at all. She was a mother who had to make a hard decision, which she believed was in the best interest of her children. Ilene didn't run off with her child in the middle of the night. She had an attorney and went through adoption procedures that involved a social worker from Yolo County. The Barlows obtained custody of the child from the court system in Alabama.

This was a poster case of favoritism by the deputy district attorney toward a father who, according to Ilene, had paid little or no child support and who the state had once claimed battered the mother of a young child. It was a case of gross overreaching by the prosecution. McGuire could have decided not to prosecute Ilene at all. This was a misuse of taxpayer funds for a political agenda and a disservice to real crime victims who needed his attention.

Ilene had no prior criminal history. She had found a safe home for Anna. Now McGuire was ruining her life by making her stand trial for placing her child with a loving Alabama family. He had it all backward. Instead of focusing on the father's conduct, he was prosecuting Ilene and bullying a family who only wanted to help.

When I heard that Frank McGuire planned to fly to Alabama in May 2005 to bring Anna back himself, I decided that I'd be there to meet him when he arrived. His trip to Alabama was a waste of taxpayers' money. The Barlows had already agreed to turn Anna over to Baldizan's mother, who was making the trip. They had previously told McGuire that it was unnecessary for him to come as well.

When I arrived at the airport in Huntsville to meet McGuire's plane, the local NBC reporter accompanied me hoping to tape the confrontation. We set up the camera in a hotel room next to the airport and Brian Barlow brought McGuire there when he got off the plane. When McGuire walked into the room to get Anna, he was surprised to find me there with a microphone on and the camera rolling.

I asked him, "Why are you wasting taxpayers' funds on prosecuting this young mother who only tried to do what she thought was best for her little girl—to place her with a loving, Christian family in Alabama so that this little girl would be safe and nurtured and loved? Why are you intervening to try to take this child back to California and why are you prosecuting this mother who your office alleged to be a battered woman?" I also asked him if he was aware that Ilene had been represented by an attorney who had tried to contact Anna's father before the adoption took place.

McGuire said I was comparing apples and oranges, but I wasn't talking about fruit. I was talking about McGuire filing a criminal case against Ilene to make a political point and to get more money for a child abduction program.

McGuire said he considered this a "most egregious case" because Anna had been taken to Alabama. I asked him why he was sending federal marshals to bring Ilene Hill back from South Carolina. I asked, "Why are you using federal funds for a crime you allege is a state crime? Is she a big bank robber?"

During my confrontation with McGuire, he had a tough time answering questions posed by the Barlows and me about why he had decided to make the case so public. I asked him what he had done to assure that the child would be safe when he returned her to California. He couldn't promise that Anna would be safe living with her paternal grandmother when her father—who still hadn't completed court-ordered anger management classes—was living in the same home as well.

Brian Barlow was furious that the DA was taking the child back to the house where this father might have unsupervised access to her.

McGuire acknowledged that Jesse Baldizan hadn't even asked for custody of Anna after being notified that the Barlows were attempting to legally adopt her. McGuire said he didn't know why. Nor did he have an answer when I asked if he was going to monitor Anna's interactions with her father to be sure that she was safe. After all, Baldizan wasn't supposed to have unsupervised visitation with his daughter until he completed his anger management classes. I was concerned that the child might be left alone with her father since he lived with his mother, who worked five days a week.

Portions of this exchange were broadcast on Alabama television that day, prompting an Alabama judge to call and tell me that I was doing the right thing. He said he believed that what McGuire was doing was wrong, and thanked me for my efforts.

Ilene was kept in four different jails for six weeks before she was finally sent back to California and placed in the Yolo County jail. This was outrageous, since she had immediately agreed to extradition and had no prior criminal history. Ironically, Jesse Baldizan was incarcerated there as well, for violating a court order.

After a hearing, Ilene was finally released on her own recognizance. She is now awaiting trial, and I am still flying to her hearings to support her and her family.

Anna was returned to California to live with her paternal grandmother while the case moved through the courts. It won't be tried by Frank McGuire. He died in a scuba diving accident in July 2005. I can only hope that his replacement is guided less by politics and more by compassion, and that—after he has had an opportunity to review all the facts—he will realize that a mistake has been made and that the case against Ilene should be dismissed.

Empowerment Lesson

Beware of government officials who think that it is acceptable to trample the rights of an individual if it will help them advance their own political agendas. The end does not justify the means. Be prepared to fight power with power. If you are a victim, develop a strong support system to help you through a crisis.

HOW TO BRING DOWN A
POLITICIAN GONE WILD

In 1992, I took on one of the biggest old boys' clubs of all—the U.S. Senate.

I had watched in horror in the fall of 1991 as Anita Hill's charges that Supreme Court nominee Clarence Thomas had sexually harassed her led some U.S. Senators to try to humiliate her publicly during hearings by the all-male Senate Judiciary Committee. Instead of rejecting Thomas, based on the testimony of Professor Hill and allegations of others who were set to testify against him but were not permitted to do so, the Senate rewarded him by confirming his nomination as an associate justice of the U.S. Supreme Court. Many women were revolted by some Senators' rejection of Anita Hill's allegations.

In 1992, during Senate Republican Bob Packwood's bid for reelection in Oregon, accusations surfaced late in the campaign that he had sexually harassed some women. The senator vehemently denied them and went on to win his race by a slight margin.

Eighteen days after the election, however, the *Washington Post* published detailed allegations of sexual harassment by ten women who had worked for Packwood or had been prospective staff members. Among their charges: Packwood had told dirty jokes; grabbed and kissed some of them; tried to take one aide's clothes off, and chased another around a table. The stories dated back as far as 1969, the first year he served in the U.S. Senate.

Packwood issued a statement saying, "If any of my comments or actions have indeed been unwelcome, or if I have conducted myself in any way that has caused any individual discomfort or embarrassment, for that I am sincerely sorry."

Well, I was sincerely sorry, too. Bob Packwood had been one of the Senate's most visible supporters of women's rights and was a strongly pro-choice Senator, unusual for a Republican. However, his vague apology just wasn't enough. Like all elected officials, he needed to be held to the highest possible standards in his workplace. I was in Hawaii giving a speech at the time the statement was released, and some women in the audience wondered why, with all these allegations, nothing was being done about Packwood in the Senate. It was a good question. I found that none of the alleged harassment victims had exercised her right to file a complaint with the Senate Ethics Committee asking for an investigation into the issue of ethical violations by a U.S. Senator.

I therefore wrote to the Senate Ethics Committee and asked it to open an investigation into the numerous allegations of sexual misconduct made against Senator Packwood. I told the committee that the American people had a right to know whether such allegations were true or false. As we had just seen the year before with Anita Hill, coming forward with such allegations wasn't easy for women. I felt that the Ethics Committee had a duty to investigate and I asked it to conduct a full, fair, and prompt inquiry into the scandal.

Shortly after I filed my request, Senator Packwood held another press conference with a further apology. He said that, previously, he "just didn't get it," but that he did now. Although he now stated that his past actions were wrong, he still refused to acknowledge the specific actions for which he was accepting responsibility; he failed to apologize to each of his victims; and he didn't offer to resign. He said he intended to seek counseling, but indicated that he did not know where to get it. I publicly offered to give him a "Gloria Allred course on sexual harassment"—free of charge.

If he had racially harassed members of his staff, he would have been forced to resign. Why was it acceptable to sexually harass women? If he really wanted to show leadership in women's rights, he should have accepted the real life consequences of his wrongful conduct. Resignation, in my opinion, was his only dignified choice.

There had already been enough lip service on the issue of sexual harassment. It was time for action, not words. Several weeks later, I was pleased that the Ethics Committee notified me that it would, based on my complaint, conduct a preliminary inquiry into the allegations. That itself was a victory, but after the Clarence Thomas–Anita Hill debacle, I wanted to ensure that women were involved in the process. I asked the all-male committee to appoint at least one female Senator to the committee investigating Packwood. That way we wouldn't have the image of "old boys" investigating "old boys," which would certainly undermine the confidence of many women in th committee's work.

I kept up the pressure on the Senate Ethics Committee throughout 1993. Although investigators had contacted hundreds of women who had worked for Senator Packwood, I was concerned that the inquiry was largely being conducted in secret. I urged the committee to hold a full public hearing, where the victims would be allowed to testify. I felt that this would increase the public's confidence in the political process and make it less easy for the old boys' club to close ranks around one of its own.

I also called on Senator Packwood to turn over his diaries, which allegedly contained details relevant to the sexual harassment allegations. Packwood had cited his right to privacy in refusing to turn them over to the Ethics Committee. As the investigation and diary battle continued, more women came forward with allegations that they'd also suffered unwanted sexual advances from Bob Packwood. One of them was Julie Williamson, who wanted to tell her story to the Ethics Committee at a public hearing.

Julie had worked in Packwood's Portland office and was talking on the phone one day when Packwood walked in and kissed her on the back of her neck. Williamson, who was married with two children, told him, "Don't you ever do that again." She told the *Los Angeles Times* that her warning had no effect. Packwood followed her into another room, where he tried to remove her clothing. Her colleagues told her, "That's just the way Bob is."

When she later confronted him about the incident, she said Packwood's response was, "I suppose you're one of the ones who want a motel room."

Julie resigned.

She came with me to Washington in October 1993, to urge the members of the U.S. Senate to vote in favor of seeking a court order to force Bob Packwood to relinquish all his diaries to the Ethics Committee. He had turned over diaries from 1968 to 1988, but had refused to turn over those from 1989 to the present.

Julie's reasons for the trip were eloquently outlined in a statement she gave to reporters. "Many of us who have brought allegations against Senator Packwood have suffered from his attempts to smear our reputations, destroy our employment opportunities and discredit us with the public. We would appreciate the opportunity to clear our names."

Julie urged the Ethics Committee to hold public hearings even though, she admitted, "I dread them. I am afraid of partisanship raising its ugly head, causing members of the panel to attempt to discredit the women to help Senator Packwood. But I stand fast in my belief that the truth can and will prevail.

"Senator Packwood's sexual misconduct has spanned his entire career in the U.S. Senate. It has affected dozens of women and their families. It is bringing discredit on the decent men and women in the Senate. We deserve better. They deserve better. Let's move forward with open, public hearings to resolve this issue, once and for all."

The Senate did vote to compel Packwood to turn over all his diaries, but both the Ethics Committee and the full Senate voted against holding public hearings. I publicly protested what I considered to be a massive and far-reaching cover-up. The decision by the U.S. Senate to conduct the inquiry in secret in order to protect one of their buddy boys from public embarrassment was a disgrace and an outrage. It was an effort to protect one man at the expense of many women who alleged that they had been victimized by the Senator. It was particularly appalling since, in the past, the Ethics Committee had always conducted public hearings when it reached this stage of an investigation.

It took two more years, until 1995, for the Senate Ethics Committee to vote for Bob Packwood's expulsion. In the interim, momentum continued to build publicly in favor of the women and against Packwood. In the end, the system was responsive to women by recommending the most serious penalty possible for sexual misconduct and other misdeeds. Unlike the result of the Clarence Thomas–Anita Hill hearings, which ultimately elevated Thomas to one of the highest judicial positions in the country, Packwood was forced to suffer the public recommendation of the Ethics Committee that he be expelled.

Apparently, Packwood saw the handwriting on the wall and assessed the political reality that the U.S. Senate would follow the recommendation of its committee. He resigned on September 7, 1995.

This was a major victory for us and a real tribute to the courage of the many women who were brave enough to come forward with their complaints of sexual misconduct. We hope the lesson he learned—that sexual harassment carries serious consequences—was noted by other members of Congress and in workplaces throughout the nation.

Empowerment Lesson

Women deserve a workplace free of sexual harassment. United women can win historic victories, even against a powerful member of the U.S. Senate. We changed history by filing a complaint and then keeping the pressure on.

IT'S NOT THE OFFICE, IT'S THE ACTION

Sometimes standing up for what you believe can put you in some awkward situations. I was an enthusiastic supporter of Bill Clinton. I first met him before he became president and saw him on numerous occasions after his election. He was extremely personable and charismatic and always very cordial to me. I liked his policies, donated to his campaigns, and defended him on my radio program and on television. I even have a picture in my office of the two of us together.

I am, however, first and foremost a feminist. I support women's rights, no matter what the consequences. In 1998, my belief in upholding the law as it applies to sexual harassment against women brought me into conflict with the legal position of the president, whose campaigns I'd supported in 1992 and 1996. The conflict involved the Paula Jones case, brought against the president by a woman who claimed that he'd sexually harassed her in 1991, while he was governor of Arkansas.

Paula Jones alleged that when she was an employee of the State of Arkansas, then-Governor Clinton had her escorted to his hotel room and, while she was there, he "lowered his trousers and underwear, exposed his penis—which was erect—and told [her] to 'kiss it.'" She also alleged that the governor, "while fondling his penis, said, 'Well, I don't want to make you do anything you don't want to do,' and then pulled up his pants."

When she later filed a sexual harassment suit against the president, it quickly turned into a political imbroglio. I did not represent Paula Jones. The case drew my direct involvement, however, when Judge Susan Webber Wright threw out Jones's suit. In her ruling, the judge said that, "while the alleged incident, if true, was certainly boorish and offensive, the court has already found that the governor's alleged conduct does not constitute sexual assault." Judge Wright concluded that "this is not one of those exceptional cases in which a single incident of sexual harassment, such as an assault, was deemed to state a claim of hostile work environment sexual harassment."

I disagreed. One act of sexual harassment, if severe, need not rise to the level of criminal sexual assault in order for an employee to seek protection under the law. I believed that, if President Clinton did what Paula Jones alleged, that act should as a matter of law be considered severe and sufficient to constitute sexual harassment. I believed that Judge Wright's definition of the term "sexual harassment" could have serious legal consequences for many other women in the future who might wish to exercise their legal right to sue for sexual harassment in the workplace. It would also send the wrong message to other men—that they could get away with an act of severe sexual harassment.

Through my organization, the Women's Equal Rights Legal Defense and Education Fund, I asked to file an *amicus* or "friend of the court" brief with the Eighth Circuit U.S. Court of Appeals to present support for my argument. I did not contact either President Clinton's attorneys or Paula Jones's attorneys about my decision. I neither needed nor sought their permission to file my brief because I did not wish to be aligned with either party; I wasn't doing this to help or hurt either of their cases. In fact, I had no opinion as to who was telling the truth about what happened in the room that day—that was an issue for the trial. My brief sought only to protect the legal rights of all women in the workplace.

I appeared to be alone in publicly voicing my opinion on this issue.

Many other women's groups privately agreed that Judge Wright's definition of sexual harassment was flawed and dangerous, but I was the first to step forward. The president of the National Organization for Women (NOW) said that the case was too politically charged and wasn't a good test for case law. While I respected NOW's decision, I disagreed.

Although I believed President Clinton had an outstanding record in the area of women's rights, I *had* to get involved. I had to do this to protect other women who could be hurt by a legal precedent that could deprive them of their legal right to sue for sexual harassment in the future. My law firm had represented more sexual harassment victims than any other private firm in the country. Our commitment to protecting victims was longstanding and unmatched.

I filed the brief in July 1998, and the Court of Appeals accepted it. Before the appellate court could decide whether to uphold or reverse Judge Wright's decision, however, Jones accepted an $850,000 settlement in the matter and the case ended. It appeared to be a win-win for both parties. For Jones, it was a significant payment, especially since she was unable to allege any significant damages. Even if she had won at trial, she would likely have received a smaller amount. For the president, it was the most expedient way of ending his involvement in further depositions, or in a trial. I think there was a substantial risk that the Appeals Court would have reversed Judge Wright's decision and sent it back for trial.

During most of the time that the president came under attack in the matter of former White House intern Monica Lewinsky, I was supportive of him. I was hosting a radio show on KABC talk radio in Los Angeles and many of my callers were very conservative. I always defended him on the air. I felt that, unless and until it was proven that he had lied under oath to the American people, he was entitled to the presumption of innocence.

I saw him at a fundraiser during this time and was about to say hello. However, instead of the very warm, cordial, and talkative person that I had come to know, he seemed to turn to stone at the sight of me. It was a total, shocking change. He seemed very awkward with me—extremely careful, cautious, and uncomfortable. As I left the event, I wondered what was going on. I soon found out.

A short time later, on August 17, 1998, President Clinton admitted publicly that he had lied about his lengthy, inappropriate relationship with Monica Lewinsky. I was heartbroken for him, for Hillary, for Chelsea, and for the nation, but my support for him came to an end when I learned that he had lied under oath and to the American people. The American people have a right to expect that their president will be honest with them, and thereby earn their trust. When he is not, it seriously undermines our confidence in both the president and his office.

It's a sad day when it is necessary to convene a Grand Jury to learn the details of the personal, intimate, sexual activity of the president of the United States. Especially troubling, however, was the fact that President Clinton had initially denied a sexual relationship with Ms. Lewinsky. I understood what was at stake. He had been a very strong advocate on issues I cared about. He was pro-choice, supportive of women's rights, and supportive of affirmative action. And yet, as head of the largest workforce in the country, the federal government, he had lied under oath. There was no way I could rationalize, forgive, or accept a lie to the American people, whether by a Democratic president or a Republican one. I could no longer support him because I do think integrity matters. That night, I went on CNN's *The World Today* and said, "President Clinton has lied to the American people, and he must resign."

My comment drew criticism from some members of the National Organization for Women, but I do not regret it. While I give President Clinton the credit that he rightly deserves for eight years of peace, progress, and prosperity, this issue of integrity was one that certainly left him with a flawed record.

It now appears that his wife, Senator Hillary Rodham Clinton may run for president in the near future. Despite my disappointment with President Clinton's behavior, I fully support her candidacy and hope that she will be the first woman president of the United States of America.

Empowerment Lesson

Standing up for integrity has its price, but it's one worth paying. Don't sacrifice your integrity because people you know have compromised theirs.

CHAPTER 4

You Can Catch a Fallen Star

Taking on Celebrity Bad Boys

MARV ALBERT AND THE BLONDE BOMBSHELL WITNESS

The Boys' Club likes to close ranks around one of its own when he's in trouble. Sports broadcaster Marv Albert benefited from the Boys' Club security treatment in 1997 when he was prosecuted for a bizarre sexual attack on Vanessa Perhach in a Virginia hotel room.

As she would later testify, Vanessa had a long-term sexual relationship with Albert that involved occasional sexual threesomes and women's lingerie, which he liked to wear. Vanessa testified that when she showed up at Albert's room on February 12, 1997 without a male sex partner in tow, he became enraged. She said that Albert grabbed her arms, threw her on the bed and said, "You've been a bad girl, you didn't bring anybody."

She testified that Albert pinched her cheeks to force her to perform oral sex, ignored her pleas that he was hurting her, and bit her on the back, saying, "You know you like rough sex." Later in the trial, an emergency room nurse testified that she found almost twenty bite marks on Vanessa's back when she came to the hospital.

When criminal charges of forcible sodomy and assault were first filed against him, Albert angrily proclaimed his innocence. He told his bosses at NBC and Madison Square Garden, where he sportscasted New York Knicks basketball games, that nothing like that had ever happened. They stood behind him.

There was a lot at stake. If convicted, Albert faced five years to life in prison.

He continued to deny the allegations all the way into a Virginia courtroom in October 1997, where his defense was apparently to paint Vanessa as a liar. That's when my client, P. J. Masten, in a surprise appearance, took the witness stand to tell her story.

Right before P. J. took the stand, according to press reports from the courtroom, Albert, his family, and his attorney had been laughing and chatting among themselves, evidently figuring that the trial was progressing in their favor. P. J.'s testimony changed that atmosphere significantly.

P. J. testified that she'd gotten to know the sportscaster in the early 1990s when she worked as a Hyatt Hotel VIP liaison and he traveled with the New York Knicks. In 1994, she said he asked her to come to his hotel room to help him send a fax; when she arrived, the door was open and he called to her to come in. As she stood in the bar area, looking out the window, "I heard a door close behind me," she testified. There was Albert, dressed in panties and a garter belt.

"He was exposed and aroused," she told the courtroom. "I was in shock and didn't know what to do. I'd never seen anything like this."

Albert told her he was tense and began to rub his body against hers, and then, as he pushed her head toward his crotch, he bit her on the neck, she testified.

This wasn't the first time P. J. had suffered through Albert's idea of a romantic tryst. She told the court that the year before, he'd invited her to a party with the Knicks. When she arrived, she found only the sportscaster.

"He started asking me weird questions, sexual questions," she testified. "He started to kiss me and instead of kissing me, he bit my lip."

Then Albert allegedly asked her if she could find another man for a sexual threesome, but she refused. P. J. testified she also declined his request for oral sex and that her refusal drew another bite on the neck.

The details of P. J.'s testimony were sickeningly similar to those offered by Vanessa Perhach, with one added detail: when P. J. grabbed his hair to push him away, "it lifted off."

Apparently Marv's "coverage" extended from play-by-play to a loose toupee.

For P. J., it was a brave appearance. Albert and his attorneys already had spent a lot of time prior to the trial attacking the judge, the prosecutor, and the victim. Albert's lawyer, Roy Black, not only fought to have her testimony excluded, but tried to tarnish P. J.'s reputation as well. He suggested that she had made up her story after reading about the case in the press. Nothing was further from the truth. In fact, P. J. had complained about Albert's behavior immediately after it occurred. She believed that, as a public role model, Albert shouldn't be allowed to send a message to young people that you can do whatever you choose and get away with it. There should be consequences for what he had done.

I believe P. J.'s testimony was an act of courage that served as an important example and inspiration to many other women in similar, difficult situations. Her actions showed them that they can contribute to the criminal justice system's efforts to bring to justice men who have committed acts of violence against women. P. J.'s testimony might have persuaded members of the jury that Albert had engaged in a pattern of conduct that enhanced Vanessa's credibility. It also helped to refocus the trial back on the issue of violence against women and helped the jury understand that there might be more to this case than allegations that Marv

Albert wore women's garter belts and women's underwear. Wearing such clothing isn't a criminal act. Biting a woman who does not consent to such behavior *is*.

The media dubbed P. J. the "bombshell witness" of the trial. Many legal commentators suggested that they found P. J. to be extremely credible and thought that her testimony was powerful.

Well, Marv Albert also must have thought that her testimony was significant. The day after she testified, before the courtroom proceedings started, the prosecutors offered Albert a deal: Plead guilty to misdemeanor assault and battery charges and we'll drop the more serious felony charge of forcible sodomy. In the wake of P. J.'s testimony, he decided to take it. His attorney said it was to stop the "parade of embarrassment" his client was suffering, not because he'd actually committed the crime.

Albert was immediately fired by NBC and resigned from his Madison Square Garden job.

At his sentencing, Albert offered a ridiculous excuse for his behavior toward Vanessa. "In the past, there was consensual biting," he claimed. "I'm sorry if she felt she was harmed."

The judge ordered Albert to get counseling and to "stay out of trouble" for the next year, but he received no jail time. If he made progress in his counseling and stayed crime-free, the judge ruled, then the criminal case would be dismissed and Albert's record would be erased.

I was appalled. There used to be a saying in the law that "every dog gets one free bite." This shouldn't apply to men who are convicted of battery against women. These men should be appropriately punished for their criminal acts. I thought Albert should have been sentenced to some time in jail. The purpose of sentencing in a criminal case is punishment, deterrence, and rehabilitation. I didn't believe that releasing Marv Albert on probation adequately satisfied any of those goals.

Some people thought Albert would take his "Get Out of Jail Free" card and disappear. Not Marv. Within two months of his sentencing, he appeared on shows like *20/20* and *Larry King Live* trying to polish his image by tarnishing the reputations of the women he'd attacked. Vanessa Perhach was "trying to extort me," he told Barbara Walters. He denied P. J.'s allegations and attacked her character. Of course, Albert's denials were not under oath, whereas P. J.'s allegations were.

It seemed to me that Albert was attempting to revise history by using a combination of doublespeak, denials, sympathy ploys, and unwarranted attacks on others. P. J. Masten had testified under oath to the specifics of what occurred between her and Albert; whereas he hadn't taken the stand at all. Now Albert was launching verbal missiles at P. J., perhaps to promote his career and for selfish economic motives. I feared that his widely publicized statements could have a chilling effect on victims of crimes by other celebrities.

This type of character smear by the rich and powerful and their highly paid legal frontpeople can deter women from coming forward to cooperate with the criminal justice system. Both P. J. and I spoke out publicly against Albert's verbal attacks. We wanted to demonstrate that we would not be deterred by Albert's self-serving war of words.

"How can [Marv] benefit from therapy if he still hasn't taken responsibility for his actions and instead blames everyone else for what has happened to him?" P. J. asked in a public statement. "In my life I have seen many injustices and I have often stood by silently. For the rest of my life, I do not intend to sit quietly by again when I see an injustice meted out or when I am a victim of it."

Albert had many friends in the media who were anxious to help him. They were part of the Old Boys' network. Some of them might have worried that the wrongs they had inflicted on certain women in their own lives would become public and that they might find themselves in legal and career nightmares similar to Albert's.

Still, P. J. and I weren't totally alone. At least one columnist was repulsed by Albert's conduct. "The guy probably hasn't gone to the dry cleaners yet to pick up the suits he wore to his trial, but he's already in the middle of a round of high-profile media appearances designed to begin the image-healing process," Richard Roeper wrote in the *Chicago Sun-Times*. "You might think a guy who less than two months ago pleaded guilty to BITING A WOMAN might be a little embarrassed and would show some humility and remorse, but not Marv."

After a year in counseling, Albert reappeared in public to announce that he had been rehired by Madison Square Garden. Its president said that Albert had been a loyal employee for more than thirty years and that they considered him to be "part of the family." P. J. and I were shocked, angered, and disgusted by the news. Obviously, loyalty to the Old Boys' network meant more to them than protecting women from violence. Since injury to women didn't seem to be a consideration to Madison Square Garden officials, I wondered what they planned to do next. Would they offer O. J. Simpson a job at Madison Square Garden as well?

Albert apologized to his fiancée, his family, and friends, and said what he did was wrong. His apology to Vanessa Perhach was weak. He never bothered to apologize to P. J. Masten at all. Instead, he made a transparent attempt to cast himself as the real victim, saying "I went through a nightmare." However, I believe that sympathy should be reserved for crime victims, not those convicted of assault and battery against women.

Madison Square Garden officials said they had talked to Albert's counselor and felt reassured that he wouldn't attack again. His criminal conviction was expunged from the record. Later, NBC hired him back as well. How could they have so much confidence in a man who had never publicly taken full and specific responsibility for his actions or publicly apologized to his victims?

Not only did Albert receive minimal punishment from the criminal justice system, but he was rewarded by being allowed to resume his prestigious career less than a year after he was convicted. It was a slap in the face to victims of violence. Marv Albert shouldn't have been sentenced to sit temporarily on the sidelines—he should have spent some time in jail. It's extremely disturbing to me that protecting Marv Albert seemed to take priority over protecting women from violence. Still, I was very proud of P. J. for stepping forward to testify in this case. Had it not been for her courage, Marv Albert might never have pled guilty to a crime.

Empowerment Lesson

Step forward when you can help with information on a criminal (or civil) case. When a woman supports another woman, it can make a difference in setting the record straight and obtaining a conviction.

TOMMY LEE'S MOTLEY TO-DO

Mötley Crüe singer Tommy Lee is no stranger to breaking the law, but like so many other celebrity bad boys, he seems particularly adept at avoiding all its consequences. It's not just because he can afford expensive lawyers either; it has a lot to do with the justice system, from the district attorney all the way through the courts.

I became involved with Lee in the fall of 1996 after he attacked my client Henry Trappler, a freelance photographer, outside the Viper Room nightclub in Los Angeles on September 29. That night, Henry was standing outside the Viper Room with his camera when Lee came out of the club. With no provocation whatsoever from Henry, Lee attacked him and grabbed his camera. He threw Henry to the ground so hard that he suffered multiple fractures of the pelvis and a fractured rib. A bystander recorded the incident on videotape. Henry was hospitalized for four days, was housebound for a number of months, and required crutches to walk.

Although law enforcement had a copy of that tape, several weeks went by before the district attorney's office filed a charge against Tommy Lee. Even then, it was weak—a misdemeanor charge of battery with serious injury. The police had recommended that the DA file a felony charge of assault with force likely to produce great bodily injury, but it was obvious that then-DA Gil Garcetti had a two-tiered system of justice—one for celebrities and one for everyone else. If my client had thrown Lee to the ground, I firmly believe that Garcetti would have thrown the book at him and broken speed records to hold a press conference announcing his tough prosecution of anyone who victimized a celebrity. In Los Angeles especially, it seems that politicians value relationships with celebrities more than with the average working person. After all, who can be more useful to them in the long run?

At the time, I even found a mailer from Garcetti to his supporters seeking to network with "influential people" they might know.

Garcetti's double standard for justice went even further in this case. He was videotaped telling celebrity photographers, "You guys are not very sympathetic." His statements, and his decision to file a lesser criminal charge in the Lee case, in effect, declared open season on working photographers. He seemed to be sending a message to celebrities that the district attorney's office would not use the full force of the law to protect photographers who are hurt by celebrities.

Garcetti's behavior prompted me to write to California Attorney General Dan Lungren asking him to investigate the DA's failure to file felony assault charges against Lee. I also filed a civil law suit on behalf of my client against Tommy Lee in October 1996, alleging assault and negligence.

In January 1998, Lee pled no contest in court to the misdemeanor charge. Although I urged the judge to sentence him to jail for at least as long as my client had to spend in the hospital and on crutches, the court gave him only twenty-four months of probation. Lee was also ordered to pay $17,500 in restitution to my client and was required to seek anger management counseling.

Evidently the counseling didn't work. The next month, Tommy Lee struck again. In February 1998, he was arrested after allegedly assaulting his wife Pamela Lee Anderson while she was holding their seven-week-old son. Lee's sentence of no jail time unless he violated probation in the Trappler case had been completely inadequate. It was obvious that the judicial system and the DA had failed, in the Henry Trappler case, to make it clear to Lee that he was not above the law. He seemed to be under the impression that if you could beat a drum, you could beat a human being.

I contacted the district attorney's office to urge them to request an immediate hearing on the issue of whether Tommy Lee's probation should be revoked because of the current allegations involving the attack on Pamela Lee. In March, during a court date where Lee paid my client $17,500 in restitution, the judge revoked his probation. Lee tried to shake Henry Trappler's hand outside the courtroom but I discouraged it. "Say you're sorry in court in our civil case," I told him. The next month, as the civil case was headed for trial, Lee settled it, taking one item off his very full legal plate.

In May, during the formal hearing on the probation violation, the judge decided some jail time *was* appropriate. He ordered him to spend six months in the county jail and the remainder of the time on probation.

Had Tommy Lee been sentenced to jail the first time for his assault on Henry Trappler, Pamela Lee Anderson and their child might have avoided his assault, and the court system could have been spared the time and expense it took to address Lee's disregard for the law and the courts.

Empowerment Lesson

Exposing a double standard of justice is important. Victims of celebrities should receive as much sympathy and respect as do celebrities. If elected officials do not make celebrities accountable, celebrities may victimize others in the future.

You can fight fame. If you are injured by a celebrity, understand that you have rights, too. Fight back in the civil justice system to receive compensation and demand that the criminal justice system make the celebrity accountable.

THE PAKISTANI CRICKET STAR
PLAYS GAMES WITH PATERNITY

It never ceases to amaze me how some fathers can be so casual about shirking their parental responsibilities.

Consider Imran Khan, captain of the Pakistan National Cricket Team, who led his country to the World Cup championship in 1992. In 1987, Khan met Sita White, the daughter of the late British industrialist Lord Gordon White, and the two began a year-long relationship. Even after it ended, Sita, who lived in Beverly Hills, continued to see her old boyfriend on and off.

Sita said in 1991, when she met with Kahn in Los Angeles, she told him she wanted to have his child. According to Sita, he was enthusiastic about the idea, particularly about having a son. Shortly thereafter, Sita became pregnant. She called Khan at his London residence to tell him the news. Sita remarked that he thought it was "great" and hoped it would be a boy.

Four months later, an ultrasound revealed that Sita was carrying a girl. She said she was shocked by Imran Khan's negative reaction.

Still, according to Sita, they continued to talk during her pregnancy and even discussed potential names. Sita rejected the suggestion that they call their daughter Sherbano, which means "tigress" in Pakistani. They decided on Tyrian Jade, in part because the initials "TJ" stood for "tiger joy."

Tyrian was born at Cedars-Sinai Hospital in Los Angeles on June 15, 1992. Sita said that she called Khan that day and put the phone next to her baby so he could hear her cry. Khan wanted to know who the baby looked like and seemed pleased to hear that she looked like him.

Imran Kahn and Sita talked periodically by phone over the next few years. Imran Kahn had by now relocated to Pakistan. According to Sita, he never made an effort to see Tyrian or contribute anything to the child's support, although he did inquire about his daughter's well-being and asked that she be raised with love and discipline. Sita told her daughter about her father and explained that he lived a great distance away.

In 1996, Kahn decided to run for Pakistani prime minister, but Pakistani law dictates that a person who has fathered a child outside of marriage is ineligible to serve as prime minister.

Sita had never asked Imran Kahn for one penny of child support, but she wanted him to acknowledge that he was the father of her child. Sita retained me to help establish paternity and we filed a motion in Los Angeles County Superior Court. We also discussed with the press our view that no election, no high office, no political position should be more important than a father's relationship with his child. In fact, anyone who denies his own child doesn't deserve the right to enjoy political power. Tyrian had a right to know who her father was. We wanted him to agree to a blood test immediately, to put the issue to rest once and for all, but he neither took the test nor acknowledged his child during his political campaign. The Pakistani press went wild with the story.

Imran Kahn lost his bid for prime minister. I'd like to think that the Pakistani people made an important statement by not electing a man who refused to acknowledge his child in order to win political power.

Even though he didn't take the blood test, the court issued a default judgment in 1997 declaring him to be Tyrian Jade's father.

Sadly, Sita died suddenly in May 2004, leaving Tyrian Jade without a mother or father with whom the child could live. According to published reports, Imran talks to his daughter once a week, but will not have her live with him. He reportedly is supporting a bid by Sita's sister, Carolina, to be her guardian.

Empowerment Lesson

Nothing—neither fame nor political power—should be more important than your own child. There is no excuse for denying paternity and mothers should fight to make sure that their child's paternity is established as a matter of law.

MY THREE ROUNDS WITH MIKE TYSON

Somebody had to hold Mike Tyson accountable. That's what I felt when I read that Tyson would be allowed to seek the heavyweight boxing crown despite a prison sentence for raping a woman—a crime for which he has shown little or no remorse.

In 1992, Tyson was convicted of both rape and criminal deviate conduct. The victim was eighteen-year-old Desiree Washington. The message of this verdict was clear. The jury didn't care that Washington had gone to his hotel room willingly in the early hours of the morning or that she sat on a corner of his bed to watch television. She still had the right to say "No" or "Stop," and he had a duty to stop in his tracks once she said it.

He didn't stop, and that's why he was guilty of rape.

The victory for women was that one woman's word against a rich and powerful man was finally taken at face value. One woman's word was believed. She may have lost her fight with him in the bedroom, but not in the courtroom.

For his part, Tyson didn't seem to care, telling the judge, "I didn't hurt anybody—no black eyes, no broken ribs." Tyson seemed to think his acts against women could be judged by the rules of boxing. The fact is, rape hurts women even if there are no black eyes and broken ribs. Desiree Washington suffered from Tyson's acts of violence and continued to suffer from his arrogant disregard for her rights.

If Tyson wanted to be a role model, he should have bowed his head and apologized to Desiree Washington and every other woman he had hurt, and told other men that they must respect a woman's right to say no. Instead, as soon as he was released from an Indiana prison—after serving only half of a six-year sentence—he wanted to return to boxing and regain its top title. It looked as if the Nevada Athletic Commission was going to let him.

Although I wasn't representing a client, I couldn't stand by and see him rewarded for his actions. In March 1996, I wrote to the Athletic Commission asking that it change the rules and ban those convicted of rape or any act of felony violence and/or sex crimes from competing for the heavyweight boxing crown. Young people look to our country's athletes as role models. What kind of role model is a man who raped a woman?

We shouldn't help to glorify or reward rapists or anyone who inflicts violence outside the ring. The best lesson for young people to grasp is that if they violate the law by hurting another human being, there will be consequences both inside and outside of the criminal justice system. I thought that banning Mike Tyson from this competition would be the best way to send a message to the world: Women aren't punching bags or objects for a sexual knockout.

My organization, the Women's Equal Rights Legal Defense and Education Fund, asked the Commission to hold a hearing on this request where I could testify, but they ignored it. They gave Tyson permission to fight Evander Holyfield in 1996. Holyfield knocked him out in the eleventh round.

During a rematch in 1997, Tyson displayed his true colors and made headlines during the fight, when, to the horror of the millions watching, he bit Holyfield's left ear. Still, the referee let him continue the fight and Tyson subsequently gnawed off part of Holyfield's right ear.

I went to the Nevada Athletic Commission's hearing on the matter in July 1997, where I gave *them* an earful: Had the Athletic Commission banned convicted rapists from boxing, as I had requested earlier, Evander Holyfield would have his ears intact. I asked them not to side with those for whom greed was a paramount motive. I asked that they ban Tyson from competing for the heavyweight boxing crown. This time they listened to me and others who expressed outrage. The commission revoked his boxing license and fined him three million dollars for biting Holyfield's ears.

Eventually Tyson returned to the ring—and to his other activities as well. With Mike Tyson, it was obviously not a matter of *if* he'd strike again, but *when*.

In August 2001, I finally got directly involved with Tyson after yet another allegation of rape surfaced, this time from a woman who said that Tyson had raped her on July 16, 2001, at his rental residence in the Southern California mountain resort town of Big Bear Lake. Tyson was training there in preparation for an upcoming fight in Denmark.

The district attorney's office of San Bernardino County issued a press release indicating they would not prosecute Mike Tyson on an allegation of rape because they believed "that the case cannot be proven beyond a reasonable doubt—based on currently known information."

I represented the woman alleged to be the victim of Mike Tyson. She was a fifty-year-old grandmother who lived in California and worked as a cashier in a retail store. At every stage of the investigation by both the sheriff's office and the district attorney's office, the woman cooperated to the best of her ability. The same cannot be said of Tyson, who reportedly refused to be personally interviewed by law enforcement, raising the question of what, if anything, he had to hide. While he declared his innocence on television, my client cooperated with law enforcement and was interviewed by them. I called on Tyson to do the same. Apparently he chose to send his attorneys to talk to investigators rather than appearing himself.

The DA's office indicated that four prosecutors, including one who specializes in sex crimes, had reviewed this case and that they all reached the same conclusion. What the DA's office failed to disclose is the shocking fact that, in their "countless hours" of investigation, their deputy district attorney who specializes in sex crimes never once interviewed the alleged victim.

Even worse, when my client and I did meet with the deputy DA's about this case in San Bernardino, the sex crimes deputy DA was absent from the meeting. When I inquired about her absence, I was simply told she couldn't make it. Further, when I asked whether or not it was the policy of the San Bernardino County district attorney's office to have sex crimes prosecutors meet with victims before making a filing decision, the DA's office responded that they would not answer that policy question, because they knew where I was going with it and they felt that I would use it against them.

Obviously, I believe that the sex crimes prosecutor—rather than a deputy DA who doesn't have the special training, experience, and emphasis—should interview alleged rape victims. It was improper in my judgment not to allow face-to-face or even telephone contact between the sex crimes prosecutor and the alleged victim before reaching a final filing decision. Such failure also raised a substantial question about the rights of women who alleged they were raped and what protections were really being afforded them in San Bernardino County.

The DA's refusal to disclose the reason for this failure was troubling, and just one of many issues that I had with the process in this case, which I believe was flawed. Here are just a few of the many flaws: No photographs were taken of the alleged victim's genital area at the hospital's emergency room; investigators failed to obtain the alleged victim's clothing during their emergency room visit; no female law enforcement officer or female deputy DA was present when a follow-up interview and interrogation was conducted of the alleged victim by a male deputy DA, a male detective, and a male investigator; and the alleged victim felt that the questioning was hostile.

At many stages of the process, my client indicated that she felt a negative attitude toward her and that she was being treated as a suspect rather than as a potential victim. For example, she indicated that she was threatened with prosecution if she accepted money from Tyson during the investigation. She had no such intention. If such threats occurred, I believe they were improper and raised serious questions about sensitivity and respect for alleged victims of sexual assault in the criminal justice process.

I learned that the DA's office had released my client's medical records to a defense doctor without our client's permission or any legal obligation to do so. Considering this to be a serious invasion of our client's privacy, we questioned why the DA did it. We were given to understand that this was not the normal procedure in Los Angeles County. I felt that the San Bernardino DA's approach was far less protective of the rights of alleged victims than was Los Angeles County's.

The woman went to the hospital emergency room the day after the incident. Her medical records from the examination indicated tears and lacerations to her genital area. From my discussion with the DA's office, it appeared to me that the issue for the DA was whether it was consensual sexual intercourse or rape. In a case where the accused has a previous rape conviction, there should be close scrutiny, and I believe that a jury should be permitted to decide.

I believe the integrity of the criminal justice process was severely compromised in this case, making the ultimate result inevitable. I raised these issues because I was concerned about how future victims of sexual assault, especially by high-profile men, could expect to be treated in San Bernardino County.

Mike Tyson, a convicted rapist who bit off part of Evander Holyfield's ear and has since been convicted of assaulting two motorists, is a free man today.

In the latest investigation, it was the integrity of the process, not Mike Tyson, that went down for the count. However, it's not over until it's over. Men and women alike should continue to speak out about the facts of Mike Tyson's record to make the system more responsive and protective of others in the future.

Empowerment Lesson

Go as many rounds as necessary to make a violent predator accountable.

Let public officials know that their excuses for inaction are exposing members of the public to continued risk of harm. If you have the facts and ideas for action, speak out at public hearings, even if you are the only one speaking out against the celebrity.

AVOIDING FALLOUT FROM
ROBERT BLAKE'S MEDIA STORM

Sometimes the web of interest that surrounds high-profile cases ensnares innocent people who had nothing to do with the event.

I briefly became involved in both the criminal and civil cases involving television actor Robert Blake. In 2001, Blake was accused of murdering his wife, Bonny Lee Bakley, as she sat in his car near a restaurant in Studio City, California. Blake said his wife was shot while he walked back to the restaurant to retrieve his gun. Bakley's death left the couple's child motherless.

I had represented Robert Blake's former wife, Sondra Kerr Blake, in a family law case in the 1980s. As the media frenzy grew around the Blake/Bakley murder case, two national tabloids published stories that described in detail the allegedly violent and abusive relationship between Sondra and her ex-husband, Robert Blake. As a result, Sondra and I were deluged with calls from the press asking for her response to these stories.

Sondra is a very private person and, for the past twenty years, has consistently refused to discuss the personal details of her relationship with Robert Blake. Although she was offered money for her story, she did not want to comment on Blake's criminal case outside of a legal proceeding. As her attorney, I supported her decision.

Sondra was subpoenaed to testify during the murder trial. At the trial, she wasn't asked about any details of her marriage to Blake. Instead, she was asked about and testified to one incident when she saw Blake and congratulated him on his marriage to Bakley and on their baby. In her testimony, she said that he pushed her up against a wall and told her that the baby was real, but the marriage was not.

Robert Blake was acquitted of murdering Bonny in March 2005. However, just as the estate of Nicole Brown sued O. J. Simpson in civil court following his criminal court acquittal on charges that he murdered his ex-wife, the Bakley family filed a wrongful death suit against Blake. In that civil case, Sondra was again subpoenaed to testify. The questioning took place in my office for most of the workday.

The testimony was different, however, because the plaintiff's attorney asked numerous questions about Blake and his behavior during his nineteen-year marriage to Sondra. Ultimately, however, the judge decided not to allow Sondra's deposition testimony into the civil trial.

It took a great deal of courage for Sondra to disclose personal details of her marital relationship, especially because Mr. Blake was sitting across from her in my conference room as she testified, but she did it.

I admired Sondra's grace under pressure and was happy that she did not have to relive her marriage to Robert Blake publicly in the wrongful death civil trial.

On November 18, 2005, the civil jury found Mr. Blake liable for the death of Bonny Lee Bakley and awarded her children $30 million. It was similar to the result in the cases involving O. J. Simpson. Simpson was found not guilty of murder in the criminal case but liable in a civil case for causing the death of the woman who had been his wife and who was the mother of his children.

Civil cases require less proof than criminal cases; a criminal jury may acquit a celebrity, whereas a civil jury may want to make a celebrity accountable.

Empowerment Lesson

If you are married to a high-profile person, you may find that if and when your marriage ends, public interest in your relationship remains high.

In addition, although you may have an expectation of privacy about certain events in your relationship, you may find that that privacy is invaded if you are subpoenaed to testify in a court case and the judge determines that your testimony is relevant. Seek the advice of an attorney about which questions you are required to answer and which ones you may refuse to answer.

If you do sell your story, your credibility will be attacked as biased by an economic motive. Weigh this downside before deciding whether or not to give interviews. It is better to preserve the integrity of your testimony by not speaking about it before you testify. That is the best way to maintain your dignity, credibility, and the respect that others will have for you.

PRINCESS DIANA, THE MODEL KELLY FISHER, AND THE FROG WHO WISHED TO BECOME PRINCE CHARMING

On August 14, 1997, I held a news conference that was covered around the world because it involved a beautiful international model named Kelly Fisher and her engagement to a man who had recently been seen kissing Princess Diana. As I said at the news conference that was held in my office with Kelly Fisher and her mother, Judith Dunaway, it was a tale of romance and betrayal. Here is what I said that day:

> We are here today to announce the filing of a lawsuit this morning in L.A. County Superior Court, Santa Monica branch, on behalf of Kelly Fisher against Dodi Fayed.
>
> Until a week ago Ms. Fisher, of Malibu, California, was engaged to Mr. Fayed and publicly wore his ring. Mr. Fayed asked her parents for permission to marry her in November of 1996 and her parents consented to the marriage. Mr. Fayed confirmed his commitment with a gift of an engagement ring in December of 1996 and then with another ring several months later. Numerous friends and Kelly's family were aware of the engagement.
>
> Ms. Fisher and Mr. Fayed met in Paris in July of 1996. They began dating and fell in love. They spent a great deal of time together during the following year. They stayed on many occasions at the Beverly Hills Hotel, the Pierre Hotel in New York, various hotels in London and Paris, on family yachts in the South of France, and with his family in apartments in London and in Paris.
>
> Long before she met Mr. Fayed Ms. Fisher was a successful and busy model who had been actively working in the modeling field

since the age of 17. Ms. Fisher had appeared in various magazines both in the United States and in Europe and was a well established and respected model who was very much in demand. At Mr. Fayed's request Ms. Fisher placed her career at risk by curtailing her acceptance of modeling assignments on the strength of promises that he made to her. Mr. Fayed wanted Ms. Fisher to put her career in second place behind him and to spend more time with him and less time on her modeling career. Because she loved him and trusted him and relied on his promises she agreed to substantially limit her bookings, engagements, assignments and employment opportunities.

Ms. Fisher loved, trusted and believed in Mr. Fayed. In return he took her love and gave her every indication that they were going to get married and that he would fulfill all of his promises to her. In the end he betrayed her and has humiliated her in the eyes of her friends and family and numerous others who were aware of the relationship and have now seen the evidence of his public betrayal of Ms. Fisher. To compound matters, Ms. Fisher learned about Mr. Fayed's betrayal not from Mr. Fayed but instead from the "kiss photo" that was published and circulated around the world to Ms. Fisher's utter dismay, shock, and shame.

This was especially devastating to Ms. Fisher because just a few weeks earlier she was on Dodi's yacht in St Tropez and had every indication and belief that they would marry in the near future. He told her that he had purchased a home that they would live in together in Paradise Cove, Malibu, California and he brought her to the home to see it and told her to start shopping for furnishings. If the time period reported by the media of "the kiss" in St Tropez is accurate then it would appear that it was at the same time that Mr. Fayed was spending at least part of his days and nights with Ms. Fisher in an intimate relationship. Mr. Fayed needs to take responsibility for the woman that he "left at the altar" and treated with such total disrespect.

We are going public with this information because we care about Princess Diana and her future. We would like the Princess, who has suffered greatly in the past, to know of Ms. Fisher's experiences with Mr. Fayed so that she can make an informed decision regarding her future and that of her children. Ms. Fisher is willing to meet with the Princess anywhere in the world, on a confidential basis, at which time Ms. Fisher would provide the Princess with a great deal of information which we believe the Princess would find to be important but which is not being made public at this time.

We think the Princess should know what has happened with Ms. Fisher and how she and her family have suffered and are suffering. Suffice it to say that they wish they had never met Mr. Fayed. We care about Princess Diana and believe that she is entitled to all information which may be relevant to life choices which she may make for herself and her children.

We wonder whether Dodi Fayed has told the Princess that he was engaged to Ms. Fisher at the time that he and the Princess were alleged to have been kissing and hugging in the south of France and that Ms. Fisher was nearby on a yacht owned by the Fayed family. We wonder if he told the Princess that he had given his fiancée two engagements rings and that they had spoken about getting married in a private ceremony on August 9th, 1997.

This is a situation which is all too common. A young woman who fell in love, changed her life to suit a man whom she trusted and loved—a man who wheedled and wormed his way into her family and gained the trust of her parents and siblings, gave her an engagement ring, promised to marry her, and who led her emotionally all the way up to the altar and abandoned her when they were almost there. He threw her love away in a callous way with no regard for her whatsoever.

There is a story about a Princess who was once married to a Prince who betrayed her and turned into a frog. This may be a case of a frog who wishes to become a Prince Charming. Mr. Fayed may be able to afford princely clothing and act as though he is of royal blood, but beneath that exterior there is no prince, only a frog in prince's clothing, or should I say Harrod's clothing?

This was a story of romance, and it is now a tale of betrayal.

Mr. Fayed who once produced "Chariots of Fire" has now caused his fiancée to endure an emotional trial by fire.

Ms. Fisher is emotionally devastated and traumatized by Mr. Fayed's mistreatment of her. She is unable to speak to the press today because she breaks down in tears whenever she begins to relive what she has personally suffered. She did, however wish me to set the record straight and explain some of what she has endured as a result of her relationship with Mr. Fayed.

I commend Kelly on her courage in filing this lawsuit and in finding the strength to appear today. We look forward to asserting, protecting and vindicating her rights in a court of law.

Kelly's mother, Judith Dunaway added:

I can only say that I am terribly upset by the way Dodi Fayed has treated my daughter Kelly.

During the course of their relationship, Dodi telephoned me frequently to tell me how much he loved Kelly and to discuss with me his plans for their future, and how much he wanted Kelly to be the mother of his children.

It was at my other daughter's wedding last November 1, 1996 when he asked me for permission to marry Kelly. He and Kelly appeared to be very much in love and he appeared to be a kind and responsible person who would love, honor and care for my daughter and respect her, her family, and her career. Unfortunately, we now know that appearances can be deceiving.

No one's daughter deserves to be treated as my daughter was. Kelly loved him, trusted him, and has been treated very cruelly by him. Dodi Fayed should be ashamed of his treatment of Kelly, and he has not only hurt her, but my whole family. He had integrated himself into our family and I considered him a friend.

I love Kelly and support her in her effort to achieve the justice she deserves.

Unfortunately, although this story was widely covered in the United Kingdom and elsewhere, Princess Diana never took Kelly up on her offer to meet, and therefore never received the confidential but important information from Ms. Fisher that we thought Princess Diana should have.

Instead, on August 31, 1997, the Princess's life tragically ended when the car in which she was riding with Dodi Fayed crashed in a tunnel in Paris, France. I was in my office when I received calls from the press informing me of the terrible crash. Everyone wanted a comment from Kelly, but Kelly was devastated by the news and went into seclusion.

Finally on September 1, 1997, I held a news conference and stated:

> In light of the tragedy that has occurred and out of respect for the Fayed family's loss, Kelly Fisher has decided that she will not pursue her breach of contract lawsuit against Mr. Fayed. She filed the lawsuit on August 14, 1997, against Dodi Fayed because she felt that Dodi had made a specific financial promise to her and she believed that he should have to live up to his promises, since she had significantly curtailed her modeling career based on his promises. She also felt that he should honor the check which he had written to her and which had been returned from the bank stamped "account closed."
>
> However, out of respect for the tragedy and tremendous loss the Fayed family has suffered, she has authorized me as her attorney to dismiss her lawsuit against Mr. Fayed. Although she does have the legal right to pursue the lawsuit against his estate after his death, she is voluntarily choosing not to exercise that right.
>
> Kelly suffered greatly because of the break-up of the relationship with Mr. Fayed. She was engaged to him and they had planned to marry August 9, 1997. Kelly loved Dodi very much and is devastated by his loss and that of Princess Diana. Nothing is more important than the life of a human being. In light of this enormous tragedy, Kelly forgives Dodi for all of his past injustices against her and she will try to go on with her life with the loving support of her family and friends.

She also wishes to state that she admired and respected Princess Diana. The world has suffered a great loss with the Princess's tragic death and Kelly's prayers will be for the Princess's children, for her family, and for Dodi Fayed.

Since that time, two inquiries were opened into the tragedy that caused the deaths of Princess Diana, Dodi Fayed, and the driver Henri Paul, and the injury to bodyguard Trevor Rees-Jones. The first inquiry by the French authorities led to the questioning of many who knew Dodi Fayed, including Kelly. She fully cooperated with the investigation because she felt that it was her duty to provide any facts that could help investigators get to the truth of why that crash might have occurred.

Similarly, when Scotland Yard contacted Kelly in connection with their coroner's inquiry, Kelly fully cooperated and provided them with all information that might be relevant to their inquiry. I was very proud of her for that.

The British coroner's conclusions have not yet been made public, but many people are awaiting his report. As for Kelly, she has gone on with her life. She is still a beautiful international model who is very much in demand, and she has my continued respect and admiration for her dedication to the truth about her relationship with Dodi Fayed.

Empowerment Lesson

It is inevitable that most of us will be hurt in our personal relationships at some time in our lives. If you are a woman in love, you may be particularly vulnerable because you want to trust your partner with your heart, your body, and your life.

If a promise is made but not kept, take this as a warning sign that danger may lie ahead. Demand an explanation for a broken promise. If the explanation is suspicious or inadequate, let your partner know that you do not accept it. If it is an important promise that can adversely affect your economic position, find out if you have any legal rights to enforce the promise and then make a careful decision as to whether or not you wish to exercise those rights.

Your partner's failure to keep an important promise should be a red flag signaling that he may not be deserving of your trust, and that if you continue a relationship with him, you will likely be hurt again.

CHAPTER 5

Fight Back at Work

DEBBIE THORNE VOLKERT AND THE DOUBLE STANDARD

Before I started my law firm, I considered working for the Los Angeles County District Attorney's office. During my job interview, the recruiter asked me several sexist questions: What would I do if my daughter became sick while I had an important case in court? What if I became pregnant? They even asked about abortion. I answered them, but after thinking about it, I went back the next day and told the interviewer to tear up my application.

Even though I really wanted to work for the DA's office, I concluded that the interviewer's questions raised red flags about their treatment of women that I should not ignore. I didn't take the job. (Ironically, years later, that interviewer ran for a judgeship and called to ask for my endorsement. He'd forgotten about the interview, but I hadn't. I endorsed his opponent, who won.)

I started my own law firm to help other women and minorities fight employment discrimination. Debbie Thorne Volkert was one of the women I was particularly proud to represent. Thanks to her willingness to fight for justice, some job interview questions will never be asked again.

In 1978, Debbie, who was working as a clerk at the El Segundo, California, police department, decided to apply to be a police officer with the city. She was required to take a physical agility test and a psychological examination. She passed those and was ranked second overall on the eligibility list. Also as a condition of the job, she was required to take a polygraph test. To this day, I don't understand what the questions she was asked had to do with her fitness to be a police officer.

She was asked, "When was the first time you ever had sex?" She was asked if she'd ever had an abortion or miscarriage and, if so, what the father's name was. She was asked what birth control pills or devices she used, and even about the regularity of her menstrual cycle.

Debbie answered truthfully. During the interview she also revealed that, before she applied for the job, she'd had an affair with an El Segundo police officer.

Debbie didn't get the job. The male law enforcement officer, however, got to keep his. It was clear that the city was applying different moral standards to women than to men, and we sued over this unconscionable fishing expedition into Debbie Thorne Volkert's private life.

It was a hard battle that took over eight years and a trip to the U.S. Court of Appeals, but we won it. The Appeals Court found that Debbie had been denied the job because of sex-stereotyped assumptions about women not having the strength or ability to be police officers. The court also found that El Segundo officials had applied different moral standards to women than to men, and ruled that to be illegal.

Was the long battle worth it? Absolutely. We not only won an important victory in Debbie's case, but the court placed new restrictions on a governmental employer's right to ask questions about private, off-the-job sexual activity. It set a new precedent across the country and was immediately cited in at least twenty cases nationwide.

Debbie told reporters, "No one should have to go through what I went through to get a job. My privacy was deeply invaded, and that can never be undone. Nothing will ever make up for the career I lost, or for the pain and embarrassment I suffered, but this decision gives us all a measure of protection against the kind of nightmare I endured."

Debbie's courage gave women and men new protections against invasions into their right to privacy, and new opportunities for employment without having to sacrifice that right.

Not long after this case, another woman came to me and related an equally bizarre experience. She said that when she applied for a job as a secretary with a local community college, she was required to take a physical examination that included a breast exam. I went to a meeting of the college's board of trustees and asked one question: "Why does she need a breast exam? She isn't required to type with her breasts."

The requirement was immediately eliminated.

Empowerment Lesson

Everyone enjoys a zone of privacy. You are not required to answer questions about your sex life in order to get a job.

NOT PART OF THE JOB DESCRIPTION

In 1989, Julia Williams went to work as a Safety Police Officer for Los Angeles County. After a year, she accepted a position at the county's Museum of Natural History, where the Chief of Safety Police was Hugh Crooks. In 1992, Julia alleged that she was sexually harassed by Chief Crooks. We filed a lawsuit alleging sexual harassment and retaliation. In her complaint, Julia alleged that in July of that year, after the two had taken a fraud awareness class, he attempted to kiss her after he drove her home. She also alleged that the following month, at Black Family Reunion Day, Crooks grabbed her breast and told Julia he wanted to have sex with her.

In September 1992, Crooks went further, according to Julia's lawsuit. As she guarded the home of the museum director, Crooks came to the house and attempted to have sexual relations with her. As Julia later testified, Crooks pushed her onto a bed at the residence and put his hands under her clothing and fondled her breast. Just as Julia thought she was about to be raped, another officer arrived at the residence and Crooks stopped.

Julia testified that after she complained to Crooks's boss at the museum, she was transferred to another museum. She believed this to be a retaliatory act.

In 1995 after the trial of our case, a jury awarded Julia $150,000 in damages, even though she hadn't lost her job or been demoted as a result of the harassment.

It was an important verdict because it established that a jury regarded sexual harassment and retaliation to be extremely serious, even if the victim did not lose time from work and was not fired. A victim who is brave enough to come forward and report the wrongful conduct deserves compensation, and employees need not leave their job in order to sue their employer.

The verdict sent a message to women that they have a right to a workplace free of sexual harassment. Supervisors have no right to grab their breasts, make lewd sexual statements about their bodies, or suggest that they would like to engage in sexual intercourse, if such advances are unwelcome to the woman who is the target of such sexual conduct.

The verdict also emphasized that employees should be able to come forward with a sexual harassment complaint without fear of retaliation. Many women fear asserting their rights because they think that their employers will label them as troublemakers rather than recognize them as victims. Laws protecting employees from retaliation allow them to assert their rights without fear of economic consequences.

In this case the jury sent a message to Los Angeles County that it had failed in its responsibility to protect Julia Williams from both sexual harassment and retaliation after she complained of it. Government should set an example of what the law requires of both the public and private sector, and this jury found that Los Angeles County failed in that task when it transferred Ms. Williams after she complained and promoted Chief Crooks, the one she accused of harassment.

Julia waged a successful battle, despite the sexual harassment and retaliation that were so emotionally devastating to her. She was willing to do it, not only because of what she had suffered but because she wanted to help other women. Her courage was an inspiration to us all.

Empowerment Lesson

Victims of sexual harassment need to realize that the issue is not about sex. It's about abuse of power. Usually, the person in power is a man and the victim of abuse is a woman.

Until women are able to attain positions of power rather than being forced to continue to work in subordinate roles, the problem of sexual harassment will continue to run rampant. Our goal must be to achieve a workforce integrated at all levels with women (as well as minorities).

Sometimes, the only way to combat sexual harassment is to speak up, fight back, and file lawsuits. No woman or man is required to tolerate or respond to unwanted sexual advances from a supervisor or a coworker as a condition of employment. Suffering in silence doesn't make the problem go away. Quitting and finding work elsewhere are often ineffective solutions because very few workplaces are safe havens from sexual harassment.

If you find yourself in such a situation, keep a diary of the incidents, including the date, time of day, and specific instances of harassment. Find out if any other employees have been treated similarly.

Talk to a lawyer. Seeking the advice of a lawyer doesn't mean the next step is filing a lawsuit. A lawyer can advise you about many things, including the various time limitations that exist, should you wish to sue.

Your case may also be settled confidentially without the need to file a lawsuit. Employers may not wish to take the risk of a greater liability that might occur in a trial, and they would often prefer to settle than risk the embarrassment and public recognition that a high-level executive or a certain well-known business has engaged in or condoned sexual harassment.

If you can prove you were sexually harassed and retaliated against, you can sue even if you have not lost your job or any pay.

Find out what rights you have, whether it is still timely to assert them, and whether you have sufficient damages to make it worthwhile to proceed. Knowledge is power, and after you learn what rights you have, you can decide whether or not to exercise them.

Just remember, speak up, fight back, and—when appropriate—file a lawsuit.

THE MAN WHO WAS MAN-HANDLED

Sexual harassment doesn't just happen to women. We proved this in our case of Christian v. J & J Snack Foods Corporation, which may have been the first case of its kind in the country, in which a heterosexual male employee won a sexual harassment jury verdict against another male who identifies himself as heterosexual. Frank Christian went to work as a maintenance mechanic at J & J Snack Foods Corporation in 1993. His first six months were uneventful; but when the thirty-two-year-old came under the supervision of a new boss, Pedro Gutierrez, his workday turned into a nightmare.

According to evidence proven at the trial of Frank's case, Gutierrez frequently grabbed and slapped Frank, and squeezed Frank's genitals, saying "Suck me" or "Blow me." On one occasion, Gutierrez thrust his penis into Frank's backside. On another, when Frank was on the floor doing some work, Gutierrez grabbed Frank's head and pulled it to his own crotch.

Frank was horrified and humiliated. He didn't feel comfortable challenging Gutierrez about his behavior—after all, he was the boss. When he tried to complain to company officials, they dismissed Gutierrez's behavior as "horseplay."

The conditions at work affected Frank at home. His wife Mary was shocked at the stories he brought home from J & J. She later said, "The sexual harassment he endured hurt him and our family. I watched a man who had previously been my best friend and the best friend a father could be to his children plummet into depression. There were times when I wanted to leave but I felt that I should stand behind him and try to let him know that no matter what, I would be there."

On the job, J & J executives continued to ignore Frank's pleas for help and retaliated against him to the point where he no longer felt able to go to work.

Frank contacted our firm for assistance and we were more than happy to represent him. No one should have to go to work and be afraid that their supervisor will sexually harass them. Moreover, all employees should be able to expect that companies will take appropriate action to stop such unlawful conduct once it is brought to their attention.

We filed a lawsuit against J & J Snack Foods. During the trial, J & J tried to argue that because both Frank and his boss were married and identified themselves as heterosexuals, that there could be no sexual harassment. The jury didn't buy that defense. It ruled that J & J Snack Foods and Pedro Gutierrez were liable for sexual harassment, and that J & J was further liable for retaliation, negligent supervision, and intentional infliction of emotional distress.

The jury awarded damages totaling almost $5 million. This verdict is a significant victory for men who deserve and are legally entitled to equal protection under the law against sexual harassment in the workplace. The jury sent a message that it makes no difference whether the victim is male or female, or whether the perpetrator is heterosexual or gay. Companies must take sexual harassment complaints seriously. Employers have a duty to investigate, take appropriate remedial action to protect the victim, and discipline the wrongdoers.

I was very proud of the excellent work done at trial by my partner Nathan Goldberg and associate Renée Mochkatel.

It took a great deal of courage for the mechanic and his wife to fight back against a large company. We hope that their courage in this case will serve as a continuing inspiration to other working people that they need not cower before big corporations who have done them wrong.

Empowerment Lesson

Men and women alike benefit from strong laws prohibiting sexual harassment in the workplace. If you are a victim of harassment by a member of either gender, complain to your employer and then take appropriate action if you are retaliated against because of your complaint.

FIGHTING FOR PATIENTS WHO CAN'T FIGHT FOR THEMSELVES

Sandra Bardenilla's fight for the rights of patients in comas began on August 26, 1981, with what should have been a fairly routine patient admission to the Kaiser Medical Facility in Harbor City, California.

Sandra was the nursing supervisor in the facility's intensive care unit when Clarence Herbert was admitted in a comatose state. Doctors Neil Leonard Barber and Joseph Nejdl, after consulting with family members, ordered that food and water be discontinued to Mr. Herbert. Sandra protested to Kaiser that the patient was being left to starve and dehydrate to death, even though he was not brain dead, and even though he had been in a coma only five days and still had vital signs.

She asked that clear guidelines be provided for her nurses under these circumstances. When Kaiser refused to take this issue seriously and develop these guidelines, she felt she could not continue working at such a place and felt forced to resign.

Sandra was so concerned that she filed a complaint with the Health Department, which led the District Attorney to charge the doctors with murder. After a preliminary hearing, Judge Brian Chahan decided not to order the doctors to stand trial for murder. The judge said, "The question is, should one prolong the living or dying process by heroic efforts." He concluded that the decision should be left to the doctors, and that whether a patient with an 8 percent to 12 percent chance of guarded recovery should be given a chance was a question of philosophic determination and not a question of law.

Our law firm thought otherwise. The issue in the case was not heroic measures. The issue was whether it is a criminal act to deprive a patient, who had only been in a coma for five days, of food and water—without which he would certainly die, and in fact, did die only six days later, as any one of us would even if we were not in a coma. We believed it was an issue of ordinary care and human decency, not a question of heroics at all. We felt it was an issue of doctors playing God, and therefore not only a philosophical question, but one of life and death, and one with which the law can and must deal.

I said that if the law and hospitals do not deal with these issues, then patients will be forced to play Russian Roulette with their lives; whether they live or die or are given a reasonable time to come out of the coma will depend not on the rule of law, but on which doctor treats them. I argued that the ramifications were terrifying.

In these circumstances, it is particularly important that hospitals have guidelines for their medical and nursing staffs on the issue of terminating food, water, and medicine to patients in a coma. It is this clarification that Sandra sought, but instead of being thanked for raising one of the most important medical-ethical-legal issues of our time, her request was denied and she claims she was told to apologize to the doctors for making them angry.

This created an intolerable situation for Sandra, as she could not continue to work at a job where she believed she would be forced to place herself and other nurses in jeopardy of violating both the criminal law and the Nurse Practice Act. This forced her to resign and take a job elsewhere earning substantially less than she earned at Kaiser.

We therefore filed a lawsuit against Kaiser for breach of implied covenant of good faith and fair dealing and for wrongful discharge. Sandra sought lost wages and damages. After trial of our case by my partner Nathan Goldberg, a jury returned a verdict in favor of our client. We litigated this case because Sandra and our law firm believed that hospitals had to learn that they might be subject to civil liability unless they developed guidelines. Sandra was dedicated to the protection of patients' rights and the fulfillment of her legal and ethical obligations as a nurse.

We urged the legislature to hold public hearings to clarify the rights of a patient in a coma. We said that unless they acted, there would be chaos and terror in hospitals, for even the judge stated that his decision did not preclude the prosecution from filing similar charges in an appropriate case in the future. The question was and is one of public policy, and we all have a stake in the outcome. We felt that this case demonstrated a clear mandate for legislative action to return to nurses, patients, their families, and doctors the peace of mind that they all must have in order to survive.

Most of all we were very happy that the jury verdict in Sandra's case sent a message to other nurses that they have a right to raise significant questions of public policy involving patient care, and that legal protection exists for them in their efforts to protect and serve the community.

This issue of discontinuing food and water for a patient came back to me years later in the Terri Schiavo case. Terri Schiavo, a resident of Florida, was in what her parents believed to be a "minimally conscious state." Michael Schiavo, her husband, believed that she was in a persistent vegetative state and he asked the court for permission to disconnect her feeding tube, which would result in her death. Terri's parents, Bob and Mary Schindler, opposed the request. After a long court battle, the court set the date of March 18, 2005, for the removal of Terri's feeding tube.

As the court process ended and the legislative process failed to stop the removal of the feeding tube, a man named Robert Herring contacted me and asked me to make an offer to Terri's husband that could save Terri's life. Mr. Herring had been observing the case in the media, as millions of others had for about a year, and he was deeply moved and distressed by it.

He was a successful, socially responsible entrepreneur who had spent more than thirty years in the electronics industry as the founder and owner of HERCO Technology. In 2000, Mr. Herring sold HERCO Technology to a New York Stock Exchange listed firm. In 2003, he founded WEALTHTV, a lifestyle and entertainment television channel. As a supporter of and a believer in stem cell research and the medical breakthroughs that were occurring in that area, Mr. Herring thought there might be hope for Terri Schiavo and wondered why there was a rush to death.

Mr. Herring recognized that unless something was done immediately, Terri Schiavo was not likely to survive very long after March 18. Realizing that he was fortunate enough to be able to help, he felt that he couldn't live with himself if he did not take action. He retained my law firm to convey the following offer to Terri's husband: If Michael Schiavo agreed to transfer the legal right to decide all of Terri's current and future medical decisions to Terri's parents, Mr. Herring would pay Mr. Schiavo the amount of $1 million (subject to court approval of Terri's parents as her conservators or guardians).

The full amount was deposited into my law firm's client trust account and on March 10, 2005, we communicated Mr. Herring's offer in writing to Mr. Schiavo's attorney. This offer remained open until Monday, March 14, 2005, at 5:00 P.M. Mr. Herring sincerely hoped that it would be accepted.

We looked forward to Mr. Schiavo's response, but unfortunately he did not accept the offer. If it had been accepted, we believed it would have been a win-win situation for everyone. Instead Terri's food and water were discontinued and she died.

My client, Robert Herring, had made a creative and decisive attempt to peacefully resolve the legal dispute over Terri. Although his offer was not accepted, it was a pleasure to have represented a man of conscience who was so altruistic that he tried to save the life of a woman he had never met.

Empowerment Lesson

We all have a stake in making sure that there are laws and hospital guidelines that clarify the rights of patients who are unable to make decisions about whether or not they wish to be denied nutrition and water. Be a strong advocate for appropriate public policies and make sure that your loved ones have a written directive from you indicating what your wishes are in such circumstances.

FIGHTING AN OLD ARGUMENT

In 1993, Dr. Fawzy Salama arrived with his family in the United States to pursue the American dream. Although the Egyptian surgeon had more than twenty-two years of medical experience, he was prepared to take further medical examinations and meet residency requirements in order to work in California. However, he encountered one hurdle he had never expected—his age.

After passing his medical board examinations, Dr. Salama applied for and received written acceptance into the anesthesiology internship program at the King/Drew Medical Center in Los Angeles. After his acceptance, however, he was told he still had to interview for the internship position. It was during one of these interviews that Dr. Salama, then forty-nine, was told he was too old for the job. A faculty committee subsequently denied him the position, although it took its time notifying him about that decision.

As he waited for an explanation, Dr. Salama came to King/Drew every day to try to determine his status. One day when he arrived, security personnel handcuffed him and escorted him from the hospital premises. Shortly thereafter, he received written notice of his rejection.

Dr. Salama was devastated. He suffered a massive heart attack not long after he was told that he would not be accepted into the program. When he recovered, he contacted us and we filed a lawsuit against the medical center and Los Angeles County alleging age discrimination, violation of public policy, and breach of contract.

At trial, my partners Nathan Goldberg and John West proved that Dr. Salama's age was the reason for his rejection from the internship program. In fact, his slot had been given to a twenty-seven-year-old. The jury found that his heart attack had been caused by the discriminatory treatment he had received at King/Drew.

In December 2000, the jury awarded him $5 million in damages. Victims of age discrimination often do suffer substantial physical as well as emotional injuries. To the best of our knowledge, this case was the first in the United States in which an individual proved that an act of discrimination resulted in a heart attack, and was able to recover damages for that.

Dr. Salama showed tremendous courage in fighting back. As a result of his victory, many other employers will understand that the cost of discrimination is high and that older workers can and will fight back and win.

Empowerment Lesson

All people, even newcomers to the United States, can obtain justice in our courts when they have been victims of discrimination. They, like all Americans, are entitled to protection from age discrimination in employment.

CHAPTER 6

You Can Knock Down the Boys' Club Door

I GET THE LAST LAUGH AT THE FRIARS CLUB

Private clubs are palaces of power that carefully guard their entrances. Business deals are as likely to be done there over an after-dinner drink as they are at a conference table in a workplace. Excluding women from these clubs deprives us of the opportunity to do business on the same basis as men, and that inequality has adverse financial consequences for women.

I made this my own personal cause in 1987, with the world-renowned Friars Club, long a haven for the nation's greatest comedians and other showmen. In those days, however, I didn't find their membership policy very funny at all.

The exclusive Beverly Hills club had a roster that read like a Who's Who of Entertainment. Among the members were Bob Hope, Milton Berle, Dean Martin, Sammy Davis Jr., and Frank Sinatra. Membership also included people from all occupations—that is, if you were a man. There were no dues-paying female members of the club.

I first thought of joining the Friars Club after visiting it as a guest of a member. Not only did I fall in love with the Cobb salad, I also enjoyed the good humor and friendliness of the members I met. Plus, the club was very close to my office.

I decided I'd like to join. As word circulated that I was planning to apply, one member suggested that I consider becoming

an honorary member. I respectfully declined. It would be a dis-
honor for me to become an honorary member of a club that
discriminated against women. I wanted to become a full, dues-
paying member with all the rights and privileges that the men
enjoyed.

Comedian Milton Berle, then the president of the Friars' Beverly Hills chapter, asked me why I wanted to join the club. I mentioned the Cobb salad.

"Well, you know, you'd be the first woman member," he said.

"Oh, really?" I replied.

He said, "You knew that, didn't you?"

We both laughed. He said that he would be happy to send me
an application for full membership. First, however, I had to find
two sponsors. The first member I asked refused. He was on the
Friars' board of directors and feared he'd be seen as a trouble-
maker if he sponsored me. He suggested the well-known comedian Dick Shawn.

Dick said, "Oh, I love you! I'd absolutely be happy to sponsor
you."

I think it was one day later that he literally dropped dead on stage
during his act. People thought it was a joke, but sadly, it was not.

I went back to Milton Berle. He said, "Gloria, not only will I
make the motion for your admission, I will second my own motion. You think it's because you're a woman. Wrong. It's to lower
the average age of members of the club—because the average age
is dead."

I think it also helped that his wife Ruth was a big fan of the
Equal Rights Amendment, and I had been publicly advocating passage of the ERA.

Certainly the climate was right. The U.S. Supreme Court had
just ordered a Rotary Club in the Los Angeles suburb of Duarte,
California, to admit its first woman member, and cities around the
country were considering ordinances that would make it illegal for

large private clubs to exclude people from membership based on sex or race.

I met with the membership committee and, in May 1987, I became the first dues-paying woman member of the Friars Club. I was so proud of my new club. We still had some details to work out, like how I would use the steam room and attend the Friars' infamous raunchy, male-only "roasts." Still, my new club had accepted me voluntarily, without being compelled to do so by a city ordinance, a lawsuit, or even a threat of a lawsuit. The action showed leadership, courage, imagination, and goodwill. I thought other all-male private clubs should act quickly to follow the Friars' lead in admitting women, rather than waiting to be dragged kicking and screaming into the twentieth century. In gratitude, I gave Milton Berle a button that said, "Men of quality respect women's equality."

Unfortunately, my club's New York chapter was less welcoming. In November of that year, while in Manhattan for an appearance on *The Phil Donahue Show*, I took advantage of the Friars' reciprocity agreement, which allowed members of the Beverly Hills club to dine at the New York Friars Club. I called to make lunch reservations for myself and some clients, only to find that the privilege was reserved for male members. I was told that the New York club's policy prohibited serving women meals until after 4 P.M. This was clearly sex discrimination by a private club. Male California Friars could have lunch there, but I couldn't—for one reason and one reason only: I was a woman. I decided to do something about it.

The next week, accompanied by reporters, I again visited the club during lunch hours. Although my membership card got me in the club's huge black and gold-trimmed entrance, Frank, the maître d', told me that lunch was out of the question.

He explained that the New York club hadn't yet changed its bylaws to admit women as members, and that even women who were guests of members were excluded from lunch. Until that changed, I would be excluded.

I was insulted and humiliated that I should be treated this way because I was a woman. After being refused the right to have lunch there, I visited the offices of the New York City Human Rights Commission where I became the first individual to file a sex-discrimination complaint against a New York City private club under a new city ordinance banning sex discrimination by such clubs. Suddenly, nobody was laughing.

A club policy of exclusion based on gender is as damaging as a policy of racial exclusion, but the New York Friars Club continued to have a policy of excluding women from lunch.

Meanwhile, back in Beverly Hills, I was having other access problems. The Friars' health club policy had me pretty steamed. Although I was a full, dues-paying member, I was not allowed to use the Friars' steam room, showers, or exercise facilities. One of the reasons given was that male members often liked to steam or sauna in the nude. I suggested by way of compromise that men and women could go in appropriately clothed or that there could be separate days for men and women. Another option was to build a new facility for women. Several members made the counter-proposal that women be allowed to join men in the sauna, if they agreed to go in nude as well. I was interested in the naked truth, not in seeing naked butts in the sauna.

Other members suggested that I find another club to join.

As far as I was concerned, the fight for women's equality wouldn't end until women were permitted both in the board rooms and in the steam rooms. After many discussions at the club, there was no resolution to the discriminatory practice. I therefore became the first person to file a complaint with California's State Board of Equalization under a new statute that could deny tax deductions for club membership to members of clubs that discriminated on the basis of gender.

As a result, the Beverly Hills Friars Club decided that women could use the health club facilities as long as they gave the club 24-hours' notice—enough time for male members to "properly clothe themselves." I immediately gave notice that I planned to use the health facilities and arrived at the health club clothed in 1890s swimwear. Once I was in the steam room with the men, most of whom were naked, I took out a tape measure and sang Peggy Lee's signature song, "Is That All There Is?" Suddenly towels snapped and men covered themselves. A little tape measure can go a long way toward assuring equal rights.

Getting the New York chapter to change their men-only lunch policy took a bit more effort. Even after the city's Human Rights Commission had found probable cause to believe that I was discriminated against because of my gender, the board of directors still refused to admit me for lunch. However, they finally caved the day after the U.S. Supreme Court upheld the New York City ordinance that barred discrimination against women at clubs with more than four hundred members.

I was in Los Angeles when I heard the news about the Supreme Court decision. I immediately called the New York Friars Club and asked if they'd heard about the decision. Yes, they had, I was told. "May I have lunch there now?" I asked.

"No, you still can't."

"Is it still because I'm a woman?" I asked.

Yes, it was.

I told them to get ready, because whether they were prepared or not, I intended to come there for lunch the next day and I was not going to accept "No" for an answer. That night I took a red-eye flight to New York and, on June 21, 1988, I held a press conference outside the club to announce that I intended to go in and have lunch.

It wasn't easy. When I arrived, comedian Henny Youngman stood in front of the door and tried to block me from going inside. His remarks to me were anything but funny.

"We want privacy and they're butting in on us," he told reporters outside the club. "We have a lot of fun here and we don't want women around."

"Stay out!" he snapped at me. "Why women want to come in, I don't know. There's no reason for it. They belong in their own club and they shouldn't take advantage of a situation that's been here for many years."

I disagreed and told him so.

"How do you know? You don't deserve nothing. You look like a well-dressed blood test," he told me, referring to my red suit.

"Your personal attacks are not going to deter me or any other woman from enjoying our rights under the United States Constitution," I replied. "Mr. Youngman, stand aside, I'm coming through. You can't block progress for women."

I pushed him back and went inside. I went up to the maître d' and told him that I was there for lunch. I once again cited the Supreme Court decision, and this time he gave me a table. Poached salmon never tasted as good as it did that day when I became the first woman to have lunch at the New York City Friars Club.

In August 1988, New York Mayor Ed Koch and I held a press conference in the club to announce the settlement of my sex discrimination charge. In settlement of my case, the New York Friars Club agreed to accept women as members for the first time in its history and allow them to use the club's facilities on the same basis as men. I had won an important victory for women.

After the conference, I noticed a flyer in the club's lobby announcing a "Men Only" Celebrity Stag Luncheon Roast for Ernest Borgnine that would be held on October 20, 1988. I'd attended stag roasts at the Beverly Hills Friars Club. I remember the first time I went, the roasts had been men-only. I tried to get some women to go with me, but they were afraid that the men would be angry at them for trying to integrate all-male roasts. One roast I attended was for Arnold Schwarzenegger on March 29, 1988. There were probably a thousand men in tuxedos there—I was the only woman. I remember Judge Harry Shafer taking bets at his table on how long I would last before I left, because the jokes were so filthy. He bet that I would stay, and he won.

The New York roast was a different story. I ordered tickets, only to be told that the settlement agreement did not include the right to attend club roasts because the events featured rough language and dirty jokes. I went anyway. On this occasion, I was actually physically pushed back by a member when I tried to enter the event. He said I should "act like a lady." I was told that the roast's rough language wasn't suitable for women. Ironically, in trying to keep me out, they called me extremely unpleasant names, four-letter words having to do with women's genital areas.

The name-calling was a strategy to deter me from exercising my right to be there, but it didn't work. When I'm called names, I see it as a good thing. It means the opposition can't articulate any logical argument—all they can do is call me names. It means they've got nothing and might as well just raise the white flag.

As an attorney and an adult, I didn't need to be protected from rough language and dirty jokes. It was wrong to exclude me from the roast simply because of my gender. The roast was attended by nearly 1,500 celebrities, lawyers, judges, and businessmen. In addition to being a social occasion, the event provided an opportunity to make new business contacts. Excluding women deprived us of the opportunity to do business on the same basis as men.

I filed another sex discrimination charge with the New York Human Rights Commission. Soon that matter was resolved as well and women were admitted to the roasts. Ever since, I've been treated most cordially at the New York Friars Club. I feel very much at home there and very welcome.

And I'm still wild about that Cobb salad.

Empowerment Lesson

Both princes and princesses belong in palaces of power, but the doors won't always open unless you fight for your rights.

Find out if your city or state has a law against private club discrimination. If not, lobby for one. If so, assert your rights under it. Don't let name-calling or fear of any kind deter you from helping to open the doors of opportunity for women.

LOCKING HORNS WITH THE ELKS

You're never too old to fight back. Just ask Dorothy Jenson and five other women in their 60s and 70s who asked me to help them challenge a group of Elks who were acting more like stubborn mules by refusing to allow women into their Lodge as members. Although in 1995 the national organization of Elks Lodges agreed to allow chapters to admit women if they wanted, the Elks Lodge in Bellflower, California, liked its Elks Club just the way it was—men only. In 1999, the hardliners found out the hard way that there were consequences for their discrimination.

For more than one hundred years, the Fraternal Order of Elks had focused on a variety of social service projects, such as helping disabled children and raising drug awareness. In 1998, the organization's 1.3 million members gave more than $160 million to charity.

Dorothy Jenson, Dona Etienne, Georgia Bonacci, Mary Harding, and their friends loved the organization and its mission to help children with physical disabilities, and had donated years of service to the Bellflower Lodge. As members of the Lady Elks, they had cooked for, waited on, and cleaned up after the men, donating thousands of hours of their time. Dorothy Jenson, 77, had served as a Lady Elk for twenty-two years and had been First Lady of the Lodge twice, when her husband was Exalted Leader. She also had served twice as president of the Lady Elks. Dona Etienne, 78, had volunteered for ten years. Georgia Bonacci had been a Lady Elk for seven years. They felt they had more than earned their place as full members of the Elks.

However, each time Dorothy and her friends applied for membership they were literally blackballed. Members vote by putting forth a white ball to vote yes or a black ball to vote no. A two-thirds vote is needed for admission. Although membership in the Bellflower Lodge had been declining, the majority of Elks there didn't want women members—not even those women who had served their organization for years as members of the Lady Elks auxiliary. Qualified women had applied for membership several times and always been rejected. In May 1999, when all the women applicants were once again rejected for membership while three men were admitted with no problems, the women decided they'd had enough. No one could think of any time that a male applicant had been blackballed, but women were always voted down.

Dorothy Jenson recalled learning that they'd been blackballed "by the uproar at the Lodge when we walked in to attend an Elks dinner made and served by the ladies at our monthly meeting of the auxiliary."

Georgia Bonacci said she felt like a second-class citizen: "I wasn't good enough to be a member of the Lodge."

Dorothy was furious and later told a reporter, "I thought these men were my friends. I have known them for years and have helped them through rough times. We cleaned, washed dishes, cooked, made costumes for the annual parade, served many hot dogs. We've backed them through Elkdom."

Dorothy, who had seen me on TV, decided to give me a call. I agreed to represent them and support them in their efforts. "I don't like to be treated as dirt under anyone's feet," said Dorothy. These women were well qualified to become full-fledged Elks. The national organization's only qualifications for membership were that the applicant be a citizen of the United States, not less than 21, believe in God, and be of good character. It was obvious that the only thing that stood between the women and Bellflower Lodge membership was their gender. The matter was additionally painful because these women had voluntarily served the male members for many years. They figured they'd paid their dues. They no longer wanted to be Lady Elks; they wanted full-fledged membership.

I sent a letter to the Lodge's Exalted Ruler asking for a meeting to discuss the matter. When he didn't respond, we decided to take the matter to the national leadership during their annual convention. While 10,000 Elks gathered that July in Kansas City, Georgia Bonacci, Dona Etienne, and I protested outside with placards reading "Not All Elks Have Antlers" and "We Can Be Elks, Too." Our actions drew press coverage, which got the attention of the national leaders. Although then-president James Varenhorst made a speech urging each of the 2,200 Lodges to "embrace all American citizens into our ranks, male and female alike," he also said each Lodge was autonomous in deciding whom to admit.

In the meantime, the women and I launched a picket and protest against the Bellflower Elks Lodge with actions designed for maximum impact. We announced that the women would no longer cook, serve, or clean until women were admitted as full members. The men were left to fend for themselves.

That got their attention.

Although, technically, the women couldn't reapply for membership for six months, the Bellflower Elks leadership held an emergency membership vote the very next month, in August 1999. During that meeting, the Elks voted to make Sandra Strong, Dona Etienne, Mary Harding, Georgia Bonacci, and Rose Knight the first members in the Bellflower Lodge's history. They were inducted a day before Woman's Equality Day, the official anniversary of American women winning the right to vote. Now they had won the right to vote in private clubs as well. It was a wonderful victory, with one exception.

Dorothy Jenson, the leader of the women, did not get in. The old boys evidently couldn't stand that Dorothy had spearheaded the protest, and some of them blackballed her again. Their rejection of her was cowardly and particularly mean-spirited. It took two more years before she was admitted as a full member, but only three months after that for her to be named Exalted Ruler of the Lodge.

Because of their courage and the battle they waged, these women opened up doors of opportunity previously closed to women.

Empowerment Lesson

Women of any age can fight back and win.

Understand that your contribution to an organization should be valued. If you are making a significant financial contribution to an organization or volunteering your time to assist members with their activities, expect recognition for your participation.

Do not let clubs exclude you from membership because of your gender. Remember that you deserve equal rights but often you must insist upon them in order to enjoy them.

KATRINA YEAW AND THE BOYS-ONLY BOY SCOUTS OF AMERICA

Discrimination based on gender is wrong for victims of any age, but it especially angers me when it is directed at children. Katrina Yeaw was an eleven-year-old sixth grader when she felt its sting—and from the Boy Scouts of America—an organization that professes lofty ideals.

Katrina, who lived in the Northern California town of Rocklin, wasn't looking for trouble when she asked to join the local Boy Scout troop. She only wanted to hike, canoe, and camp with her father, a scout leader, and twin brother Daniel, a member of the troop who was enjoying learning those outdoor skills.

Katrina, a horseback rider and athlete, had tried the Girl Scouts and Campfire Girls, but she wanted more outdoor activities than they provided. She wanted the challenges that only the Boy Scouts could offer. She wanted to be an Eagle Scout, a designation with no Girl Scout or Campfire Girl equivalent. After discussing it with her father, he agreed and submitted an application to the Golden Empire Council of the Boy Scouts in April 1995.

Two months later, a terse response arrived in the mail: "Boy Scouting membership is only for boys. The Boy Scouts have no plan to restructure its programs to allow for the registration of girls, and there are no plans to conduct new pilot programs involving girls as Boy Scouts."

This certainly wasn't the policy in other countries with scouting programs. Scouts in Canada, the United Kingdom, Australia, and most of Europe allow girls under the age of fourteen to participate in integrated scouting programs. There were other girls who had tried and failed to join scouting programs in the United States. Katrina decided to stand up for all of them, and she and her family retained me to help them in that quest.

I knew it wouldn't be easy. There were at least two other cases in other states in which girls unsuccessfully sued the Boy Scouts. I wasn't deterred by those results because I believed that California law was much more protective of the rights of girls to be free of sex discrimination.

It wasn't my first case against the organization. In 1987, I had filed a suit on behalf of Phyllis Gibson, a single mother, challenging the men-only leadership policy of the Boy Scouts of America. Ms. Gibson had wanted to be able to supervise her son at Boy Scout overnight camp. There was a "daddy shortage," and if women couldn't participate as leaders, there would not be enough supervisors and many boys would not be able to attend overnight camp. Nonetheless, Phyllis was told that "adult troop leadership is a men only situation."

We filed a lawsuit against the Boy Scouts and, after we won a key court battle, the organization dropped its seventy-eight-year-old ban on female leaders supervising at Boy Scout overnight camps. Phyllis's suit proved that exclusion of women often hurts boys, and that by fighting back, women can win.

Now I wanted to do the same for Katrina. She knew it was going to take a lot of strength and courage. She knew about Shannon Faulkner's battle to be admitted to the Citadel, the men-only military academy in South Carolina. In my mind, this case was like a "junior Citadel."

"I like to hike, camp, and study nature," Katrina said at a press conference we held in August 1995. "Women can vote now and help lead scout troops, but girls cannot join the Boy Scouts. The only reason is that I was born a girl. That reason should not be allowed if I want to participate, work hard in the scout program and even become an Eagle Scout."

Her brother was equally supportive. "In school, in our community, and even in sports, I have participated in many activities with girls," he told reporters. "They can contribute just like every other person. I do not see any reason why girls cannot be in a patrol and participate in activities just like the guys do in my patrol."

We filed suit in Sacramento Superior Court on August 24, 1995, against the Boy Scouts of America and the Scouts' Sacramento-based Golden Empire Council. It was the same week as the seventy-fifth anniversary of women winning the right to vote. Nobody had given women that right; they had to fight for it, and that's what Katrina was prepared to do.

In March 1996, the Superior Court denied our request that Katrina be allowed to join the Boy Scouts while the case was litigated. We immediately appealed that decision to the California Court of

Appeals. It was tough. Media attention was intense and took its toll. Eight months after the lawsuit was filed, Katrina's brother Daniel told the *Los Angeles Times* that he no longer felt comfortable going to troop meetings: "A lot of friends still ask me at school why she's doing this and I used to explain everything about how sad it made her feel and stuff. Now I just tell them, 'Ask my sister.'"

In June 1997, the Appeals Court ruled against us as well. It decided that the Boy Scouts of America wasn't covered by California's Unruh Civil Rights Act, which prohibits discrimination based on sex, race, color, and national origin in all "business establishments."

Katrina was disheartened by the ruling. "I'm sad that my dad, my mom, and my brother can do these things together in scouting and I can't. Why? Because I'm an American girl," she said.

The ruling was disappointing, but we weren't finished. I filed a petition for review with the California Supreme Court. Katrina's petition joined two others before the Supreme Court, which was now being asked to decide whether the Boy Scouts could continue to discriminate against what the media had nicknamed the "3 Gs: God, gays, and girls." (The other two cases involved boys who did not want to say "God" in the Boy Scout Oath, and a young man who was excluded because he disclosed that he was gay.)

In the end, the California Supreme Court decided that the Boy Scouts of America is not a business and therefore could not be sued for discrimination under California civil rights law. The decision meant that our case was over and the Boy Scouts would be permitted to shut out girls from membership.

I was extremely disappointed, especially in view of the fact that a number of other courts in other states had decided that the Boy Scouts *were* a business for purposes of civil rights laws. The organization has a multimillion-dollar budget and a national catalogue from which it sells hundreds of products. It owns dozens of properties, including campsites and campgrounds, and has hundreds of employees. The California Supreme Court treated the Boy Scouts as a sacred cow by granting it a special right to discriminate—one that is not afforded to other organizations such as the Rotary Club or the Boys' Club. It was a dark day in the state's judicial history and a big step backward on the road to equal rights for girls.

There have been, however, a number of cases in this country's history where the highest court of a state or the nation has upheld racial segregation, and years later recognized the error of its ruling and reversed the decision. I will continue to fight for gender integration and against gender apartheid, and am confident that one day we will win. One day, the Boy Scouts—the world's largest, best funded, and most prestigious youth organization—will be open to our daughters in addition to our sons, and children will no longer suffer discrimination based on their gender.

Katrina Yeaw was extremely courageous to have fought this battle. She knew the road to equal rights is a long and rocky one, but she saw the goal as worth the fight.

Empowerment Lesson

Not every battle can be won, but if we don't fight these battles we will never win the war.

Remember that we are fighting for equal opportunity. Young girls should be part of our movement to win change, and adults should be especially vocal in their support of young pioneers. When our daughters stand up for equality, they need the support of their families, friends, and community.

EVEN STUBBORN ORGANIZATIONS CAN BE PERSUADED TO CHANGE

Jan Bradshaw loved to golf. After playing four years on the city courses around Yorba Linda, California, she decided to join a country club. In 1988, Jan paid a considerable sum of money,

$14,000 plus $200 per month dues, to purchase a full golfing membership at the Yorba Linda Country Club. At the time, no club official bothered to tell her that her first-class purchase would only grant her second-rate status at the club. Why? She was a single woman.

The country club's golfing rules discriminated against single women almost every day of the week, especially in the mornings, when the course was coveted due to less heat, less waiting, better conditions, and the pre-workday hours. On Sundays, men played the course exclusively until 9:00 A.M. After that, couples were granted exclusive play until noon. As a single woman, Jan couldn't get on the course until the early afternoon.

Men had the course exclusively on Wednesdays from 10:30 to 2:30 P.M., on Saturdays until 11 A.M., on holidays until 9:00 A.M., and during several men's golf tournaments that were held throughout the year. Women members had no voting privileges, and there were no women on the club's board of directors. Only on Tuesdays did women get a break—playing the course exclusively until 11:00 A.M.

Jan Bradshaw was teed off. Like all recreational golfers, she played with a handicap. At Yorba Linda's golf course, she was saddled with a gender handicap as well. Jan paid the same membership fees as the men, but received fewer benefits and rights just because she was a woman. That violated California state law, which prohibits businesses from discriminating against women.

I filed a lawsuit on Jan's behalf alleging gender discrimination by Yorba Linda and the American Golf Corporation, which owned Yorba Linda and 110 other golf clubs around the country. Their policies were based on false stereotypes about women and were having a chilling effect on the growth of women's golf as well as on the individual progress of women golfers.

The response to Jan's suit was ugly. The mother of three was treated as a pariah by other female members. Her name on the sign-up sheet was frequently erased, her picture on the club bulletin board was mutilated, and no foursome would play with her.

This from practitioners of a sport that prides itself on gentility and good manners!

It didn't take long, however, for Jan to make a hole in one. Yorba Linda settled our lawsuit and changed its policies. Women were given more equitable access to the golf course and granted full voting rights and access to positions on the board of directors.

Since then, many golf courses around the country have changed their policies. It took the courage of women like Jan Bradshaw to start the ball rolling.

Empowerment Lesson

One woman's actions can open the door for many.

Once you are a member of a club, insist on equal rights and privileges within it. Be courageous and willing to risk a backlash from men who have the arrogance to assert that they should enjoy more benefits than women within the club.

Jan Bradshaw's story reminds me of something Susan B. Anthony once said: "Cautious, careful people, always casting about to preserve their reputation and social standing, never can bring about a reform. Those who are really in earnest must be willing to be anything or nothing in the world's estimation, and publicly and privately, in season and out, avow their sympathy with despised and persecuted ideas and their advocates, and bear the consequences . . ."

You are a golfer—not a doormat. The men can step on the golf course, but don't let them step on you!

CHAPTER 7

Little Things Start Big Changes

THE CASE OF THE COSTLY SHIRT

In 1984, Los Angeles resident Julie Stark took some shirts to her local dry cleaner. Flair Cleaners charged her $2.75 per shirt, rather than $2.35, which is what men were charged to have their shirts cleaned. When she asked why, a Flair employee told her that women's shirts cost more because they buttoned right to left. Men's shirts, which buttoned left to right, the employee stated, were easier to clean.

Julie decided to perform an experiment and enlisted a male friend to help. He took Julie's shirt to Flair to be cleaned and was charged the lower man's shirt price. Later Julie took the same shirt to Flair for cleaning and was charged the higher woman's price. Talk about being taken to the cleaners!

Julie came to see me and I took her case. It was clear to me that buttonhole placement was irrelevant and that Julie was being overcharged solely on account of her gender, without any business justification at all. There were many other cleaners who engaged in unfair pricing policies based only on gender, and they cost women millions of dollars a year. We decided to file a lawsuit in order to send a message to the whole industry to clean up their business practices.

The lawsuit took less than five hours to resolve. After a press conference outside the store, where we announced the lawsuit,

Flair's vice president followed me to my car, where we resolved our differences. Flair agreed to equalize prices at its nine stores and not charge women more than men.

I turned out to be one of the beneficiaries of Julie Stark's action. Although I didn't realize it at the time, the local dry cleaner I had been using was owned by Flair as well!

Empowerment Lesson

Sometimes it only takes a small push to get a big result.

If you are being charged more for a service because you are a woman, examine the rationale that the business provides you to see if it really makes sense.

In this case, we talked with dry cleaners who did not charge more to clean women's buttoned shirts. They told us they thought that the buttonhole justification was ridiculous and not a good reason to charge women more. With this information, we were able to end the practice, so that women would no longer be "taken to the cleaners."

SAKS MAKES ALTERATIONS
TO AN UNFAIR POLICY

Dr. Muriel Kaylin Mabry fought back against what some people might view as a little matter and ended up changing the policy of an entire department store chain. In 1988, Dr. Mabry bought a dress from Saks Fifth Avenue in Costa Mesa, California, for $345. The dress needed alterations: the hem needed to be taken up, the sleeves adjusted, and a hook and eye added. Saks performed the alterations and charged Dr. Mabry $41.

The charge didn't seem right. She told the salesperson that the charge was unfair because Dr. Mabry's male friend had shopped at Saks for a suit a few months earlier and was told that if he bought the suit at Saks, the alterations would be free. Mabry said the salesperson told her that it was the store's policy to charge women for alterations and not charge men. If a man's purchase needed major work, like remaking a jacket, then it would cost a measly $7.

Lorie Anderson, who worked with Dr. Mabry, had a similar experience a month later, when she purchased a $1,500 evening gown. The dress needed alterations much less drastic than retailoring a man's jacket, but Lorie was charged $40 for them. Just days earlier, her husband had purchased a $500 suit that required extensive alterations, and had obtained them at no additional charge.

After Muriel and Lorie contacted me, I checked around and, sure enough, Saks was similarly discriminating against women when it came to alterations at the Saks stores in Beverly Hills and New York City. The store needed to tailor its alterations policy to fit customers of both sexes. We filed a class action suit in September 1988, charging Saks with violating California's Unruh Civil Rights Act, which prohibits sex discrimination by businesses. We alleged that Saks had a policy of charging women for alterations, but not charging men.

Our lawsuit forced Saks to rethink its policy and alter its pricing practices. Saks settled the lawsuit in August 1989. As part of the agreement, it changed the alteration pricing schedule at every one of its forty-five stores nationwide. Previously, women had been charged $18 for hem length alterations, $12 for sleeve length alterations, $15 to $18 for waist alterations, $10 to $18 for seam alterations, and $12 for the addition of plain shoulder pads. Now all of those alterations would be done for free, and the prices for altering shoulders, backs, and dress collars were significantly reduced. This simple policy change added up to millions of dollars in savings for women across the country.

Saks's response to this lawsuit served as a model to the industry. As a major force in American fashion, the department store demonstrated sensitivity to issues affecting women. Women can't afford to pay more for alterations than men, and shouldn't have to even if they could. Charging them more solely on account of their gender is damaging to both their bank accounts and their dignity.

In this case, Saks's alterations to its policy resulted in a perfect fit.

Empowerment Lesson

Many women have called to tell me about stores that still practice discriminatory alterations pricing policies. Often they can't find an attorney willing to take the case.

In a state that prohibits sex discrimination by businesses you could consider simply filing a discrimination case in small claims court and, if you have the facts to prove it, you will win damages and make the business review its discriminatory policy. In small claims court in many states, you act as your own attorney because attorneys are not permitted to represent clients there, but there is a limit on what you can win.

Women were created equal with men and should be entitled to equal rights under the law and in every aspect of life—politically, economically, and socially. This applies at home, in the workplace, and even in a department store.

If you live in a state that does not have a law that prohibits businesses from discriminating on account of gender, lobby your state legislators to pass such a law.

THE CLIP JOINT

I think Yael Miller may be the youngest client I've ever had in a sex discrimination case. I filed a lawsuit on her behalf in 1985, when she was just three years old. Why? The Yellow Balloon haircutting salon in Los Angeles seemed to be unfairly trimming her mom's pocketbook when it came to haircuts.

Joni Zuckerbrow-Miller took her daughter Yael and her son Ari to the Yellow Balloon, which catered to children. She asked that the same haircutter trim both of her children's hair. Although it took less time to trim Yael's hair, her haircut cost two dollars more than her brother's because the Yellow Balloon had a blanket policy which it prominently displayed in its window: "Girls' haircuts $12, Boys' haircuts $10."

Why did the cost of a haircut depend solely on gender? Wouldn't it be fairer to charge on the basis of hair length and the amount of work required for the particular haircut, rather than on the basis of gender? We sued the salon, alleging a violation of California's Unruh Civil Rights Act, which prohibits businesses from gender discrimination. Yellow Balloon quickly settled and agreed to change its policies to a gender-neutral pricing structure.

In addition, after I spoke to him, nationally known hairstylist Jose Eber voluntarily changed the pricing in his Beverly Hills salon to a sex neutral policy.

Empowerment Lesson

Mothers of young children can help protect the rights of their daughters by filing lawsuits to end pricing policies based solely on gender.

A PRICELESS CASE OF MENU BIAS

In 1980, I approached L'Orangerie, one of Los Angeles's most exclusive French restaurants, about its policy of giving women menus without any prices when men and women dined together at the restaurant. Most restaurants had stopped that practice, but L'Orangerie's Old World style owner Gerard Ferry claimed it was a French tradition to provide a menu with prices only to men, because it was assumed that men would pay the bill. Kathleen Bick and Larry Becker didn't find it quaint at all when the two arrived to eat at the restaurant. Kathleen, who had invited Larry to dinner to celebrate a business success, was appalled when he was given a menu with prices, while hers listed none.

I contacted the restaurant and spoke with Ferry's wife. I asked, "Why do you have this policy?"

She replied, "Because a woman is a woman is a woman."

My response was, "What does that mean, what does that mean, what does that mean?"

She said it was the French way. I told her that this was California, where there was a civil rights act that kept businesses from discriminating against women and that L'Orangerie's practice was discriminatory. The policy stayed in place.

We filed a lawsuit against the restaurant, which Gerard Ferry called ridiculous.

I thought their policy denigrated women and perpetuated negative stereotypes about them. Since when was it a restaurant's job to decide who would be financially responsible for a meal? The policy assumed that a woman would always be taken care of if she were with a man and that women shouldn't be worrying their pretty little heads over the price of dinner. It failed to take into account that when wives were dining with their husbands, they might want to know the cost of the meal. After all, it was paid for with community property. Further, the custom was insulting to businesswomen who entertained male clients in restaurants and were often the ones picking up the check.

To emphasize our point, we set up a table outside L'Orangerie with linen tablecloth, gold plates, silverware, a candlestick, and a rose in a vase. The picture ran in newspapers and on television and put pressure on the restaurant to change.

L'Orangerie finally stopped its unappetizing and sexually discriminatory policy and practice.

Empowerment Lesson

You can have your cake, eat it, too—and see how much it costs. Sex stereotypes should not be on the menu of anyone's dining experience.

CURTAINS FOR PAPA CHOUX'S POLICY

Suppose you were told that a restaurant's best section was off-limits to you because of your sexual orientation, or your gender?

That's what happened to Zandra Rolon and Deborah Johnson in January 1983. Zandra and Deborah, who were life partners, decided to celebrate Martin Luther King Jr.'s birthday by having a romantic dinner out. They decided to go to Papa Choux, a Los Angeles restaurant that offered such a setting. The restaurant, with its dark oak walls, low lighting, and pink lamps, featured strolling musicians playing tunes like "Stardust" and "Moonlight in Vermont." However, the pièce de résistance at Papa Choux was its six intimate, curtained booths set aside specifically for romantic dining. Deborah and Zandra made a reservation requesting one of those booths.

When they arrived, they were seated in that special section—but not for long. The restaurant manager arrived at their booth and told them that they could sit anywhere else in the restaurant, but not in those booths for romantic dining. He said restaurant policy and a city ordinance prevented two people of the same sex from being seated in that section.

"It was irritating and frightening to me," Zandra Rolon told a reporter later. "It was really scary. The back of the bus."

Deborah Johnson said that with "my being black and her Hispanic, it was like someone just slapped you down. We were in the Martin Luther King Jr. frame of mind."

They asked themselves, *What would Reverend King have done?* They said that they decided he would want them to call Gloria Allred, and pretty soon they were seated in my office.

Businesses shouldn't make stereotypical assumptions about same-sex couples. Such couples should receive the same dignity, respect, and rights afforded couples who are not of the same gender. I filed suit against Papa Choux for violating discrimination laws and asked for an immediate injunction against the restaurant, to prevent it from giving "back of the bus," second-class citizen treatment to same-sex diners.

Los Angeles Superior Court Judge Brian Geernaert was assigned to the case and arranged for a field trip to visit Papa Choux's now-infamous booths, which I dubbed the "corpus boothi." Papa Choux owner Seymour Jacoby was livid. He argued that its customers might be offended by seeing two women or two men together in a booth. He even took his case to the press, buying newspaper ads saying the restaurant "would never allow this charade" because same-sex seating in the intimate booths "makes a mockery of true romantic dining."

Jacoby had had a prior skirmish with the law. A previous Jacoby coffee shop featured a glass-enclosed jungle garden with flamingos, Japanese koi, and spider monkeys to entertain guests while they ate. That entertainment stopped when the monkeys began copulating, much to one diner's distress. When the city health department got involved, Jacoby was ordered to close his jungle paradise and send his romantic monkeys to the zoo.

His attorney wasn't very sensitive toward our case either. He told me in the hallway outside of court one day that the restaurant didn't realize my clients were lesbians because "they dressed so nicely."

In July 1983, the judge denied our request for an injunction and said the law prohibiting discrimination on account of sexual orientation was unconstitutional. His ruling sent me immediately to the California Court of Appeals, where we won a precedent-setting decision in 1984.

The court reversed Judge Geernaert's decision and upheld the Los Angeles city ordinance prohibiting discrimination based on sexual orientation, also citing the California antidiscrimination law known as the Unruh Civil Rights Act. Same-sex couples weren't going to be denied seating in the special romantic section of Papa Choux any longer. The case went back to Los Angeles Superior Court, where a new judge awarded my clients $500 in damages and ordered Jacoby to pay my legal fees.

Rather than open its booths to everyone, regardless of sexual orientation, Jacoby closed them forever on May 18, 1984, holding a mock funeral. The room with the booths was sealed and draped in black crepe. Whether Papa Choux kept or closed them didn't matter to me. The point was that if they were open, they had to be open to everyone. We were holding a celebration for the birth of a new day and a new definition of romance that would include everyone, including same-sex couples.

In the South, city-owned pools that had been open only to white children were also closed in the 1960s after African Americans won the right to have their children swim there. Later these pools were reopened to everyone. Similarly, the importance of the Papa Choux case was not what happened in this particular restaurant, but that we won new legal rights and protections for same-sex couples that applied to all restaurants, hotels, theaters, retail stores, and other business establishments throughout the state.

Empowerment Lesson

You don't have to accept second-class citizenship because of your sexual orientation. Do what Martin Luther King Jr. and Susan B. Anthony would have wanted you to do. Stand up for your civil rights and fight back.

A TOY STORY

There was a time when it wasn't widely accepted for boys to play with dolls or for girls to wear firefighter hats. I'd like to think that seven pint-sized clients whom I represented in 1979 had a lot to do with changing all that.

In those days, the Sav-On Drugstore chain had a large toy section, but the store took it upon itself to divide the toys into sections marked "Girls" and "Boys." The boys' section offered toys such as play money, doctors' kits, firefighter hats, model trucks, athletic equipment, tool kits, and airplanes. The girls' section offered toys such as dolls, dolly diapers, stoves, and nurses' kits.

My clients, seven girls and boys ages five to eleven and their parents, saw those signs as stereotypes that deterred both genders from exploring all of their interests. Two prominent psychiatrists we contacted were even more concerned and pointed out that signs like those in Sav-On could cause inner conflict in children.

At first, I tried to speak with store managers at Sav-On, and I contacted the vice-president of operations for the chain's 139 stores. He told us that the reason for Sav-On's signs was that "God made people different." He also said that it was a free country and Sav-On could have boys' and girls' toy signs if they wanted to have them. He refused to discuss the issue further.

We filed a lawsuit against Sav-On, asking for a preliminary injunction to get the gender-specific signs out of its stores. The trial was set to start on December 20, 1979.

We held a press conference outside a Sav-On in Burbank, where my clients and others changed the chain's jingle, "Sav-On is the savings place," to a new version: "Sav-On is the sexist place."

One of the boys who attended the conference told reporters he was too embarrassed to go to where the jump ropes and hula hoops were located because they were in the section marked

"Girls." Several girls worried that their section didn't include sporting goods like baseballs and bats. Another boy at the news conference asked, "Why are all the cooking sets on the girls' side? Can't boys grow up to be chefs?" A girl asked, "Why are all the money games on the boys' side? Don't girls need to know how to handle money, too?"

Media around the country carried news of the protest and lawsuit. It seemed appropriate that all of this was taking place during the holiday season, when so much interest was focused on toys and gift giving. We wanted all children to have the equal opportunity to express themselves regardless of their gender, so that they could grow and aspire to occupations that matched their interests and abilities.

At one court hearing, I held up a poster that showed an African American child looking at a store window. On one side of the window a sign read "Toys for African Americans" and underneath it was a shoeshine kit. On the other side a sign read "Toys for Whites" with encyclopedias underneath. I told the judge that this type of racial stereotyping would never be tolerated and that similar gender stereotyping shouldn't be tolerated either.

Ultimately, because of our lawsuit, Sav-On agreed to remove the "Boys" and "Girls" signs and replace them with ones that simply said "Toys." We commended the chain's officials for their flexibility and willingness to change. In time, their actions were emulated by almost every other retailer in the country.

Empowerment Lesson

Gender stereotyping can harm children, developmentally and emotionally. Don't let it happen to yours. Organize protests if necessary and make your voice heard.

THE CASE OF THE DECEPTIVE
PREGNANCY COUNSELING CLINIC

In January 1984, Shanti Friend, a young Los Angeles woman in her twenties, thought she might be pregnant. Looking in the Yellow Pages under "Clinics," she found a listing for "Free Pregnancy Testing and Counseling" and went in for a consultation.

When she arrived, she explained that she wanted to take a pregnancy test. Instead of being given a test, she was ushered into a room where she was told several antiabortion horror stories and shown pictures of fetal development. The counselor told Shanti that there were medical risks to abortion, and that it could cause her to have premature babies in the future. She was also told she risked future miscarriages if her uterine wall were torn apart during an abortion, and that she could hemorrhage to death as a result.

Shanti was horrified and frightened by the counselor's warnings. After she was finally given a pregnancy test, the counselor showed her more pictures of mutilated fetuses. Shanti left the clinic in tears.

After hearing about Shanti's and other women's experiences at these so-called "clinics," I filed a lawsuit on January 22, 1985, against the Right to Life League of Southern California, Inc. and the Pregnancy Counseling Center, South Bay, to put a stop to their practices. The free pregnancy test was no more than a "hook" to lure unsuspecting women into their centers, so that the League could counsel pregnant women against abortion. I alleged that these clinics were practicing medicine without a license.

Young women who are pregnant, single, alone, and afraid have a right to know what these centers are and who is running them before they get there. I believed that these Pregnancy Counseling Centers were potentially dangerous to women because a positive result on a pregnancy test does not necessarily mean a woman is pregnant (she might have a tumor) and a negative result does not necessarily mean she is not (she could have an ectopic pregnancy).

As a result of our lawsuit, we won a preliminary injunction in September 1985, prohibiting the centers from operating the way they had in the past. The injunction was based on the court's finding that these centers were practicing medicine without a license and operating an unlicensed clinic. To my knowledge, it was the first preliminary injunction issued in the nation against the Right to Life League for their pregnancy counseling center procedures.

In October 1989, after trial, we won a permanent injunction for unlawful business practices, unfair and deceptive advertising, violation of California's Medical Practice Act, and violation of California's Clinic Licensing Law. Los Angeles Superior Court Judge Miriam Vogel called the League's practices unfair, deceptive, and misleading.

In a subsequent settlement with us, the Right to Life League agreed to the issuance of a permanent injunction putting it out of the pregnancy-testing business and agreed not to appeal the judge's decision. The League also agreed to the injunction prohibiting their advertising in the telephone book under "clinics."

Our victory encouraged similar cases to be filed in other states as well. Because of our landmark case, the Right to Life League in California would now be forced to obey the law and women would be protected from the "hook" which had been used on thousands of women at the most vulnerable time in their lives.

Empowerment Lesson

If you feel that you have been a victim of a wrongful, inappropriate, unethical, or illegal business or medical practice, seek the advice of an attorney. By standing up and fighting back, you may help to protect many other women who may not know their rights or who are unable to assert them.

While you may have to sacrifice some privacy in order to succeed, the benefits you win may be worth the sacrifice.

PAUL JASPERSON'S COURAGEOUS CRUSADE

It's easy to forget that there was a time when AIDS was viewed like leprosy. It took heroes like Paul Jasperson to begin to raise public awareness by challenging those who discriminated against people with AIDS.

In July 1986, Paul, thirty-five, one of Los Angeles's most respected hairstylists, went to Jessica's Nail Salon in West Hollywood to make an appointment for a pedicure. After making his appointment at the front desk, Paul, who had recently been diagnosed with AIDS, ran into several acquaintances and openly discussed his condition in front of the receptionist. Jessica's Nail Salon called him later, canceled his appointment, and refused to make any future appointments for him. They told Paul they weren't accepting any new male clients.

The salon's actions were astounding to me, especially since West Hollywood had just enacted one of the strictest city ordinances prohibiting businesses from discriminating against those who were HIV positive or had AIDS. Its conduct was also a violation of California's Unruh Civil Rights Act, which prohibits discrimination in all business establishments.

The implications were serious. Irrational fear cannot be permitted as an excuse to deny rights to anyone. Experts contacted by my firm said that manicurists and pedicurists were at extremely low risk of contracting AIDS from a client. Any concerns could be addressed simply by wearing gloves.

The City of West Hollywood filed a criminal complaint against the salon owner, giving her the dubious distinction of being the first person in the nation to face criminal prosecution for denying commercial services to someone with AIDS. In turn, the salon challenged the validity of the ordinance, claiming it was unconstitutional.

We filed a lawsuit against Jessica's Nail Salon in January 1987. I wanted an injunction prohibiting it from discriminating against people with AIDS. I intended to protect their right to enjoy equal access to business establishments. Paul's case presented a unique challenge. I couldn't rest until men and women with AIDS enjoyed all the protections the law could provide.

Our civil case went to trial in February 1988. Judge Lawrence Waddington's decision was disturbing. Although he acknowledged that Jessica's had denied Paul a pedicure because he had disclosed that he had AIDS, and that West Hollywood had an ordinance against AIDS discrimination, the judge refused to issue an injunction against the salon. In his ruling, Waddington said, "There is an extremely small, but nonetheless real, risk of exposure to AIDS from the procedures of a pedicure." He ruled that Jessica's could indeed discriminate against Paul, or anyone else with AIDS, because of that "reasonable risk of harm from the afflicted person."

His decision was wrong. It ignored all the medical testimony we presented showing that pedicures and manicures could be performed safely on people with AIDS. We felt that the judge's decision could fan the flames of AIDS hysteria that were sweeping the country, and foster the mistaken impression that people who disclosed they had AIDS could be denied services by businesses in order to protect employees and other customers against the virus. Such a message could discourage people with AIDS from disclosing their condition for fear of being subjected to the same type of discrimination that Paul was forced to endure. In truth, the only way to protect the public's health (especially since many people who have AIDS don't even know that they have it) was to take the reasonable safety precautions prescribed by the California Board of Cosmetology. Then services could be provided to all persons, whether or not they had AIDS.

Judge Waddington's decision was also a slap in the face to West Hollywood, which passed the ordinance against AIDS discrimination in the first place. The city had been at the forefront of enacting laws to protect the public and people with AIDS, and other cities had copied the ordinance. The judge's failure to enforce West Hollywood's ordinance endangered those advances.

There was no valid reason why Paul Jasperson, a responsible citizen who did not hide the fact that he had AIDS, shouldn't be entitled to any service available to any other citizen, whether it was a manicure, pedicure, a dental appointment, or a meal in a restaurant.

I was so proud to represent Paul, who found the courage to fight back against fear and ignorance, and who wanted to protect both people with AIDS and the public health. My firm vowed to pursue this case, all the way to the California Supreme Court if necessary, and we started by appealing the decision to the California Court of Appeals.

This case was extremely important because we were seeking to enforce the West Hollywood city ordinance that had been used as a model for other cities. We were joined in our appeal by the ACLU and the cities of Los Angeles, West Hollywood, and Santa Monica, who filed friend of the court briefs in support of upholding the ordinance.

In May 1989, before the appeal could be heard, Paul died. The impassioned AIDS activist had devoted the final years of his life to speaking engagements, public appearances, and interviews to heighten awareness about AIDS discrimination. His joy for living, his commitment to the community, his devotion to his friends, and his quick wit and humor were an inspiration to everyone whose life he had touched. His death didn't stop my determination to see this case to its conclusion and do everything possible to win the case for Paul, who had made such important sacrifices.

After Paul's death, the salon's attorney made a motion to get the case dismissed. He argued that because Paul was no longer alive, there was no need for an injunction; the case was "moot." We fought the motion vigorously, arguing that if the court granted it, other defendants would delay AIDS-related cases until plaintiffs died, then make similar arguments that their cases should be dismissed. Laws protecting persons from discrimination on account of AIDS or HIV-positive status would be rendered meaningless. Lawyers for such victims might think it was useless to pursue such cases, since their clients might not live until the end of the long legal process. As a result, AIDS discrimination would run rampant and unchecked.

In a precedent-setting decision, the court agreed with us. The court acknowledged that the system often moved at a glacial pace and, therefore, it ruled to allow victims of AIDS discrimination to seek an injunction even after death! In December of that year, 1989, the Court of Appeals reversed Judge Waddington's decision and we won our case. It was a wonderful holiday gift. The ruling assured people with AIDS that ordinances passed for their protection were valid.

It served an even larger public purpose, too. As the court stated in our case, the West Hollywood ordinance ensured "that persons with AIDS will not be discriminated against. It encourages them to disclose their status to providers of personal services and this latter group can then take precautions against transmission. Since there is neither a vaccine nor a cure for AIDS, precautionary measures are vital to preventing the spread of the disease. It has been found that denial of services tends to inhibit disclosure of a person's HIV status, resulting in greater danger to personal service providers."

The Court of Appeals decision enabled the courts and city councils to fight back against fear and ignorance about AIDS and discrimination against people with the disease. It stands as a living memorial to Paul Jasperson. I still consider this pioneering lawsuit to be one of the most important cases our law firm has ever won.

Empowerment Lesson

Even someone who is ill can fight back and win important precedents to help themselves and others. If you believe a business has denied you a service because you have AIDS or are HIV-positive, consult an attorney in your state to determine if the law provides you with protection from discrimination. If it does, take appropriate steps to assert and vindicate your rights, either with a lawyer or in small claims court. If your state, county, or city does not afford you legal protection, lobby for change so that others may benefit from such protections in the future.

CHAPTER 8

You Can Fight
High-Profile Killers

O n June 11, 1994, I attended a beautiful black-tie event at the Beverly Hills home of Diane and Bill Ellis where a number of celebrities were present. One of them was Orenthal J. Simpson, who was there with Paula Barbieri, his woman friend at the time. Someone asked me if I'd like to meet him. Although I'm generally up for meeting new people, for some inexplicable reason, I just wasn't interested. I declined, saying that I just didn't think we had much in common. Later during dinner, he was seated at the table behind me. I kept turning around to look at him, trying to figure out why I had reacted the way I had, because it wasn't like me at all.

A few days later, on a Monday morning, I got a call from CNN. Nicole Brown Simpson, Simpson's ex-wife, had been brutally murdered on June 12. Nicole, who had divorced Simpson in 1992 after an abusive relationship, was found dead outside her Brentwood condominium along with her friend Ronald Goldman. At the time of their murders, Justin and Sydney, Nicole and O. J.'s children, were sleeping upstairs. CNN wanted me to comment. It wasn't an unusual invitation to ask me to comment on the murder of a woman, but I said, "No, thank you." I just didn't feel that enough facts were known for me to comment.

I was intrigued by my reactions to both the invitation to meet O. J. Simpson and the subsequent invitation to comment on the murder of his wife, especially given what would transpire in the months and years ahead. Eventually, as factual and legal issues developed that I felt were important to victims' rights, I did begin to speak out about the Brown-Goldman murder case.

In the weeks after Nicole and her friend Ronald Goldman were found brutally murdered outside Nicole's condominium, we learned that, in 1989, she had been attacked by Simpson. At the time, Simpson pled no contest—tantamount to a guilty plea—to the spousal battery charges filed against him. He never received any jail time.

The judge in the case, Judge Ronald Schoenberg, held a news conference to explain his actions. He claimed that the Los Angeles City Attorney recommended that Simpson not be sentenced to jail. The judge said that he simply followed that suggestion. The city attorney's recommendation was deplorable, but Judge Schoenberg's rationale wasn't much better, and I said so publicly.

Regardless of what a city attorney recommends, a judge is obligated to hand down the appropriate sentence to fit a crime. If a judge's only function were to rubber-stamp a city attorney's recommendation, then we could eliminate all judges for sentencing and just have the city attorney enter the sentence—but that isn't how the system is supposed to work. Judges can, should, and often do reject prosecutors' recommendations for sentencing and impose stiffer sentences in appropriate cases.

The initial spousal battery charge against Simpson and his plea of no contest should have resulted in serious consequences for him. The purposes of sentencing are rehabilitation, punishment, deterrence, and protection of the victim. The minimal sentence imposed on Simpson ($500, counseling, and charity work) obviously didn't accomplish any of those purposes. That sentence was an insult to battered women and sent the wrong message to men who batter their wives.

Nicole did everything she could to contain O. J. Simpson's abuse: She moved out, consulted battered women's shelters, divorced Simpson, sought therapy, documented her injuries, and called 911. Still, Simpson killed her. Nicole's death demonstrated that when domestic abuse isn't taken seriously, the violence often escalates until the victim ends up dead. The system fails to shield women from deadly domestic violence.

In our legal process defendants aren't the only ones who require protection. Victims and victims' families also need and deserve advocates. As Simpson approached his trial for double murder in 1994, Nicole's grief-stricken family grew increasingly angry as they saw false details about her life published and bandied about in the media. The Browns were enmeshed in a very high-profile case involving a celebrity who was being investigated and accused of murdering their loved one. They needed someone to keep the record as accurate as possible. They also needed someone to advise them as they proceeded through the criminal justice system, and to assist them with the issues that would come up along the way. Hence, they contacted me.

I was honored to represent the Browns in their efforts to defend Nicole's memory, help prepare them as witnesses, and assist them in their desire to be strong advocates against domestic violence. We wanted a fair trial for the victims, Nicole and Ron, and the People of California—not only for O. J. Simpson.

I became increasingly concerned that the victims might not receive a fair trial when I heard about a meeting that was held on July 19, 1994, between Los Angeles County District Attorney Gil Garcetti and prominent representatives of the African American Community. The topic was the Simpson case. Afterward, John Mack, the president of the Urban League, held a press conference to say that Garcetti had been asked not to seek the death penalty against Simpson. I found out later that Johnnie Cochran was also at the meeting, although he said at the time that he wasn't representing Simpson.

I didn't think it was appropriate for the district attorney to be meeting with members of the community to determine whether or not to seek the death penalty in a particular case. However, since he decided to meet with those who opposed it, I thought it was only fair that the DA meet with those of us who thought he should seek the death penalty.

There were precedents for Garcetti to decide to seek the death penalty. The DA had asked for and obtained the death penalty against two wives who were prosecuted for killing their husbands. Would seeking this punishment for the murder of a husband but not for the murder of an ex-wife indicate that Garcetti considered a man's life to be more valuable than that of a woman? I felt that, if he didn't apply the death penalty decision equally, his actions could be interpreted as discrimination against female spouse victims, particularly battered women.

In this case, which involved a celebrity defendant, the jury would be the conscience of the community. If the jury decided to convict Simpson of first degree murder, it, not the district attorney, should be permitted to make the ultimate decision of whether or not to recommend the death penalty for Simpson.

I could see that District Attorney Garcetti was committed to O. J. Simpson's receiving a fair trial, but the DA's decisions made me very worried about whether or not he was equally concerned with a fair trial for the murder victims. He didn't meet with my group of battered women's advocates, and in September 1994, he decided not to allow the jury the option of recommending the death penalty—even if they convicted Simpson of brutally murdering the mother of his young children and her friend. I wondered if he had concluded that Simpson's life was more valuable than theirs.

At a news conference, I said that Garcetti's decision reflected a callous and conscious disregard for the lives of Nicole and Ron. It wasn't enough that they were killed in a bloody and brutal slaying; now they had become human sacrifices on the altar of racial politics.

With this decision, the system once again failed to respect and protect the rights of Nicole Brown Simpson. It failed her in 1989 when she made numerous 911 calls, but no arrests were ever made. It failed her again when Simpson was prosecuted for the misdemeanor offense of spousal battery, but never served a day in jail because a judge decided he could go free.

The DA's office said it considered "aggravating and mitigating circumstances" in making the decision against seeking the death penalty for Simpson, but I questioned how Mr. Garcetti could have reached his conclusion if he had really considered all legally relevant factors and no political ones. There were numerous aggravating circumstances in the case that would normally justify seeking the death penalty—such as premeditation, lying in wait, and multiple killings. I wondered, *What mitigating circumstances existed that prevented the jury from having the option of choosing the death penalty if it convicted Simpson?*

In 1989, was inflicting a black eye on Nicole and leaving her in the bushes, bloody and terrified, a mitigating act?

Was fleeing from police after beating her up a mitigating act?

Was stalking and spying on Nicole after they separated a mitigating act?

Was fleeing from the authorities after he promised to turn himself in on the murder charges a mitigating act?

Was carrying a football or running through an airport in television commercials a mitigating act?

Were Simpson's career successes mitigating circumstances that trumped the fact that his ex-wife's head was practically decapitated and separated from her body? Is a pigskin on the football field more important than a wife's human skin in her own home?

I thought Gil Garcetti had chosen the cowardly way out. Although he had met with advocates of Simpson, he refused to meet with victims' rights leaders, battered women, and me. He refused because he knew there were too many questions he couldn't sufficiently answer—such as, why was he seeking the death penalty against the Menendez brothers, who were not celebrities before their prosecution, but not seeking the same penalty against celebrity O. J. Simpson?

His decision meant that every woman in Los Angeles County was now at greater risk of being beaten, battered, and killed. He had, in effect, declared open season on women and issued a hunting license to men to prey on their wives, ex-wives, and lovers without fear of the death penalty. Evidently, to obtain this hunting license, the applicant need only be male, a multimillionaire, and a celebrity (preferably an athlete) with good political connections to a DA who would be fearful of what would happen if he didn't appease an important constituency. I called on Gil Garcetti to resign because he had allowed the integrity of the legal system to be corrupted by petty political ambition and wheeling and dealing.

It was also a foolish legal judgment. If Mr. Garcetti had sought the death penalty he might have been able to have a more "law-and-order" jury. Generally, jurors who are not against the death penalty as a matter of principle are more prosecution oriented. Might Mr. Simpson have been convicted if Garcetti had sought the death penalty? It's definitely a possibility.

There were several other disturbing developments before the trial began on January 29, 1995. Media reports surfaced that Simpson had signed a multimillion-dollar book deal in which he would profess his innocence. (*I Want to Tell You* was published by Little, Brown & Co. in February 1995.) The timing hardly appeared coincidental to the Browns and me, and I went public with our concerns. Within days, the jury would be sequestered. Was the defense making a last-minute attempt to manipulate the jurors and the public with media coverage of Simpson's self-serving protestations of innocence? It disappointed us that the man charged with murdering Nicole would seek to exploit this tragedy by writing a book about it.

We also heard that the money he would get from the book would go to his legal defense fund, which seemed unnecessary. It appeared that his army of lawyers would continue to serve him even if he didn't get a big book advance. Surely, if anyone needed the proceeds from his book, it would be his children, Sydney and Justin. Therefore, on behalf of the Brown family, I asked that Simpson put all of his book's profits toward the care and support of his children. I also demanded that the defense team stop their efforts to manipulate public opinion.

The defense team didn't seem to care what the Brown family thought. In fact, it wanted the Brown family as far away from the jury as possible, and introduced a pretrial motion to have them barred from the courtroom. The request itself wasn't unusual; attorneys often ask that witnesses be barred from the courtroom so that they will not be influenced by the testimony of other witnesses. What was different here was that the witnesses they were trying to exclude were also members of the murder victim's family.

Denise Brown spoke out angrily about the motion, asking if the defense team was "afraid that the jury will be reminded through our presence that a real human being, my sister Nicole, was brutally murdered and that she has left behind a family who grieves for her still and misses her more than words can say? How unfair is it for the family of a murder victim to be treated this way? Who are the victims, anyway?"

I agreed with Denise that the family had a legal as well as a moral right to be at the trial. I appeared before Judge Lance Ito on January 17, 1995, to argue against the motion. The defense claimed that members of the family were "making faces" in court, but there was no indication that this was true—no instance of them being admonished by the judge for such behavior. The defense also argued that testimony of some of the witnesses might be influenced or tainted by the Browns' presence in the courtroom. I believed that, by attempting to shield the jury from the presence of

Nicole's family, the defense was trying to dehumanize and depersonalize Nicole, so that she just became a name in the courtroom—not a human being that anyone should care about.

I told Judge Ito, "Apparently, the defense wants to take away from Nicole's family the little they have left of Nicole—the truth, the whole truth and nothing but the truth about her life and her tragic death. The Brown family wants to understand what happened to their sister and daughter. They don't want to read about it in the newspapers six months later. Why should the family of the murder victim have fewer rights than a hundred million people in this nation, who can turn on their television sets and see this case? Why should Nicole's family have fewer rights than Mr. Simpson's family and Mr. Simpson himself?"

Judge Ito agreed with me, denied the motion by Simpson's defense team, and allowed the Browns to remain in the courtroom.

The defense, however, continued its efforts to keep the jurors shielded from the reality of Simpson's role in the death of Nicole and Ron. Prosecutor Marcia Clark had taken to wearing an angel pin, as had many of Nicole's supporters. The defense asked Judge Ito to order her to stop wearing it. They seemed to be worrying about symbols while the prosecution was focusing on justice. I suggested that the defense stop whining and complaining and get on with their jobs; they would do well to join the search for justice rather than engage in petty posturing designed to obscure the fact that two human beings had become murder victims.

There were more sobering developments. During the trial, jurors were going to be taken for "walk-throughs" of Simpson's Brentwood house, and of Nicole's condominium, where she and Ron Goldman had been murdered. We had issues with the procedure on both occasions. Out of respect for Nicole and Ron, the Brown family did not want Simpson at her condominium. We asked Simpson to respect the feelings of the family and not set foot on the property where the murders occurred. We asked him to stay outside with the sheriff's deputies who guarded him while the jury walked through the crime scene.

There was no question that Simpson had been to the condo many times and knew this property from every angle. We had no doubt that, even if he were not present for the jury walk-through, his army of attorneys would adequately protect his interests when they visited the murder scene. We simply asked that Simpson respect Nicole's memory by staying away and urged him not to batter the feelings of her family as he battered Nicole during her short life, and before her untimely death. Finally, his attorneys agreed.

The jury also visited Simpson's home. During that visit to Simpson's Rockingham Avenue estate, Simpson—who was accused of a bloody and heinous double murder—was not required to wear handcuffs, leg shackles, or an electronic device that would have stunned him, should he have attempted to escape from custody. I wanted to know why Simpson was receiving such preferential treatment. In the past, when police confronted him about beating Nicole and indicated that they were going to arrest him for spousal battery, he reportedly left his house. This was the same man who fled after he learned that police were about to arrest him for the murders of Ron and Nicole. He had to be chased on the freeway, as millions watched on TV, before his ultimate capture.

Simpson was not free on bail; on any other day, he was an inmate at the Los Angeles County jail. If he were O. J. the ordinary plumber, truck driver, or factory worker on trial for double murder, would he have been permitted to roam free? Of course not. In the past—to my knowledge—all defendants in double murder cases were required to wear handcuffs, leg shackles, or some other type of restraint when on a tour with a jury.

Why not O. J. Simpson? Why did this convicted wife batterer and accused double murderer get such velvet glove treatment? Was it because he was a celebrity, a football legend, or a multimillionaire?

Were there two classes of justice—first class for celebrities accused
of homicide, and second class for everyone else accused of homicide? Who made this decision, and why? How could it possibly be
justified? In my mind, it could not.

Wasn't it enough that Simpson had the largest list in the history
of the Los Angeles County Jail of so-called "material witnesses" who
were allowed to visit him frequently while he was in jail? Wasn't it
enough that he was allowed to sit in jail with an author who helped
him write a book from which he stood to make in excess of a million
dollars, due to the notoriety of the crimes with which he was
charged? Wasn't it enough that he had practically unlimited access
to a telephone, television, and an exercise bike—access that was far
more than other inmates enjoyed? His fellow inmates even nicknamed his cell "the penthouse at the blue bar hotel."

Apparently all these special privileges weren't enough. He was
now being treated as a nondangerous man who just happened to
be charged with a double murder. He could be free of the re-
straints and requirements to which other alleged murderers were
subjected. I wondered what was next. Would he be permitted to
sign autographs outside the crime scene? I thought this special
treatment was an insult to Nicole's memory and had dangerous
implications for anyone who believed in equal justice under the
law. It was painfully clear that there was a double standard in play.

Was the trial only about O. J.? What about Nicole and Mr.
Simpson's prior history of violence toward her?

During her appearance on the witness stand, Denise Brown
testified powerfully for the prosecution. She tearfully told jurors
details of her sister's humiliation and physical abuse by her then-
husband. Once, she recalled, O. J. had grabbed Nicole's crotch in
a bar, telling onlookers, "This belongs to me."

She further testified that, on another occasion, he smashed
Nicole against a wall of his house, then—literally—threw her out
the door.

The day Nicole was murdered, Denise testified, she saw her ex-brother-in-law at a dance recital. "He had a very bizarre look in his eye, it was a very far-away look."

She showed great courage on the witness stand. It was not easy for her to relive the painful memories of what she had seen Nicole endure.

We were angered by criticisms from people who said the Browns should have done more to protect Nicole. Every family with a loved one who has been abused wishes that it could have done more to protect that family member. The Brown family was no different. Rather than assess blame, I suggested that anyone who cared about abuse should focus on putting a stop to it. In spite of their grief, the Browns were doing everything they could to prevent future acts of violence against others by establishing the Nicole Brown Charitable Foundation for family violence intervention. They should have been commended and supported for those efforts, not criticized during a time of personal crisis and heartbreaking grief.

Another woman who was criticized during the trial was prosecutor Marcia Clark, who came under attack for issues involving her personal life and her role as a working mother of two young children. Marcia's estranged husband asked a court to award him primary custody of the couple's two young sons, saying that his ex-wife spent most of her time involved with trial work. These attacks were painful to watch for a number of reasons. Marcia Clark had a right to privacy about her personal life. I also saw these charges as similar to ones made on many single working mothers.

There appears to be a disturbing trend in this nation to try to force single moms to choose between their children and their careers. If they take their careers seriously, they are labeled as bad mothers. If they spend time with their children, they are labeled as people who can't be serious about careers outside the home. This is a sexist double standard. No such guilt trip is imposed on men, who are generally not forced to choose between their children and their jobs. Marcia Clark was the latest victim of this backlash against women.

Although some fathers seek custody of their children for legitimate reasons, others use their children as pawns to gain bargaining leverage in a divorce. They want a larger share of the marital property, or don't want to pay more child support. Some simply want vengeance and attack a mother in her most vulnerable area—the possible loss of custody of her young children. The court's job is to determine what is in the best interests of the children and the court must never be guided by improper motives of any party.

In support of Marcia Clark, I said publicly that I hoped that these custody decisions would be based on all the facts and not on any sexist stereotypes. I also said that I hoped no working mother would be punished for deciding that *both* her children and her career were important. I also delivered a dozen roses for Marcia Clark to the district attorney's office on behalf of many single working moms who wanted to show Marcia their support.

In March 1995, the Simpson fund-raising machine again surfaced. We learned that Simpson, while sitting in his jail cell, was signing Leroy Neiman prints that would be sold, and the proceeds given to him. The Browns and I felt it was outrageous that a man charged in a double murder was trading on that notoriety. The arrangement was just the latest example of how Simpson was receiving special treatment by the criminal justice system.

We believed that the profits from the Neiman print sales should not have gone to Simpson, but to the taxpayers who had been forced to pay for his incarceration and his expensive trial. In the alternative, he could have sent the profits to his children, the innocent victims in this tragedy.

The outcome of the O. J. Simpson criminal case, the so-called "Trial of the Century," is etched in history books. The not guilty verdict that was delivered on October 3, 1995, was troubling to me because I felt that the jury did not take sufficient time in deliberations to thoroughly review all the evidence in this case. I felt that it was a sad indictment of the criminal justice system and could have serious consequences.

Other attorneys and potential jurors witnessed the success of Simpson's defense, whose main thrust appeared to be the race issue. I was certain that this would encourage other efforts in the future to confuse and perhaps openly influence juries to consider matters outside the scope of what may be legally permissible. The jury listened, but did they really *hear* Nicole's voice from the grave? It was a tragic day for all victims of violence.

I believe that this was another case like countless others throughout the country in which a woman was victimized by violence, and justice was not served. The verdict sent a clear message that money, power, and celebrity can make a difference, and that the system still fails to respect the civil rights of murder victims.

Millions of women continue to be beaten, terrorized, seriously injured, and killed by men who say they love them, but who use, abuse, and hurt them. Like Nicole, many of these women are young mothers whose children also suffer. These mothers have a right to expect that the justice system will be there to protect them and punish those who abuse them and destroy their self-esteem, their spirits, their bodies, and their lives. They have a right to expect that they can be safe from violence in their homes and in the streets, but often they are sorely disappointed. Many women never report these crimes to authorities because they fear the system will not impose any real consequences on their abusers; they fear going to the authorities will only incite anger and retaliatory abuse.

I look forward to the day when our legal system begins to be more accountable to women. I don't want the verdict in the Simpson case to deter women from standing up for their rights and fighting the injustices against them.

Within days of the jury's decision, O. J. Simpson, who had decided not to take the stand to give his side of the story, made arrangements to sit for a one-hour interview with NBC, his former employer. I was appalled. If Simpson wanted to talk, why didn't he testify under oath in the criminal case? Did he want to avoid the penalty of perjury? Did he not want to be cross-examined? Was he afraid he might get caught in lies and inconsistencies?

To their credit, the Brown and Goldman families did not accept the verdict as the end of their crusade to seek justice for Nicole and Ron. They filed a wrongful death lawsuit in civil court against Simpson, on behalf of the estate of Nicole Brown and Ron Goldman.

As that case proceeded, Simpson accepted an offer to go to England in May 1996, to appear on British television and address students at Oxford University. Press reports suggested that Simpson would receive substantial monies from some of the appearances. A British publicist was quoted as stating that Simpson "will be treated like any other star who comes into the country."

I was revolted. It was easy to understand why Simpson wanted to leave the United States, but it was almost impossible to fathom why people of good conscience would subsidize the trip of a convicted wife batterer and man accused of double murder. The fact that Simpson was acquitted of the criminal charges against him did not change the fact that Judge Ito found there to be substantial evidence on which the jury could have convicted Simpson, nor did it change the fact that a civil case against him for wrongful death was pending.

I felt that, instead of subsidizing a trip abroad for Simpson, payment should have been made to the Nicole Brown Charitable Foundation to help prevent family violence. Rather than having dinner with Simpson, as the Oxford students were planning to do, I suggested that they contribute to shelters that provide dinners for battered women. Rather than helping Simpson try to repair his damaged public image, they should assist mothers to find safety from husbands who have broken their bones and destroyed their lives. Asking questions about the murders of Ron and Nicole should not be turned into a parlor game, a device to boost ratings for new television shows, or an excuse for an intellectual academic debate with the man accused of the brutal murders. Many people seemed to forget that the murders were real tragedies that affected real human beings and left long-lasting scars.

While Simpson was planning to go to England, the Internal Revenue Service alleged that he had failed to pay all his taxes. I became concerned for his children's economic future. Rather than flying to England on a shameless, self-serving, first-class ego trip, Simpson should have been addressing his debts to the government and dedicating his time to guaranteeing some economic security for his children.

The next stop on Simpson's public relations rehabilitation tour was one of the most disturbing to me. On June 27, 1996, the Stop the Violence Foundation held a fund-raiser at Simpson's Rockingham estate. Reportedly a portion of the funds raised that night were to be used to help fight spousal abuse. I didn't believe that any organization dedicated to stopping violence should use an admitted wife batterer like Simpson to assist them in raising funds—especially in a place where a murder victim's blood had been found.

Simpson was obviously engaged in a massive attempt to restore his shattered public image. He didn't appear to be concerned about showing respect for the murder victims, Ron and Nicole. Rather than attending a fund-raiser, I publicly suggested that Simpson participate in long-term counseling to address his problems with anger control, violence, and issues related to violence against women.

Not only was he convicted in 1989 of spousal abuse, but even after the murder trial he was quoted as saying he wanted to knock the chip off Marcia Clark's shoulder. I thought Simpson still presented a serious risk of harm to women.

In my mind, paying for a ticket to that fund-raising event at Simpson's estate was akin to paying blood money. I asked people instead to contribute to Nicole's foundation, which already had an established record in the field of spousal abuse. In June 1996, it had already contributed $150,000 to organizations that help battered women.

It was equally preposterous of the Brookins Community African Methodist Episcopal Church in Los Angeles to make Simpson an "honorary member," which it did in July 1996. The Bible says, "Honor thy father and thy mother." It doesn't say honor a wife batterer. Simpson was not a saint or a role model for nonviolence. He was not a civil rights leader or a national hero whose record should be honored.

"The church should pray *for* him, and even pray *with* him," I said at the time. "But pray, do not honor him. Pray that he will publicly acknowledge the extent and scope of the violence that he inflicted on Nicole. Pray that he will enter long-term meaningful counseling to assure that he will never again inflict violence on another human being. Pray that he will stop his public relations campaign which appears to be designed to make the public 'forgive and forget.'"

A church spokesman said he didn't think it was a crime for a man who had been acquitted to go to church. I didn't think it was a crime to go to church, either. However, I reminded the church that it *was* a crime for a man to beat his wife, and for that I thought it was shameful to give any kind of honor to Simpson. Such honors should be reserved for those who help women, not hurt them.

O. J. Simpson's seemingly endless photo opportunities were wearing thin. Posing next to a Bible, a minister, an altar, or even well-meaning churchgoers wouldn't change history's record.

Shortly before jury selection in his civil trial began, in September 1996, Simpson initiated another disturbing legal maneuver—he initiated a court action to regain custody of his children. He wanted to wrench them from the security of their grandparents' home and transplant them to his estate, where their mother's blood had been found.

Why was he attempting to change custody now, I wondered. Was he trying to influence prospective jurors by sending them a message that he was a loving father and family man, who—because he loved his children—could not possibly have killed their mother? If that was his motive, then he certainly did not deserve custody.

Sydney and Justin had been living with the Browns for more than two years following their mother's brutal murder. They enjoyed and benefited from the love of their grandparents, aunts, and cousins. I was concerned about the emotional scars that they might suffer if they were abruptly ripped out of that caring environment and forced to move to a new home and a new school to live with Simpson, who had never before been the primary caregiver. Stability and security are important in the lives of all children, and particularly to these children who were suddenly awakened in the middle of the night and removed by police from a murder scene where their mother's body had been discovered lying in a pool of her own blood.

What would happen if custody were given to Simpson and a jury found that he was liable for the death of Sydney and Justin's mommy? Of course, that's exactly what did happen, and ultimately the Court of Appeals reversed the lower court's decision, which had given custody to Simpson. By then, however, it was too late. The children appeared to want to stay with the only parent they had left.

In November 1996, a group named Christian Women for Justice held a fund-raiser at the Hollywood Park Casino to help O. J.

pay his legal bills in the civil trial. Approximately three hundred people paid $40 per person to attend. Of all the good causes to which people could have contributed—O. J. Simpson's wasn't one of them. What did the golf-playing, jet-setting, party-going Simpson tell the event organizers about his income and his assets? Did he tell them whether or not his attorney's fees and costs in the civil case were being paid by his insurance company? Did he detail how much money he'd received from speaking fees, interviews and his book and video? Did he tell them how much equity he still had in his multimillion dollar Brentwood estate? Did he reveal to them how much money he made from the sales of his autographed memorabilia? Did he explain how blood matching his was found at Nicole's condominium after the murder?

This charitable organization could have raised money for many poor African American men who couldn't afford attorneys' fees in true discrimination cases, where they really had been the victims of injustice. Instead, they chose to raise money for a wife beater. I questioned their priorities.

Meanwhile, the Simpson saga wasn't finished.

On November 22, 1996, an incident occurred during Simpson's testimony in the civil trial that led me to call for an investigation by the Los Angeles County District Attorney's office. Simpson, testifying under oath, was being examined by Daniel Petrocelli, the attorney for the Goldman family. He gave the following answers to these questions about his altercations with Nicole Brown Simpson:

Petrocelli: "And how many times, Mr. Simpson, in the course of these physical altercations did you hit Nicole?"
Simpson: "Never."
Petrocelli: "How many times did you strike Nicole?"
Simpson: "Never."
Petrocelli: "How many times did you slap Nicole?"
Simpson: "Never."

Petrocelli: "How many times did you kick her?"
Simpson: "Never."

Simpson's clear and unequivocal denial that he had ever hit, struck, slapped, kicked, or punched Nicole shocked many people, particularly women, for a number of reasons. One of the reasons was sitting right next to him: a photo of Nicole which showed her with a cut lip, swollen face, blackened eye, bruises, and a welt over her right eye—injuries that she had allegedly incurred as a result of the 1989 incident involving Simpson.

He pled no contest to that charge, which is tantamount to a guilty plea. The jury had heard Nicole's frightened voice in a 911 tape, with Simpson's voice raging in the background. The jury also knew of Nicole's diaries in which she alleged abusive behavior by Simpson. They knew of witnesses who alleged that Nicole told them of Simpson's abusive behavior, and of witnesses who had seen it directly.

It is an offense to all women that someone can be criminally prosecuted for spousal battery, plead no contest to that crime, be sentenced for it, and then get up on the witness stand and, in essence, deny that he did it. He said the injuries occurred while he was "wrestling" with her. I believed that it was just as wrong for a convicted wife batterer to deny under oath that he had beaten his wife as it was for Detective Mark Fuhrman to have denied using racial epithets.

Victims of domestic violence were outraged and urged me to demand an investigation into whether Simpson should be prosecuted for perjury for giving those answers. I believed that there was sufficient evidence for the Los Angeles County District Attorney to investigate the matter. The question was, would District Attorney Gil Garcetti, who had almost lost his reelection campaign after losing the Simpson criminal case, be too intimidated to ever again investigate O. J. Simpson? I wanted him to conduct a proper investigation into what was probably the most public testimony that anyone has ever given in a court of law. If it was a lie, it brought our system of justice into total disrepute. If there were ever a case in which the system must demand the absolute truth, this was it.

Garcetti didn't pursue it. When a *Los Angeles Times* reporter asked a spokeswoman from his office why, the spokeswoman replied that no one had ever sent the office any transcripts of the testimony. This was obviously an excuse. The DA's office could have ordered transcripts, but failed to do so. I ordered a copy of the entire transcript of Simpson's testimony and sent it to Garcetti. I even marked the specific pages in question. Nicole's sister, Denise, stood by in case they needed her to testify. Still, nothing happened. It seemed patently absurd and unjust to me. Detective Fuhrman was prosecuted for perjury for denying under oath that he had used a racial epithet many years before the People v. Simpson criminal trial. Even if he had used such an epithet, his denial was arguably not material to the murder case against Simpson. Simpson, on the other hand, was not being investigated for his unbelievable testimony about Nicole in a trial where his statements were material to the issues being litigated.

There was injustice upon injustice in this case. In December 1996, a judge in Orange County refused to wait for the verdict in the ongoing civil trial before making a decision on custody. She also declined to hear evidence of murder allegations against Simpson. She awarded him custody of his children—which was a heartbreaking decision for the Browns. I was very upset and disturbed by the judge's ruling. Although I had not represented them in the custody/guardianship case, I felt that the judge could have maintained the status quo. There would have been no danger to the children in allowing them to remain with the Browns until the verdict was reached in the civil case.

The system had failed Nicole. Now it had failed Sydney and Justin as well.

On February 4, 1997, a jury of O. J. Simpson's peers in the civil case found him legally responsible for the deaths of Nicole and Ron. They ordered him to pay compensation to the Goldman family and to his own motherless children (because they were the beneficiaries of Nicole Brown Simpson's estate). This verdict was even more significant than the one in the criminal trial. Every member of the jury knew Simpson had already been acquitted of the murders, yet still found him liable. Simpson could no longer run and hide from his past.

One has to wonder what the outcome might have been in the criminal case had that jury been presented with the wealth of new evidence that was brought forward at the civil trial, including Simpson's noncredible testimony. Our system of criminal justice gives every advantage to the accused, including the right not to take the stand in a criminal case. In the civil case, however, Simpson enjoyed no such advantage. There he could not invoke his fifth amendment privilege against self-incrimination because he had been acquitted criminally and double jeopardy prevented him from ever being prosecuted for those same murder charges. He had to testify and the jury in the civil case had the opportunity to hear him explain his activities on the night of the murder—putting his story and credibility to the test. He failed miserably.

This time Simpson and his legion of lawyers and spin doctors were not able to hide the simple truth from this jury of courageous men and women from his community. Everyone now knew the truth about what happened on the night of the killings. Nothing can bring back Ron and Nicole. No amount of money can soothe the pain that the families will always suffer from their loss, but justice was nonetheless sweet on this day.

O. J. Simpson is a disgrace to humanity.

May the souls of Nicole Brown Simpson and Ronald Goldman rest in peace.

Empowerment Lesson

If you are the victim of a crime, you (or your estate if you are deceased) have the right to file a civil lawsuit against the perpetrator, whether or not he is convicted of a crime. In that lawsuit the burden of proof is lower, which means that it is easier to prevail. If you win the civil case, unlike in the criminal proceeding, you can be awarded money damages to compensate for your losses.

Of course, no amount of money can ever really compensate for the terrible loss of a loved one by wrongful death or murder. A civil lawsuit, however, is one way to vindicate the truth and help make the wrongdoer accountable.

CHAPTER 9

You Can Fight Rapists and Other Sexual Predators

LORI BROWN AND THE SERIAL RAPIST

Justice isn't automatic. Lori Brown learned that lesson the hard way. Bringing her rapist to justice took eight years of working through a legal system that often seemed unresponsive to the victims of this serious crime.

In 1978, Lori moved to California from Iowa while her fiancé Stewart Nelsen stayed behind to finish up his master's degree. Shortly after she arrived, she met Gary Wayne Brown (who was not related to her). He seemed at first to be "no one you would be fearful of," she said later, but what she described as his "day and night personality" emerged quickly when she found herself locked in a bedroom with him. There, he forcibly raped and orally copulated her. She reported the crime to the police and identified Gary Wayne Brown as her attacker, but the district attorney's office inexplicably decided not to prosecute.

One night after her fiancé arrived in California, Lori got a call from a woman who also claimed that Gary Wayne Brown had raped her. She told Lori that there were at least five other women who had also complained to the police. Stewart Nelsen was shocked and frustrated by these stories and by the legal system's inaction in Lori's case. The shock turned to anger a few days later when Stewart drove through the neighborhood where Lori had been assaulted. She had told her fiancé the address of the house where the incident occurred and given him Brown's description. When Stewart saw

Gary Wayne Brown walk into the street, he became so emotionally upset and distraught that he hit him with his car.

I represented Stewart. He was prosecuted for hit and run, assault with a deadly weapon, and battery. He pled no contest and was sentenced. He received no jail time, but was fined and ordered to pay the medical bills of the man who raped his fiancée. I sympathized with Stewart Nelsen's plight. He and many other men whose loved ones are assaulted are the forgotten victims of the trauma that rape inflicts. The system treats them with little sympathy and gives them no support. Whereas Stewart was ordered by the criminal justice system to pay damages to Gary Wayne Brown, no one had ordered the rapist to pay damages to his victims.

Since the criminal justice system was unresponsive to Lori Brown, we turned to another branch of the courts and filed a $2 million civil lawsuit against Gary Wayne Brown for assault and battery, rape, intentional infliction of emotional distress, and false imprisonment. Perhaps the civil side of the court system would at least provide Lori with her day in court and a judgment against the rapist for damages.

Despite the civil case, however, we still wanted Gary Wayne Brown to be criminally prosecuted. We were concerned about the possible risk of harm to other women. I kept urging the district attorney to prosecute him, but the rapist remained free. Inevitably, he raped again. This time his victim was a woman named Roberta, who had read about Stewart's case and contacted the police. A third alleged victim surfaced as well.

Finally, the DA decided to prosecute, but there was a delay of more than a year in getting these three cases into court. When the trial finally did take place, it was one that would never be forgotten. The victims asked that I be present as their attorney to give them moral support and legal advice. The defendant's attorney had a different strategy in mind. He had me excluded from the courtroom, stating that he planned to call me as a witness—but he never did.

The defense attorney's strategy was to try to convince the jury that the case represented a conspiracy by me and the women's movement against his client, and that we were only in it for the money, as evidenced by the $2 million civil suit that I had filed against Brown on Lori's behalf. Even worse, in an effort to paint Lori and the others as women who wanted sex, the defendant's attorney made an outrageous, tasteless, and totally uncalled-for remark to the jury in his final argument. He said that, because Roberta had an IUD birth control device and wasn't wearing underwear at the time of the rape, she "was like a 7-Eleven market, open twenty-four hours a day, ready for action anytime." This is just another example of the unjustified trauma that the legal system continues to inflict on rape victims.

The remark was callous, shocking, and should be condemned by all decent people. Fortunately, the jury didn't buy the defense's disgusting argument. They convicted Brown of the rapes of Lori Nelsen and Roberta, although they did not find him guilty of the charges brought against him by the third woman. He was sentenced to state prison in 1981. As soon as he was released in August 1986, we went forward with the civil trial. Lori was awarded $2 million in general damages and $3 million in punitive damages.

Lori's story was so compelling that it became a 1990 NBC television movie, *Without Her Consent* (Melissa Gilbert played Lori, Bebe Neuwirth played me).

Empowerment Lesson

It is important to file a police report if you have been raped, whether or not you think the case will be prosecuted. Other victims may come forward and the police will have more evidence, which will help make the rapist accountable. You can gain access to courts by filing a civil lawsuit. Help protect yourself and other women from becoming victims by doing your part. Your actions in the criminal and civil justice systems can send this message to rapists: It is not a question of *if* you will be caught; it is only a question of *when*.

A RAPIST IS A RAPIST, REGARDLESS OF THE VICTIM

As Lori's case proves, it is sometimes difficult even for the girl next door to get the authorities to prosecute when she reports a sexual assault. Just imagine how much courage it took for my client Rhonda DaCosta—a prostitute—to get her sexual assault case to court. Rhonda believed that even prostitutes have a right to say no and that rape laws were there for their protection. That was before she met Los Angeles Superior Court Judge Gilbert Alston.

In 1985, Rhonda DaCosta was a woman in desperate circumstances. She needed money to care for herself and her small child. Why else would she be working as a prostitute, offering to perform oral sex for $30? Unfortunately, Rhonda picked the wrong customer when she agreed to such an activity with Daniel Zabuski. She didn't know it at the time, but Zabuski already had a disturbing police record. In 1979, he had been convicted of bribery while working as a jailer in the South Gate, California, police department. According to press reports, he'd been demanding sexual favors from female prisoners. In 1983, he'd been convicted of sexually molesting a young girl under the age of 14.

On July 10, 1985, Zabuski picked up Rhonda in his car, where she agreed to perform oral sex for $30. Evidently, Zabuski wasn't satisfied. Rhonda later testified that he became "extremely violent" and forced her to engage in sexual intercourse and sodomy. Then he stole $150 from her.

Zabuski was charged with rape, sodomy, and grand theft. His criminal trial was held in a Pasadena courtroom in front of Judge Gilbert Alston. During this trial, Rhonda felt victimized again—this time by the judge. Zabuski denied that he forced himself on Rhonda and took her money. He said she wanted to have anal and vaginal intercourse. Before the jury could hear the rest of the case and decide whether Zabuski was guilty of rape and sodomy, Judge Alston decided to take matters into his own hands. He dismissed the case, saying it wasn't the court's job to "resolve the contractual dispute between a whore and her trick and I'm not going to do it."

Later in his chambers, he told the *Pasadena Star News*, "The law was set up to protect good people—you, my wife, my daughters, my granddaughters. It doesn't protect a street-walking prostitute from a contract gone awry. This case shouldn't have been filed. A whore is a whore is a whore."

It was at this point that Rhonda contacted me. I was appalled by the judge's comments. This case wasn't about contract; it was about rape and every woman's right to say "No." Judge Alston had, in effect, declared open season on prostitutes. Rapists and those who beat and murder prostitutes could interpret this to mean that they now had a license to rape, beat, and kill because the criminal justice system would not be there to protect prostitutes or to give them access to justice. He seemed to be telling rapists that if they committed sexual acts on these women, against their will, that the law would protect them by denying the victims access to the courts. Evidently, these women weren't entitled to protection of the law from acts of rape and sodomy.

Further, if rapists thought they could rape prostitutes, then all women were at risk, because defendants could allege in the future that they should not be prosecuted for raping a woman whom they thought was a prostitute. By suggesting that rape laws were established only to protect "good people," Judge Alston was also opening the door to investigating the behavior, morals, and sexual history of every rape victim who filed charges to determine who

was a "good" person and who was not. That is specifically prohibited by California law.

The judge's comments provoked immediate criticism from me,
as well as the Pasadena Rape Hotline, the Los Angeles Commission on Assaults Against Women, the San Fernando Valley Rape
Crisis Service, Pacific Asian Family Services, the Rosa Parks Sexual Assault Crisis Service, at least two law professors, and a number of deputy district attorneys.

His remarks and decision could not go unchallenged. In May
1986, I filed a complaint with the California Commission on Judicial Performance, which had the power to investigate and discipline judges in appropriate cases, and I called on the Los Angeles
County Commission on Women to investigate the matter. I asked
them to pass a resolution affirming that all women deserved equal
protection under the law, and that no man under any circumstances has a right to engage in acts of sexual intercourse with any
woman without her consent.

I also filed a civil suit on Rhonda's behalf against Daniel
Zabuski alleging assault and battery, assault and battery by rape,
and intentional infliction of emotional distress. I filed the case because Rhonda DaCosta deserved access to our justice system and
I believed that the civil courts and judges would provide her that
access. Rhonda DaCosta filed the case because she wanted other
women to know that they had rights, even if they had engaged in
prostitution. She wanted them to know that they could and should
fight back.

Daniel Zabuski's attorney tried to get our civil case dismissed.
However I was successful in persuading a different judge that our
case was not about a contract, but about a rape—and he permitted
us to proceed. It became an important victory for Rhonda and a
significant statement by the justice system.

In October 1986, the Commission on Judicial Performance
notified me that it had taken "appropriate corrective action" as a

result of my complaint. However, because of Commission rules protecting judges, this corrective action would not be made public. "Your bringing this matter to our attention has served a useful purpose," the Commission wrote. I believed the Commission's action to be supportive of rape victims and a rebuke of Judge Alston. I released the letter to the media, and considered the matter closed.

I was therefore stunned several days later when I learned that Judge Alston's response was to question the authenticity of my letter from the Commission. He even went so far as to tell one television station that he couldn't "rule out the possibility of forgery." Instead of acknowledging that his statements about "whores" were despicable, he chose again to reinforce them. "I feel no remorse for having refused to sugarcoat the truth," he told the *Los Angeles Herald Examiner*. His comments were "absolutely true," he told the *Los Angeles Daily News*. Judge Alston's response was as ill-conceived as his original comments, once again causing many rape victims to lose confidence in the justice system. I filed another complaint with the Commission.

Tragically, Rhonda died before her civil case could be heard at trial. Still, in her fight to spare other women similar trauma when pursuing sexual assault cases, she'd won an important victory.

I remained concerned that Daniel Zabuski was free and that all women, not just prostitutes, were in danger because of Judge Alston's decision. It didn't take long for my worst fears to become a reality. In 1991, Zabuski pled no contest to trying to rape a girl and sexually assaulting an eighteen-year-old woman. Under a plea agreement, he was sentenced to ten years in prison instead of fourteen.

At the time the deputy district attorney on the case said Zabuski would "pose an extreme danger to society . . . when he is released from prison." His words were prophetic. In 2000, Zabuski was released after nine years and resumed raping women with a vengeance, this time using the Internet to lure his victims. He attacked three women in just six months. He beat one, threatened to kill her, forced her to perform oral copulation, and raped and sodomized her. He was described at the time by police as a "high-risk sexual predator."

Finally in 2002, Daniel Zabuski was put away for eighty years to life.

Gilbert Alston retired from the bench in 1991. I wonder whether he ever realized that by letting Daniel Zabuski walk out of his courtroom, he imperiled all women, not just "whores." His wife, daughters, and granddaughters could have been victims, too.

Empowerment Lesson

If you feel that a judge has made inappropriate comments from the bench, get a transcript or record of the remark and file a complaint with your state's Commission on Judicial Performance.

Stand up for victims' rights even if the victim has an occupation or lifestyle that you would never choose. Until all victims are guaranteed equal access to the courts, nobody in society is safe.

THE PILLOWCASE RAPIST AND THE HOLLYWOOD ASSAULT

In the mid-1970s, Los Angeles was terrorized by the "Pillowcase Rapist," so named because he put pillowcases over his victims' heads to conceal his identity. When Reginald Muldrew was arrested and identified as the Pillowcase Rapist, authorities believed he might be linked to some 200 rapes from 1976 to 1978. However, he was later convicted of only four rapes, burglary, and robbery. He served sixteen years in prison, a relatively short time considering the enormous pain and suffering he inflicted on his victims.

While in prison, Muldrew refused rehabilitation. Psychiatric authorities considered him to be mentally disordered and a danger to the community. Despite those concerns, he was released in 1995. His release was mandated by law, for he had served his entire twenty-five-year sentence (with time off for good behavior).

At the time, I wrote to California Attorney General Dan Lungren asking that he commit himself to informing the public about Muldrew's whereabouts if he registered as a sex offender in California. California law required that he register with police or sheriffs if he resided in the state, but in those days before Megan's Law was passed, law enforcement was not required to notify the public if a sex offender moved into a community.

Muldrew never registered. Instead, he moved to Gary, Indiana, to live with his brother. In August 1996, he was back in jail after being arrested on burglary charges. He had been hospitalized after being beaten by a group of men. They said that they caught Muldrew with a purse taken from a woman who had been assaulted a short time before. Police suspected that Muldrew broke into the woman's home, held her down with a pillow, and took her purse. In a separate incident, they also suspected that he had broken into another woman's home, put a sheet over her head, and fondled her.

I went to Indiana with two young women who wanted justice for Muldrew's alleged victims. We wanted to do everything possible to see that Muldrew was charged as a career criminal, if the evidence supported it. One of the young women who accompanied me was D'Anza Bringier, who had been a high school student in 1978 when she helped capture Muldrew by hitting him with a golf club as he attempted to rape her mother. The other, Virginia Watson, had been a student at the University of Southern California in 1978 when she was attacked by the Pillowcase Rapist. He gave her two black eyes and cut her behind the ear with a knife during the assault. We met with the police, hoping that the information we provided to the authorities could help in the criminal prosecution of Muldrew.

Muldrew was charged with six felonies, including a count of "criminal deviate conduct." During his trial, a mother and daughter testified about Muldrew's break-in at their home. They alleged that he touched the daughter's breast and put his finger in her anus, then grabbed a sheet and put it over her head. The mother said she stopped the attack by hitting him with a hoe. They had identified him in a police lineup.

In April 1997, however, the jury acquitted him of all criminal charges. The jury had not been permitted to hear about his prior criminal record in California, nor about prison authorities' concerns that he remained a danger to the community. Muldrew was a free man, but his victims weren't done with him.

Later that year, it looked as if the Pillowcase Rapist was about to strike again—this time using Hollywood as his accomplice. A group of women who had survived attacks by Muldrew in Los Angeles and Gary, Indiana, contacted me. They were infuriated by news reports that Reginald Muldrew had sold the rights to his story to a Hollywood production company. Virginia Watson, who had gone with me to Indiana in 1996 to assist the police in the criminal case there, was particularly outraged. "Why would anyone want to own the rights to the life story of a convicted sex offender who, to my knowledge, has not received any rehabilitation and may have a very short fuse ready to explode at any moment?" she asked during a press conference.

Why weren't producers interested in the survivors' stories or their points of view? The production company's executives and Muldrew's Indiana attorney were forced to make statements explaining their flimsy motives. His attorney claimed the movie would examine why he committed the crimes, not glorify his attacks. The Hollywood producer claimed he was only interested in "finding out the truth about all of this."

This photo was taken of me when I was five or six and still believed in fairy tales.

My high school graduation photo, 1959

was a high school English teacher for many years. Here I am with my students at Benjamin Franklin High School in Philadelphia.

Feminist attorney Gloria Allred beneath signs directing customers to boys' toys and girls' toys.

Children's crusade against sexism

Rita Milla and I announce the filing of a lawsuit against seven Catholic priests and the Catholic Archdiocese of Los Angeles, alleging sexual abuse by the priests and asserting that one of them fathered her child.

Outside of L.A. County District Attorney Ira Reiner's office, I lead a protest criticizing his lack of child support enforcement efforts.

President Ronald Reagan presented me with the 1986 President's Vo
Action Award for outstanding volunteerism for my work on child sup

Un
Pac
a c
Se
ing
cla
h

My client Vicki Ann Guest and I explain to Joan Rivers why we sued Guest's school district after she was barred from cheerleading because of the size of her breasts

At a "Take Back the Night" rally in Santa Barbara, I hold hands with my client Lori Brown Nelsen, a survivor of a sexual assault by Gary Wayne Brown. He was convicted and we won a $5 million verdict against him after a seven-year battle.

I sued state Senator John Schmitz after he issued a press release attacking Jewish women, lesbians, Protestants, and me.

Outside of the New York Friars Club, I hold up my membership card and celebrate, becoming the first woman permitted to have lunch there.

Over the years I participated in many pro-choice rallies and voice
my passionate support for keeping abortion safe and lega

President Bill Clinton and
me at a fund-raiser. Later,
when I learned that he lied
under oath about the
details of his relationship
with Monica Lewinsky, I
said that he should resign.

For fourteen years I was a talk show host on KABC Radio in Los Angeles.

Amber Frey, my law partner Nathan Goldberg, and I leave the courthouse after Amber testified in the case of People v. Scott Peterson.

Model Kelly Fisher and I explain to the press why she sued her ex-fiancé, Dodi Fayed Shortly thereafter, Fayed was killed in a tragic car crash with Britain's Princess Diana

Actress Hunter Tylo and I discuss her pregnancy discrimination case against the pr͏ ducers of *Melrose Place*. We won a multimillion dollar verdict for her at tri͏

At a radio talk show host conference in New York City, I met then-Governor George W. Bush. When I asked him if he supported the passage of the Equal Rights Amendment, he responded, "Oh, is that coming back?"

I confer with my clients LaDonna and St. James Davis, the human "parents" of Moe the chimpanzee, at their arraignment in West Covina, California. We were successful in getting the criminal case dismissed.

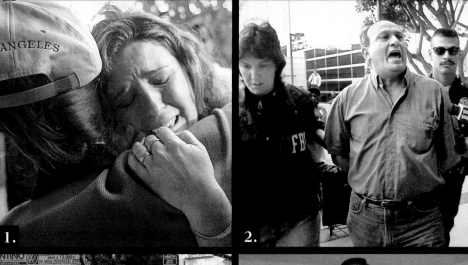

1. Teri Martinez sobs on my shoulder after Carlo Ventre is arrested by the FBI for kidnapping her niece, Santina. Ventre was later convicted of international parental kidnapping and faced a hearing in Italy on a charge of "voluntary murder" in the death of Teri's sister, Toni Dykstra. 2. Carlo Ventre is arrested and taken into custody by FBI Special Agent April Brooks immediately upon his arrival in Los Angeles. 3. I confront one of Carlo Ventre's attorneys in Rome, Italy, while holding up a photo of Toni Dykstra and their child, Santina 4. Milt Dykstra with his twin daughters, Toni and Teri. The day that this photo was taken was the last day that Milt saw his daughter Toni alive.

My client, Sylvia Guerrero, mother of "Gwen" Araujo, a seventeen-year-old transgender teen who was murdered, joins me in speaking to the press outside the Hall of Justice in Fremont, California.

In Loving Memory of

Eddie "Gwen" Araujo
Feb. 24, 1985
Oct. 03, 2002

Poster of "Gwen" Araujo, who was murdered after she was discovered to have male genitalia.

Defendants (left to right) Jose Merel, Michael Magidson, and Jason Cazares face the judge at the first of their two criminal trials. Merel and Magidson were ultimately convicted of second degree murder in the death of transgendered teen "Gwen" Araujo. The jury deadlocked both times on Cazares.

Our clients, Diane Olson (left) and her life partner, Robin Tyler, with me and my law partner John West, as we enter the courtroom where John and I argued that it is unconstitutional to deny same-sex partners the right to marry in California. The Superior Court judge agreed.

Dorothy Jensen holds back tears as she is installed as "exalted ruler" of the Elks Lodge in Bellflower, California. We had waged a two-year battle to win the admission of women into the lodge.

Gina Ocon and I celebrate our victory in her custody case. She had won a scholarship to Harvard and fought for the right to move away with her child to complete her education.

I walk to the courthouse with some of my fifty-seven clients who sued Hooters restaurant, alleging that, when they applied for a job there, they were secretly videotaped removing their clothes to change into uniforms. The man who videotaped them was prosecuted and ultimately convicted.

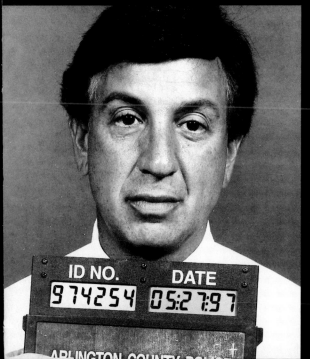

ID NO.
974254

DATE
05:27:97

ARLINGTON COUNTY

Marv Albert shortly after being
arrested for assault on a woman

Michael Maroko (left) and Nathan Goldberg founded our law practice with me thirty years ago. They are still my partners and our law firm is named Allred, Maroko & Goldberg.

I am very proud of my daughter, Lisa Bloom, shown in this photograph with me in 2004.

We turned the heat up on this production company—way up—and in June 1997, a group of Muldrew's alleged victims and I had a lengthy telephone conversation with the production company representative. By then, the story seemed to have changed.

The representative emphasized that his company had no intention of producing a movie or book with the Pillowcase Rapist and would never be involved in any such deal. He also stated that neither Muldrew nor his attorney had been paid compensation for their rights.

Survivors who were present shared with the representative the pain that they had suffered at the thought that the Pillowcase Rapist might profit from his crimes, or from describing those crimes from his point of view in a television movie. The survivors of the Pillowcase Rapist had suffered enough. Our efforts brought the proposed movie to a halt.

Muldrew hasn't been heard from since.

Empowerment Lesson

D'Anza Bringier helped to capture a rapist. You, too, can learn when and how to fight back against sexual predators by taking self-defense classes. If there are other victims of the same predator, remember what Mother Jones once said, "Don't agonize—organize!" Join together to track rapists who are released from prison but learn to do it safely and legally.

DESIRAY BARTAK AND THE HOUSE OF HORROR

Many children are sexually abused by their fathers, stepfathers, godfathers, uncles, or other members of their immediate family every day. I had firsthand experience with this sad fact when a brave pre-teenager contacted me. Around Christmas 1992, I received an unforgettable letter—one that reinforced my will to fight for victims' rights. Although she was just a child when she wrote to me, Desiray Bartak had already encountered more heartache than an average adult.

On the Fourth of July 1990, Desiray spent the night with her godfather, Richard Streate, and his family. She was ten years old. Streate was Desiray's father's best friend, and his daughter was Desiray's friend. While sleeping that night in a guest bedroom, Richard Streate entered the room, pulled down Desiray's underwear, fondled her vagina and thrust his fingers inside of her. Desiray alleged that he attempted to molest her again in August 1991.

Desiray was shattered. Richard Streate was her godfather. He was supposed to love and care for her as if she were his own child. Instead, in those few moments in the dark, he ripped away her childhood and changed her life forever. For almost a year after the first attack, she told no one, although she began to suffer from depression and an eating disorder.

After the second attack, Desiray's mother finally learned what had happened. One of the most painful things for a parent to hear is, "Mommy, I was molested." Together, they decided to bring to light Richard Streate's dirty secret. Desiray reported the incidents to the Los Angeles County Sheriff, and on October 26, 1992, Streate pled guilty to committing lewd acts upon a child. One of the reports filed with the courts recommended probation without any jail time.

Desiray personally contacted me to represent her at Streate's sentencing to argue that he should be incarcerated and she also retained me in a civil case. "When I hired Gloria," she later told a reporter, "I told her I wanted $500 for every bad dream, $1,000 for every bad day, and $1 million for touching my vagina." On January 5, 1993, we filed a civil lawsuit against Richard Streate for child sexual abuse, sexual battery, assault, intentional infliction of emotional distress, and negligence. Desiray took this action because she believed that children who are abused shouldn't be terrorized into silence by their abusers. Instead, they should learn their rights, break the silence, and fight back.

Two days later, at Richard Streate's sentencing in the criminal matter, Desiray bravely decided to step out from behind the cloak of anonymity that the law offers to children of her age and state publicly how his actions had affected her. She may have been the first child-abuse victim ever to waive her anonymity in a California molestation case. Going public was Desiray's idea. I was reluctant to have her do so because she was a child, but ultimately she and her mother persuaded me to support her decision. She didn't want Richard Streate on probation; she wanted him in jail. She wanted to encourage other abused children to speak up and not be ashamed that they were victims, and she firmly believed that speaking out would help her healing process.

"He has made my life a living hell these past two-and-a-half years," she told the judge. "I have been made fun of, told to keep quiet, been called a liar, and accused of making it up for attention. People say, 'In time things will get better,' but no one can give me back the time I spent crying, the time I had suicidal thoughts, the time I spent without sleep; the time my life was so bad, I dressed in black, painted my face black, and pretended to be an invisible person, with no life, no friends, no family."

She begged the judge to give Richard Streate the maximum sentence without parole, saying "I will not feel safe until he is in prison."

During my statement to the judge, I asked him to put himself in Desiray's place.

"Your Honor, let us imagine the terror that a ten-year-old girl feels when she is away from both of her parents. It is night. It is dark. There is silence. The child is sleeping. Suddenly, there is a large man by her bedside. He leans over her. What is more vulnerable than a sleeping child? He places his fingers inside of her. He moves them around, not just once, but continually, for ten minutes. Ten minutes of terror for a now rudely awakened and frightened child. Now some may say ten minutes is not a long time, but Your Honor, ten minutes to adults like you and me is not the same as ten minutes to a ten-year-old child who is being sexually abused by her godfather. It was not ten minutes of fun. It was ten minutes of horror."

I asked the judge to tell Streate to hold up the fingers that he put inside Desiray.

"Those are not little fingers," I continued. "They are large and they are attached to a large adult male's hand. Now let's think of those fingers in this little child's vagina for ten minutes and imagine her terror. What would one minute of terror be like with those large fingers inside a little girl in the middle of the night in the dark. . . . Let's close our eyes for one minute and think of it. Now let's multiply it by ten for what was then a little child away from her Mommy and Daddy, who suddenly, and without warning, was having her childhood stolen from her. He made what was to be a safe house into a house of horror for a little girl."

The judge didn't give Richard Streate the maximum sentence, but he didn't let him walk out of the courtroom either. Streate was sentenced to three years in prison.

In January 1994, my daughter, Lisa Bloom, and I went to trial on Desiray's civil case. There, Desiray won a $2 million judgment against Richard Streate. We viewed that as the court's recognition of the seriousness of the injury he inflicted on her.

Richard Streate was to be released from prison on August 17, 1994, after serving only 18 months of his sentence. Desiray, her mother, and I contacted the governor of California and the Department of Corrections to try to prevent his release. We requested a medical psychological evaluation and a protective order for a distance of 100 miles—we were granted 35 miles. Desiray asked that he be required to wear a monitoring ankle bracelet. It was the only way she would feel safe during his three-year parole.

When asked how it felt to know that Richard Streate was out of prison, she replied, "I wish the Judge would have taken me seriously in 1993 when I begged him at his sentencing to drop the plea bargain so I could go to trial and let a jury decide." That plea bargain had not stopped Desiray's pain and anguish. It's obvious we need tougher sentencing for child sexual abuse. It is obscene that criminals often serve a longer term in prison for writing a bad check than for molesting a child.

Richard Streate changed his name to Kyle Hochstrasser while in prison and quickly disappeared after his release. I believe a law should be passed prohibiting those who have committed crimes against children from changing their identities, because the public should have a right to know who the perpetrators are.

Still, Desiray won a substantial victory through her bravery and willingness to serve as an example to all children who are abused. Desiray and her mother went on to publish a national newsletter for victims of sexual abuse and appeared on numerous talk shows. She was even honored by then-First Lady Hillary Rodham Clinton with a National Caring Award.

Desiray remains my heroine. I was so touched by a letter she wrote to me and my daughter. In her letter, she wrote, "Dear Lisa and Gloria, Thank you for giving me my life back." Her strength still inspires me and thousands of others.

Empowerment Lesson

Make sure your child knows how to fight back.

Children everywhere should be taught to say "No" to anyone who is touching them in an uncomfortable or inappropriate way or place.

They should be encouraged to tell you, a parent, a close friend, teacher, counselor, or someone that they trust if something like this does happen.

Most important, children need to know that it's never, ever their fault, and if they confide in you, you will believe them and not blame them for the abuse. Let them know that if they are threatened or told to keep the abuse a secret, that they still must tell you and that you will keep them safe.

Teach them that there are legal ways that they can fight back against their abusers, and that it is the child molester who should be ashamed of his conduct—not the child.

RITA MILLA AND THE SEVEN PRIESTS

Sometimes justice takes a very, very long time.

Rita Milla's horrifying sexual ordeal perpetrated on her by seven Catholic priests is shocking even by today's standards, when the lawsuits against the Catholic Church for abuse by priests are legion; but Rita's story began more than twenty years ago, when almost nobody believed that a priest would molest a parishioner. At that time, the idea that seven priests—all of whom had taken vows of celibacy—would break those vows and engage in sexually inappropriate and wrongful behavior with a deeply religious and trusting young woman seemed unimaginable.

Rita was a devout Catholic raised in a low-income Hispanic family in the Los Angeles suburb of Carson. Her life's ambition was to become a nun and she was actively involved in St. Philomena Church from an early age. She was a member of the choir, helped teach young children in the church's religious school, and enjoyed playing the guitar for Mass. She was shy and dressed modestly.

Rita Milla practically worshipped the priests at St. Philomena and regularly took confession with Father Santiago Tamayo and

Father Angel Cruces. Father Tamayo soon made it clear that he had more than a spiritual interest in his young parishioner. In 1978, when Rita was only sixteen, Tamayo began to make sexual advances toward her in a private room in the back of the church. He even reached through a broken screen and fondled her breasts during confession.

Two years later, Father Tamayo had intercourse with his virgin parishioner—but he didn't stop there. On many occasions, the priest told Rita's parents that he wanted their daughter to accompany him to several convalescent homes. Instead, he took Rita to his brother's apartment and engaged her in various sexual activities.

He then brought in Father Cruces to have sex with her in January 1980. By April 1980, Tamayo introduced her to two more priests, who also had intercourse with her. Over the next two years, Tamayo instructed her to have sex with even more priests— ultimately seven in all. Rita's spiritual adviser, counselor, and confessor told her they were only human and they were lonely; it would be of great service to them.

Why did Rita do it? As she once explained in a newspaper interview, "I felt they would know what is a sin . . . and the difference between good and evil." The priests told her that sex was a God-given activity, ethically and religiously permissible, but that she should never tell anyone about her relationships with them. One night, four of the priests took her to a Venice Beach motel and took turns having sex with her; she didn't feel she could say no. "I was brought up to be obedient," she said later.

One day in 1982, Rita had sex with both Father Valentine Tugade and another priest in the church rectory. It was the only time the priests didn't use condoms, and she got pregnant. She didn't know which of them was the father.

When she told Father Tamayo, he first suggested an abortion, even though that violated Church tenets. When she declined, he cooked up a plan to send her to the Philippines. He told her she could live in his brother's house, give birth to the baby, place the child for adoption, and return to the States without telling anyone about the sexual activity, her pregnancy, or the birth of her child. The two priests bought her plane ticket and arranged for her passport. Father Tamayo told Rita's parents that she was going abroad to study nursing and that he would send Rita money for support.

During her seven months in the Philippines, Rita received less than $450 from the priest to support herself. She suffered from malnutrition and almost died during the C-section delivery of her daughter Jacqueline in October 1982. While Rita was in the hospital, a Philippine church official came to visit her. When she told him her story of the priests' sexual abuse and her pregnancy, he promised to help. He told her, however, not to tell anyone else. Six months later, no help was forthcoming.

After returning to Los Angeles with her baby daughter, whom she decided not to place for adoption, Rita met with Father Tamayo. Again, he told her not to tell anyone what had happened, and another priest suggested that Rita resume having sex with him.

In July 1983, Rita went to see the Los Angeles Archdiocese and told an official there that her baby's father was a Catholic priest, and that she had been abused by six other priests. The official promised to investigate and instructed her to keep it a secret. Four months later, he told her there was nothing he could do. Was he trying to delay, with the hope that it would then be too late for Rita to file a case?

At that point, Rita came to see me. There *was* something I could do. In 1984, we filed a lawsuit against the Catholic Archdiocese in Los Angeles and against Father Tamayo and the six other priests, charging them with civil conspiracy, breach of fiduciary duty, undue influence, fraud and deceit, and clergy malpractice. To my knowledge, it was the first case in the United States where a female victim had gone public alleging that she had been sexually abused by multiple priests.

Rita took tremendous personal risks and showed enormous courage by going forward with her lawsuit. She and her family had been completely victimized, but she found the courage to fight back. Rita and her mother wanted to file the lawsuit to protect other young women from the pain and suffering caused by priests who abuse their positions of trust. Rita's mother felt that Catholic parents had a right to expect a high standard of conduct from the priests to whom they entrust their children, and that this trust must not be betrayed. They also wanted the Church to establish a policy of financially supporting children fathered by priests.

We didn't intend the case to be an attack on the Church or its priests, but we did think it was important for all professionals (whether priests, doctors, teachers, etc.) to face consequences when they abused their positions of trust. Rita, who had once been eager to become a nun, lost all faith in God and the Catholic Church. I thought this case was so extraordinary that it merited an investigation by the Vatican. How could seven priests take advantage of a young girl and condone this conduct if this was not a widespread practice among priests? Further, how could two bishops of the Catholic Church have failed to take any meaningful action in this most serious situation, when they were made fully aware of the allegations?

The Los Angeles Archdiocese owed the public an explanation of how such egregious moral failures could have occurred, and it owed an explanation to Catholic parents about what steps it would take in the future to protect their children so this would never happen again. Instead, on the day we filed the lawsuit and held a news conference, all seven priests mysteriously disappeared from their parish offices. The Los Angeles Archdiocese wouldn't provide addresses for them. Reporters tried to interview church officials for comment, but were told repeatedly that no church official was available to talk.

Within the next month, another Los Angeles bishop, during an appearance on Los Angeles's predominant Spanish language station, described Rita as "a person of bad reputation" who had engaged in "very bad actions even with altar boys." The broadcast was seen by Rita, her family, friends, and neighbors, who were devastated by the attack.

Rita had never had a date or even kissed a boy before being sexually victimized.

In 1987, the California Court of Appeals ruled that, from the Church's point of view, it wasn't foreseeable that a priest would sexually abuse a parishioner. In addition, they ruled that Rita had waited too long before filing her lawsuit and that the statute of limitations had run out. The Court wasn't going to permit Rita to go to trial. It appeared that neither the Archdiocese nor the priests would ever have to answer for their conduct.

Although the Court refused to allow the civil case to proceed, we still wanted to establish paternity for Rita's child so that the child would know who her father was. However, we hadn't been able to locate any of the seven priests to serve them with the legal documents necessary to proceed with the case. Rita was devastated, but she did not give up hope.

Her faith and patience were rewarded in 1991, when Father Santiago Tamayo surfaced with a shocking confession. The Roman Catholic priest contacted me and I persuaded him to hold a news conference in my office in Los Angeles to apologize publicly to Rita. She had been telling the truth all along, he said. "I had her full trust and confidence, yet I got sexually involved with her," he told reporters. "I failed as a pastor to rescue her from getting involved with the other priests."

Tamayo also revealed the even more appalling fact that the Los Angeles Archdiocese had played a role in trying to cover up the priestly wrongs. He had the documents to prove it. *Los Angeles Times* staff writer Patt Morrison, who for years stood alone in her exemplary reporting on this case, obtained copies of letters and detailed them in a front page story. A 1984 letter from the Archdiocese enclosed a check for $375 to Tamayo, who had fled to the Philippines, asking "that you do not reveal that you are being paid by the Los Angeles Archdiocese unless requested under oath." In my opinion, this money was in exchange for Tamayo's silence and for staying away from the United States, since he was performing no priestly service for the Los Angeles Archdiocese in the Philippines.

In 1987, Tamayo wanted to return to California, but the Los Angeles Archdiocese advised him against it. "Our lawyers also inform us that you are liable to personal suits arising out of your past actions. . . . Such suits can only open old wounds and further hurt anyone concerned, including the Archdiocese."

Although Father Tamayo had now admitted his involvement with Rita, the Archdiocese took no action to discipline or counsel him, nor did it take any action to restrict him from continuing his priesthood in the Philippines. We thought it was time for the Church to acknowledge its responsibility to victims such as Rita. We felt that the Church's actions (and lack thereof) demonstrated a callous disregard for the harm inflicted on Rita, her child, and her family. Furthermore, I thought it was the height of hypocrisy for the Church to preach family values while taking an active role in assisting priests who abuse their positions of trust.

All that then-Archbishop Roger Mahony had to say publicly was that the events happened before his arrival at the Archdiocese in 1985. He said it was the responsibility of the priests to apologize, but not the Church. As for the payments to the priest to stay out of the country, he said, "I don't think it was a matter of cover-up, precisely."

A Church spokesman told the *Los Angeles Times* that the Archdiocese had wanted Tamayo to stay abroad out of concern for its members: "When people see their priest being accused of some sort of misconduct, there's a great deal of hurt among many, many people. . . . We're not in the business of hurting people, we're in the business of healing people."

How did the Church heal Rita Milla? Did truth and justice mean nothing to the Church? I thought the Church should worry more about innocent victims, and less about protecting its image and perpetuating the myth that its priests can do no wrong. Tamayo pleaded with the other priests to come forward and accept responsibility for their actions. None did, at least not immediately.

In 2002, when Rita Milla was forty and her daughter, Jacqueline, was nineteen, scores of sexual abuse lawsuits began to be filed against priests. I held a press conference in my office and again demanded that Roger Mahony, now Cardinal Mahony, help Jackie learn the identity of her father, since the Cardinal said that he wanted to help the victims of priests. "Help us find the father, Father," I said.

In a letter I wrote to Cardinal Mahony, I pointed out that, despite his statements that he had arrived at the Archdiocese after the sexual incidents between Rita Milla and the seven priests had transpired, he had been copied on the 1987 letter to Father Tamayo telling the priest to remain abroad. It was time for the Church to develop policies to help, not hurt, victims of sexual abuse by the clergy, and to provide support for the children of priests. Such children are truly children of the Church.

I asked him to fully and publicly acknowledge the Church's role in transferring and concealing the priests when Rita Milla's lawsuit was filed. I wanted full disclosure of his knowledge of the Archdiocese's role in discouraging Father Tamayo from returning to California. I asked him to help Jackie find her father. I wanted him to compensate her for the loss of her parental relationship with him, which occurred because the Church helped the priests disappear.

Although Mahony's spokesman, Tod Tamberg, stated, "We are very open to assisting Ms. Milla in her attempt to locate her father," the Church did nothing to assist us in our search for Jackie's father; it continued to stonewall us instead of providing the information that we sought. In addition, Cardinal Mahony refused to meet with Jackie and Rita, the victims of the priests, and did not provide one cent of compensation or support to them for the harm that they suffered.

With no help from the Church, we found Father Valentine Tugade, who was living in Fremont, California. (*People* magazine found Father Angel Cruces, who was a priest at Holy Cross Church in Manhattan. His comment to the magazine was, "Talk to the Archdiocese's lawyers in L.A.") We made numerous attempts to serve Father Tugade with a paternity lawsuit and were finally successful in serving him. We then asked the Court to order that Father Tugade take a DNA paternity test. He did and the results were 99.99% probability of paternity (the highest possible result). After the DNA tests results were delivered, on July 31, 2003, Los Angeles County Superior Court Judge Rolf M. Treu signed the legal judgment declaring Father Valentine Tugade the father of Jackie Milla. That legal judgment is now final.

What was Tugade's response? He told *People* magazine, "We had intercourse with her, a lot of us. . . . I repented a long time ago." He said he didn't owe Rita an apology. Despite his comments, we were all very happy that the day had finally come when Jackie at least knew the identity of her father.

The battle was not over, however. We still felt that the Archdiocese of Los Angeles and the Church should be held accountable to Rita for the harm that its priests had inflicted on her. An unusual bill, SB 1779, was introduced into the California legislature which would extend the statute of limitations to provide access to the courts for many victims of childhood sexual abuse by priests or other clergy. We sent a letter to Governor Gray Davis asking him to sign the bill and notified the press that we planned to hold a news conference outside the governor's office on July 11, 2002, in support of it. When we arrived at the news conference, representatives of the governor came out and told me that he had signed the bill into law at midnight (after I notified the press of my planned action at the governor's office).

This was an important victory for us because Rita's case against the Church had been barred largely based on a statute of limitations—the limited time period within which a lawsuit can be filed. Now Rita and other victims could have their day in court against the Church and those who had sexually abused them. This was particularly important in Rita's case because Rita had first gone to the Church for assistance, rather than to a lawyer, because she believed that the Church would help her. Instead of assisting her, the three Bishops who knew of her plight engaged in a pattern of delay and cover-up. They ran out the clock and then said that there was nothing they could do for her.

The Church should not, under any circumstances, be able to benefit by its own wrongdoing by abusing the trust of victims and then hiding behind the statute of limitations. If the Church knows, has reason to know, or is otherwise on notice of any un-lawful sexual conduct by an employee and fails to take reasonable steps and implement reasonable safeguards to avoid future acts of unlawful sexual conduct, we believe that it should be held ac-countable.

The new law opened the courthouse door (at least for a short time) for victims who had it shut in their faces in the past. Be-cause of this new law, we are once again pursuing Rita's case in court. Rita and Jackie have displayed enormous courage and re-fused to give up their battle for truth and justice. We will continue our legal battle for and with them until they receive the full mea-sure of justice that they deserve.

Empowerment Lesson

You can fight those who betray your trust, but you must persevere. People in power will often attempt to cover up their wrongs. Be ready for a David and Goliath battle that could take many years. Remember, often it's these long, hard-fought battles that yield the most important victories for victims.

CHAPTER 10

Beware of Bigotry

MEL MERMELSTEIN FIGHTS
THE HOLOCAUST DENIERS

When Mel Mermelstein arrived in our office in 1980, he still had tattooed on his arm the number A-4685, put there by the Nazis during World War II. Mel was a Jewish survivor of the Nazi death camps at Auschwitz-Birkenau and Buchenwauld.

The rest of his family hadn't been as fortunate. His father worked himself to death as a slave laborer for the Nazis, and his brother was shot and killed during a death march between concentration camps. On May 22, 1944, Mel watched helplessly as his sobbing mother and sisters were led to their deaths in Auschwitz's gas chamber No. 5, and then he saw the smoke curl out of the chimney as they were murdered.

Thirty-five years later, on November 20, 1980, having endured this hellish experience of human atrocity, Mel was shocked to receive a letter offering him $50,000 if he could prove that "Jews were gassed in gas chambers at Auschwitz." The letter came from the Institute for Historical Review (IHR), an organization that contends the Holocaust was a hoax. The letter further threatened that, if he did not accept the offer "very soon," the Institute would "publicize this fact to the mass media."

Fueled by his fury at these assertions, Mel decided to take them up on the offer and he formally accepted it on December 18, 1980. He submitted his recollections of his family members' deaths and eyewitness accounts of thirteen other death camp survivors.

He also produced hair and ashes of cremated Auschwitz prisoners and Zyklon B gas crystals used in the gas chambers. An IHR panel rejected his evidence and refused to pay the reward. It continued to assert the nonexistence of the Holocaust in its publications. It also published an open letter to Mermelstein, suggesting that he and other survivors were Nazi collaborators who perpetrated "the extermination hoax."

To stop the lies and the distortion of history, and to make a legal record for future generations, Mel decided to sue. He wanted to vindicate the memory of his family and the families of the six million Jews murdered by the Nazis.

My partner Michael Maroko took on the case, for very personal reasons. His parents were also death camp survivors. In February 1981, Mel filed a lawsuit against the IHR, its founder Willis Carto, and the Liberty Lobby, another group founded by Carto. Not all Jewish groups greeted Mel's lawsuit with applause. Some organizations feared that by appearing to dignify the IHR's claim with litigation, he was playing into the Holocaust deniers' hands, but Mel believed that future generations would be harmed if he didn't take a stand. "Resistance to tyrants is obedience to God," Mel said at the time, quoting Thomas Jefferson.

Mel won his first victory in October 1981, when a Los Angeles Superior Court judge ruled that the fact that Jews were gassed to death at Auschwitz was "indisputable."

In July 1985, Mel's courageous action was vindicated. Shortly before the trial was to start, we settled the case with the IHR, and it was ordered to pay Mel $90,000—$40,000 more than their original offer.

More significantly, the IHR agreed to make a formal, written apology. Willis Carto, his wife, and the other named defendants in the lawsuit stated that they "formally apologize to Mr. Mel Mermelstein . . . and all other survivors of Auschwitz for the pain, anguish and suffering he and all other Auschwitz survivors have sustained relating to the $50,000 reward offer."

We also forced them to acknowledge, on the record, the judge's ruling that Jews were gassed to death at Auschwitz and that the reward offer was abusive to survivors of Auschwitz.

Our victory in the case sent a clear message to those throughout the world who attempt to distort history and inflict misery and suffering on Jews. Survivors of the Holocaust would fight back through the legal system to protect themselves and vindicate the truth about their lives and the history of World War II. With this case, we brought these formerly influential and powerful defendants to their knees.

While others might have rested on this accomplishment, Mel wasn't done just yet.

There was one defendant who didn't settle, so my partner Michael and I proceeded to trial. Ditlieb Felderer, a Swedish citizen and member of the IHR's editorial advisory committee, had been sending despicable literature to Mel ever since he submitted proof of his family's deaths at Auschwitz.

Over a period of years, Felderer sent a "Jewish Information Bulletin" that he published, which stated that the Holocaust was a hoax and continually challenged Mel to prove Jews were gassed to death at Auschwitz. One Felderer publication said Mel was "peddling the extermination hoax" and called him "a racist and exterminationist." Another mailing taunted Mel's beliefs by including hair that Felderer claimed was the "hair of a gassed victim" and a condom that supposedly contained the semen of Jewish gas chamber victims. In another, Felderer said that, instead of a death camp, Auschwitz was a place where "ice cream was served" and where "there was a first-class kitchen with expert cooks, children had toys to play with and they had special playgrounds, there was a modern swimming pool for the prisoners, there was a Red Cross" and "a special football ground."

Felderer had other legal problems during this time as well. In 1982, he was prosecuted in Sweden for violation of its criminal libel laws. Mel flew to Sweden to testify at the trial. The Swedish court convicted Felderer of persecution of a minority and sentenced him to ten months in prison.

In January 1986, our civil trial against Felderer began in Los Angeles Superior Court before a jury of twelve. During the trial, from which Felderer was absent (he never answered the complaint), Mel testified about his personal suffering at the death camps and about the many atrocities perpetrated by the Nazis against the Jews. We won the case when an all-Christian jury awarded Mel $5.2 million in damages for libel and intentional infliction of emotional distress. Mel trembled and choked back tears as the clerk read the decision. Michael and I were overcome with emotion.

This case was extremely important to my partners and me. The record we made in these lawsuits was sent throughout the world and remains a written memorial to the six million Jews murdered by the Nazis and to the courageous survivors of those death camps. It will serve as a testament to future generations that the truth will live forever and as a reminder of our hope that Jewish people will never again suffer another Holocaust.

Later, I was profoundly disturbed when a TV movie made of Mel's story portrayed his attorneys as Irish Catholics. It distorted the historical record about the role that Jewish people played in winning the case. Mel's Irish Catholic lawyer had filed the case, but ended up withdrawing from it. Jewish lawyers in my firm then took the case and spent thousands of hours and three years litigating it, before we won it.

In an editorial I wrote for the *Los Angeles Times* about the movie, I said that Jewish people are entitled to the truth about Jewish history. Stereotypes that portray them as not caring about other Jews, or as not having the courage or sense to stand up for each other, are not only harmful to the self-esteem and pride of the Jewish community, but to the very existence of the Jewish people.

It was ironic to have litigated a lawsuit against those who wanted to revise history about the Holocaust, only to find ourselves then having to respond to a TV version of the same lawsuit that appeared to revise history about who won the case. Jewish lawyers fought and won an important battle for a Holocaust survivor and the world had a right to know that!

Empowerment Lesson

Even the most vulnerable people, such as Holocaust survivors, can and will fight back.

Let this be an inspiration to you. If you have been victimized so much in the past that you no longer feel you have the strength to fight, reach down within yourself and remember this: If Mel could fight back and win after having suffered unimaginable horrors, you too can find the necessary strength to meet your challenges.

"GWEN" ARAUJO—TRANSGENDERED TEEN
DEAD AT SEVENTEEN

From an early age, the child who was born Eddie Araujo Jr. felt like a female trapped in a male's body. In his early teens, he expressed those feelings to his family in Newark, California, who accepted his transgender status—that Eddie self-identified as a woman. They supported him and continued to love him when he dyed his hair pink, dressed as a female, and began calling himself "Gwen"—after his favorite singer, Gwen Stefani. From then on, most members of his family considered Gwen a she, and I will refer to her that way as well.

Dressing the way that she did was an expression of her identity. She was being honest about who she felt she was and had every right to project a self-image not associated with her biological maleness. Her mother knew her to be a sweet and loving spirit, as did her siblings, many aunts, uncles, and friends. She was extremely bright and touched many lives.

Others were less tolerant. Gwen often didn't go to school because she felt ostracized by her teachers and other students. She felt that her teachers did not appreciate her uniqueness or her skills. Some of them even made fun of her. She felt that she didn't have the full opportunities enjoyed by other students because of the way she was treated.

Gwen's sister, Pearl, often intervened when other kids picked on her sibling. To Gwen's family, it didn't matter what she wore; they knew her as their kind and gentle sister, daughter, niece, and grandchild who loved and trusted people, had a passion for Monarch butterflies, and enjoyed cooking for her family. She took a caring, protective role with her family and checked the doors and windows each night to make sure they were secure. She was searching for acceptance and wanted to believe that others would give it to her.

Her search and her life ended October 3, 2002. That night, the seventeen-year-old put on a stylish denim skirt and went to a party, just blocks away from her home. She never returned. Instead, she was brutally killed by individuals who decided that she would pay the ultimate price for what they believed was her deception. According to the criminal trial testimony of one of those individuals, Jaron Nabors, when he and three other young men at the party learned to a certainty that the pretty girl (with whom two of them had recently had sex) had male genitalia, Gwen was slapped, kneed, choked, and hit with a can and a skillet. A rope was tied around her neck and she was strangled. The young men then drove 150 miles away to the foothills of the Sierra Nevada mountains and buried Gwen's body in a shallow grave—"Tony Soprano style," according to testimony by one of the defendants in the criminal case. Jaron Nabors agreed to plead guilty to involuntary manslaughter in exchange for an eleven-year prison sentence if he testified truthfully at trial. The other three men were charged with murder.

The funeral was attended by over a thousand people from the Latino working-class community and media from around the country came to cover it. The church was filled to overflowing. Inside the funeral home, Gwen's mother Sylvia honored Gwen by having her dressed the way she would have wanted: in a skirt, blouse, and makeup. Later, she had her child's name legally changed to Gwen.

Gwen's mother, Sylvia Guerrero, and other relatives asked me to represent their family. I was shocked that anyone could think they had a right to terminate someone's life because of his or her sexual identity. I believed that Gwen had been targeted and murdered because of *who she was,* a factor over which she had no control. It is exactly the same as someone being murdered for being black, or Jewish. Gwen had a right to be who she was; she had no duty to live a lie to conform to someone else's standards. Unfortunately, honesty and courage cost Gwen her life.

The district attorney charged the men not only with murder, but with a hate crime. The killers' strategy during the first trial, which began in May 2004, was thought by many to be a so-called "gay panic" or "transpanic" defense. Previously, two of the defendants had had sex with her, allegedly thinking at the time that they were having anal sex with a girl. Defense attorneys claimed their clients went into alcohol and drug-fueled "shock and panic" when they realized that Gwen had the anatomy of a male.

Jury deliberation lasted almost three weeks. On June 22, 2004, the jury announced that they were deadlocked, but not because the gay or transpanic argument worked. The district attorney indicated that the entire jury voted in favor of a murder conviction for the three men, but were deadlocked over whether it was first or second degree murder. The DA immediately announced that the case would be tried again.

The good news was that the jury didn't buy that gay panic or transpanic argument. They felt it was murder and refused to come back with a verdict of manslaughter or acquittal.

A retrial of the three young men was conducted in 2005. After three months of testimony, the jury found two of the men guilty of second degree murder in the death of Gwen Araujo. Their names were Michael William Magidson and Jose Antonio Merel. The jury deadlocked on the third defendant, Jason Cazares, and did not find the hate crime allegation to be true as to any of the defendants. On December 16, 2005, Jason Cazares entered a plea of "no contest" to voluntary manslaughter.

Empowerment Lesson

Everyone has a right to live their lives free of violence. Gwen was a teen who happened to be transgendered. She had not yet had an operation to change her anatomy but was planning to do so. Help to educate the public about the fact that such individuals are not choosing to be transgendered any more than others are choosing to be gay or heterosexual. It is instead a matter of their sexual orientation and sexual identity.

Stand up for minorities, whether or not you are a member of that group. Transgendered individuals should not have to pay with their lives for being who they are.

OUR FIGHT FOR EQUALITY IN MARRIAGE

On February 12, 2004, with Valentine's Day around the corner, two couples applied for marriage licenses in Beverly Hills. Both couples were in loving, committed, long-term, stable relationships.

I was there when both couples were turned away. California law, they were told, defined marriage as the union of a man and a woman. These couples did not fit that legal definition. I immediately announced that I would be filing a lawsuit on behalf of the couples challenging the state statute as unconstitutional.

Robin Tyler was a nationally known lesbian rights activist and leader. Her life partner, Diane Olson, was the granddaughter of former California Governor Culbert Levy Olson. Reverend Troy D. Perry was the first openly gay member of the Los Angeles Human Rights Commission and a past delegate to the White House Conference on Hate Crimes. He and his partner, Phillip Ray DeBlieck, were legally married in Canada in July 2003. They wanted the same legal recognition in California. Both couples wanted to marry for the same reasons that heterosexual couples wish to marry. They are in loving, committed relationships, and they wish to signify that to their families, their community, and to each other by assuming all the legal rights and responsibilities that the law recognizes in "marriage."

They turned to our firm for assistance. We believed that refusing these couples state licenses to marry denied them their constitutional rights. We thought that the state had no compelling interest that justified excluding same-gender couples from the marriage relationship. Several weeks later, we filed a lawsuit against Los Angeles County challenging the denial of the two marriage licenses. We argued that the statute relied upon by the county was unconstitutional because it violated constitutional guarantees of equal protection under the law, due process, the right to enjoy and defend life and liberty; the right to acquire, possess and protect property, and the right to pursue and obtain safety, happiness and privacy. We also sought recognition of Reverend Perry and Mr. DeBlieck's Canadian marriage in California. We wanted an injunction that would compel the county to issue those licenses.

We hoped our legal action would pave the way for other same-gender couples who wished to marry. The issue is not about being relegated to the back of the bus; it is about not being allowed to get on the bus at all. Every day that these couples are denied the right to marry is a day when they are being irreparably damaged by the denial of their fundamental constitutional rights. The days of accepting a "separate and unequal" status—or domestic partnership rights, which provide only some legal, economic, and social benefits of marriage, but not all—are now long past for lesbian and gay couples who wish to marry.

Our clients were the first in the state to file a lawsuit challenging the constitutionality of the marriage statute that purported to ban same-gender marriage. We vowed to fight this matter all the way to the California Supreme Court, if that's what it took. The Court had to decide whether the California Constitution would protect same-gender couples from discrimination and second-class citizenship under the law.

At the time, there were other lawsuits filed in San Francisco challenging the legality of San Francisco Mayor Gavin Newsom's decision to issue marriage licenses to same-gender couples before the court had a chance to rule on the constitutionality of the marriage law. That was a different legal question than ours. Our case challenged Los Angeles County's *denial* of a marriage license and went to the core of the question of the constitutionality of the law defining marriage as a contract between a man and a woman.

Still, all the cases were consolidated and brought before San Francisco Judge Richard Kramer, where my law partner John West and I argued our case in December 2004.

On March 14, 2005, we won a historic victory when Judge Kramer issued his decision. I was particularly pleased that the Judge adopted many of the arguments that I had made to him. He agreed that the statutes were unconstitutional and a violation of the equal protection clause of the California Constitution. In rejecting the State's argument, Judge Kramer stated, "The state's protracted denial of equal protection cannot be justified simply because such constitutional violation has become traditional."

He also rejected the arguments that marriage was primarily designed for procreation, recognizing that there can be procreation without marriage and marriage without procreation.

He also dismissed the State's arguments that because same-gender domestic partner rights provide benefits similar to those enjoyed by married couples, there is no denial of equal protection.

Citing the historic Brown v. Board of Education decision that struck down segregated schools, Judge Kramer stated, "The idea that marriage-like rights without marriage is adequate smacks of a concept long rejected by the courts—separate but equal."

We were very proud of our clients, who were the first in California to file such a lawsuit. We recognize that the struggle has just begun and that, ultimately, the case will be appealed to the California Supreme Court. As promised, we intend to pursue the case to a final resolution that guarantees all same-gender couples in California the right to marry.

Empowerment Lesson

If you are gay or lesbian, you need not accept laws which force you to accept second-class citizenship and which deny you rights enjoyed by others. Political action—such as applying for a marriage license even if you know that you will be denied it—helps the public understand that you feel that you should be entitled to the same legal rights that others enjoy. Following the political action with a lawsuit will ultimately compel the courts to answer the question of whether or not your state constitution requires that you enjoy equal protection under the law.

Minorities have never been given their rights. They have always had to wage a political and legal battle to win them. It may take many years, but I am confident that one day this battle will be won.

CHAPTER 11

Motherhood Is Powerful

WOMEN IN CHAINS

When I first took this case, I had to check my calendar. The policies at the Sybil Brand Institute women's jail sounded like something from the fourteenth century, not Los Angeles in 1980.

Los Angeles County sheriff's deputies were chaining pregnant women inmates to beds, laundry carts, and other pieces of furniture while they were in labor and when giving birth. The department, then led by Sheriff Peter Pitchess, claimed the practice was necessary to prevent female prisoners from escaping from the County USC (University of Southern California) Medical Center, where they were taken to deliver their babies.

I was horrified by the practice. As someone who had given birth to a child, I also knew that it was preposterous to think that a woman in the midst of labor and childbirth had the time, the inclination, or the physical ability to make an escape! If security was an issue, why not just lock the delivery room door, or have an officer present?

On behalf of Sharon Larson and other inmates who did not wish to give birth in chains, our firm sued the Sheriff of Los Angeles County. Sharon, who was thirty-four years old, had been convicted of prostitution and was incarcerated in the Los Angeles County Jail for violating her parole. Her violation was simply that she had been found within the borders of Hollywood after having been ordered to stay out of that city. Sharon was nine months pregnant when we filed the suit. She'd heard about the chains and was terrified of being shackled while she was in childbirth.

We filed for an immediate injunction against the practice and I went to court on my birthday, July 3, 1980. We were not the only ones who felt that the practice of chaining pregnant women during childbirth was medieval and inhumane. The case generated widespread public outrage. Los Angeles Superior Court Judge Jerry Pacht, who heard our case, said that if what we alleged was true, then the practice was "barbaric."

The Sheriff's Department agreed to halt the practice, but only on an "experimental" basis. We wanted more. Although Sharon was allowed to give birth later that month, free of chains, we wanted a permanent end to the pain and degradation suffered by women forced to give birth in chains.

Four years later, we settled the case when the Sheriff's Department formally agreed never again to restrain pregnant inmates during labor or delivery. That result, which we fought for and won, was the best birthday gift I had ever received.

Empowerment Lesson

Even women who are pregnant, chained, and in jail can fight back and win victories. Although they have been convicted of a crime, they should still be afforded the right to be treated as human beings. Security concerns cannot justify cruel and inhuman punishment.

Prisoners can challenge authority if their rights have been violated, and if they do so in a timely and appropriate manner.

GET CREATIVE TO GET CHILD SUPPORT

Single mothers who cannot collect adequate amounts of child support often lead lives of quiet desperation. They are the true "desperate housewives." Often they cannot pay their rent, put enough food on the table for their children, take their children to the doctor, or buy shoes, clothing or medicine for their little ones.

When fathers don't pay their court-ordered child support on time or in the amount they are ordered to pay, their children suffer. Millions of mothers face this problem every day. It is the number one reason that mothers are forced into poverty and onto the welfare program, Aid to Families with Dependent Children (AFDC). Compounding the problem is the fact that the system often fails to assist these mothers in collecting their child support in a timely and meaningful way. Deadbeat dads think they can get away with avoiding their responsibilities—and too often they are right.

I've had plenty of personal experience with the problems that single moms encounter when trying to collect child support. After my divorce, the father of my child was sporadic in his financial support. Eventually, his inadequate and irregular child support checks stopped coming altogether. Unable to afford an apartment, I was forced to live with my parents.

I did not want to go on welfare, so I consulted an attorney and commenced legal action to force my daughter's father to meet his child support obligations. It wasn't a battle I wanted to fight but I felt that I had no choice. My child needed the support. Her father had the ability to pay and I refused to feel guilty about asserting her rights. Ultimately, the man who had once been my Prince Charming was sent to jail for failing to pay his court-ordered child support.

Years later, when I became an attorney, my personal battle for child support inspired me to work to improve and change the system to help other single moms with their own support dilemmas. I knew from experience how hard it was for mothers to obtain orders for child support and to enforce them once they were made. It was while fighting these battles that I realized I needed to be creative in drawing attention to the issue.

On Mother's Day, 1978, I launched a campaign to pass a "Parental Responsibility Bill" in California. I organized a mother's march and sent apple pies to state legislators with labels that read: "Supporting Your Children Is as American as Apple Pie." California passed the bill, which enabled custodial parents to get a wage assignment (forced collection from the parent's wages of the child support owed) as soon as the delinquent parent missed one month's payment of child support. After the bill passed, I heard that then-Governor Jerry Brown had indicated he might veto the bill. I took immediate action. Accompanied by some angry single mothers who had problems collecting child support, I went to the governor's office in Los Angeles and hung diapers on a clothesline that said, "Sign the Child Support bill." Our event received widespread media coverage. Brown signed the bill. It became law in 1980 and was the first of its kind in the nation.

Despite the bill's passage, I remained concerned that so many mothers were still unable to collect their court-ordered child support on time, or in the amount ordered, or both. I knew that it was important to keep pressure on elected officials to help the children. I therefore made it a practice, whenever possible, to meet with new district attorneys in Los Angeles County to discuss ways to improve child support enforcement.

District attorneys were and still are very important in this process. Many mothers are unable to afford the help of private attorneys and depend on the county district attorney to help them collect support that their children are owed. DA's have a legal duty to assist the public without charge. Often, however, they fail in this responsibility.

In 1985, I had an appointment to meet with newly elected Los Angeles County District Attorney Ira Reiner. Before his election, I had encountered Mr. Reiner at a reception and told him that I'd like to meet with him about child support enforcement in the event that he won his race. He had invited me to do just that. On the day set for our meeting, I went to his office. I planned to propose an innovative child support amnesty program to offer deadbeat parents immunity from prosecution if they agreed to pay their delinquent child support payments. My research found that a similar county program in another state had improved child support collections. I also told the media about my meeting and my proposed amnesty program.

When I arrived at Mr. Reiner's office, his receptionist told me that the district attorney was not going to be able to meet with me.

"What do you mean he is not going to meet with me?" I asked her. "I have an appointment. He said he would meet with me. If he has an emergency, of course I'll be happy to reschedule and come back another time."

She said, "Well, I can't make another appointment."

"That's not acceptable," I told her. "I'll sit here in the office until he calls in and at that time, please tell him that I am here and that I'm waiting to have another appointment made."

I sat there all afternoon. At the end of the day, the receptionist still said that she would not be able to make another appointment. Again I told her that this was unacceptable.

Finally she said, "If you don't leave by the end of the day, you're going to be locked in all night."

"Fine," I said. "Lock me in. This is too important. He needs to discuss child support enforcement."

So, they locked me in.

I called my daughter and told her I wasn't going home because I was locked in the district attorney's office. There I stayed. In the middle of the night the telephone rang in one of the offices, so I answered it. It was a reporter from the local radio station.

"We're just calling to see if you're still there—oh my gosh, you *are* still there! I can't believe this!"

The next morning the media arrived, and so did some mothers who had child support problems. All day, they sat there with me in his office.

At the end of the second day, the district attorney's staff seemed to have decided that I was on my way to becoming a martyr and they asked me to leave. When I wouldn't, they summoned some law enforcement personnel, who literally picked me up and threw me out of the building. A photo of me being thrown out of the district attorney's office over child support appeared on the front page of the *Los Angeles Daily News* the next day. Even though I had been physically ejected, the following day I came right back like a boomerang to the DA's office. I sat there all day again. It was getting to be a bigger and bigger story. At some point on that third day, I spoke with the former DA of Los Angeles County, Robert Philibosian, who offered a creative solution. He said that if I would shut down my sit-in, he would get me an appointment with James Stockdale, the acting Secretary of Health and Welfare for California, who oversaw child support programs throughout the state.

I left Ira Reiner's office and went up to Sacramento to meet with Mr. Stockdale, who thought my amnesty proposal was an excellent idea. He said he'd call other district attorneys in other California counties to see if they wanted to try it. In a very short period of time, we had five DA's ready to try the idea in their counties—Los Angeles was not among them. Eventually, I convinced eleven other counties to do what DA Reiner refused to do. As a result, the state recovered millions of dollars in child support, much of which helped moms to care for their kids.

As a result of my efforts, I was nominated for the President's Volunteer Action Award, which I received in 1986 from President Reagan at the White House. That year, I was the only person in the nation to win that award from the president for volunteer action on child support.

I found out later that my arrival at the White House caused some panic among the president's staff when they realized that Gloria Allred would be coming up to the stage to receive an award from President Reagan and the First Lady. Of course, there was a huge amount of press on hand to cover the event, and the president's staff didn't know what I might say when I got onstage. They feared that I might make a statement of protest on some issue and embarrass the president. They asked what I planned to do and suggested that I just smile and accept the award.

I said, "Excuse me, but you invited Gloria Allred, and I seriously doubt that you would ask this of the other people. You just need to trust me, but if you don't want me to go up and accept the award, I won't. However, if you do that, I may have a comment to make later about why I didn't go up to the stage to accept my award from the president."

They wisely decided to let me go onstage. I smiled, and accepted my award without further comment. Afterward, when all the other recipients were taken to meet the press, I was kept behind to look at portraits on a wall, an obvious ruse. When I finally went to meet the media, they were gone.

What the president's staff didn't know was that I would never have said anything critical of the president at that time, because I would not have taken the risk of embarrassing the two people who had nominated me for the award and shown such confidence and trust in me. On the other hand, I would never have compromised myself by promising what I would or wouldn't do and allowing the president's staff to set conditions on me for accepting an award that I had won.

Years later, Ira Reiner and I agreed to meet—not in his office, but in a coffee shop on Sunset Boulevard—to see if we could resolve our differences. He ended up appointing me cochair of his child support enforcement committee for Los Angeles County, and soon the amnesty program was successfully instituted there as well.

Some time later, I called an elected county official to make an appointment with him about another subject. When I arrived in his office, he told me, "I had to see you. I was afraid if I didn't, you'd arrive at my office with a sleeping bag."

My fight for stronger child support enforcement continues. I've testified in the legislature, I've lobbied, I've filed lawsuits. There is still a long way to go, but we are making inroads.

Empowerment Lesson

Sometimes you should just refuse to take "No" for an answer. "No," is still a communication. Keep talking and get creative until that answer changes to "Yes." Do everything that you can that is legal and nonviolent to win change.

STOLEN EGGS, A STOLEN SON

Imagine waking up one day to find that you were a parent to a child you never knew existed. I can understand how this has happened to more than a few men—but how could it happen to a woman?

Jane Doe confronted this nightmare in 1995, when she discovered that she was the mother of a seven-year-old boy. This unusual saga began in 1985 when Jane, then thirty-eight, longed to have a child but was unable to conceive. Her doctor referred her to Dr. Richard Asch, a fertility specialist at the University of California at Irvine's Center for Reproductive Health.

Under the supervision of surgeon Dr. Jose Balmaceda, a so-called "GIFT" procedure was performed. Balmaceda would "harvest" Jane's eggs and fertilize them with sperm from her husband.

Before the surgery, Jane was asked whether she wanted to donate any extra eggs taken from her body to other women. She said no. She asked that her extra eggs be fertilized with her husband's sperm and stored, so that she could avoid the discomfort of further fertility shots that the procedure required. After her surgery, Jane was told that a total of sixteen of her eggs had been taken. Four of them had been fertilized with her husband's sperm and were returned to her uterus. Of the remaining eggs, only about half were viable. Jane was told that those fertilized eggs had been placed into storage, as she requested.

In 1995, a newspaper reporter called Jane to tell her that at least one of her fertilized eggs had been taken by a doctor at the clinic and been implanted without her knowledge or consent into another woman, who had given birth to a son. The child Jane had always wanted was now seven, and he didn't even know that she existed. When Jane came to see me, my partners and I were horrified by her story. We felt that it was one of the most callous acts ever to have been inflicted on a woman. Did these doctors believe they had the right to play God?

Jane was not alone—almost one hundred other prospective parents had suffered similar thefts by the doctors at the UCI fertility clinic—but her case was among the most painful and emotionally gut-wrenching to emerge from the scandal. Her stolen egg had produced a child. In this regard, she appeared to be unique. The saga was complicated by the disappearance of all the clinical and laboratory records relating to the disposition of her eggs, along with the disappearance of Dr. Balmaceda and Dr. Asch, who fled the country.

The scandal made international headlines and raised significant biomedical, ethical, and legal issues. How could the system allow patients' eggs to be taken and transferred to others without the knowledge and consent of the women from whom the eggs were taken? What did the clinic operators know and when did they know it? Why did oversight systems fail to prevent such a biomedical nightmare? Would the clinic operators compensate the patient if a child had been born?

We filed a lawsuit against the AMI Medical Center of Garden Grove, UC Irvine, the doctors who ran the infertility program, and others, alleging negligence, fraud, intentional infliction of emotional distress, conversion, and negligent and intentional spoliation of evidence. Other women sued as well, but none of the alleged victims were in the particularly painful position in which Jane found herself, having only just discovered the existence of a seven-year-old son. The university ultimately paid out nearly $15 million to settle seventy-five cases. Jane received a substantial settlement, which was close to the maximum for this type of case, but of course no amount of money would be sufficient to compensate for all that she suffered.

Of greater importance to Jane was that she was able to confirm through DNA testing that the young boy was, in fact, her biological child. Although Jane had never met her son, she was able to receive pictures of him and talk on the telephone to the only mother the child had ever known. She took comfort in the fact that he was growing up in a family that loved him and provided him a positive, supportive home. Putting what she believed were the child's best interests first, she decided to allow him to continue to live with his "family" of seven years.

I hope that no other women will ever have to face such a difficult and heart-breaking decision again.

Empowerment Lesson

We place our faith and trust in doctors believing that they will help us and do us no harm. In most cases, they are worthy of our trust. Occasionally, however, there are physicians who violate the Hippocratic Oath, and violate us in the process. In those cases, have the courage to stand up against those who have hurt you. Consult legal counsel if you believe that your doctor has committed malpractice.

SOMETIMES MOMS NEED TO MOVE ON

Wendy Burgess wanted the best life possible for her children. In 1996, recently divorced and with primary custody of her kids, Wendy wanted to move a mere forty miles away from her ex-husband. The distance from Tehachapi to Lancaster, California, was slight, but the benefits to Wendy and her children would be great. Before her divorce, Wendy and her ex-husband both worked at the Tehachapi state prison, but now she was offered a better paying position at the state prison in Lancaster, which would allow her to give their kids a better quality of life.

Wendy's ex-husband fought the move. The courts initially agreed with Wendy, but then the California Court of Appeals reversed the decision. At that time, California law said that parents who had previously been awarded primary custody of their children could lose that custody simply because they—in good faith—wanted to relocate.

When Wendy contacted us and asked us to represent her, we decided that a relocation of the law's priorities was in order. There were numerous good faith reasons why a parent would need to move after a divorce—such as remarriage to a spouse who lived in a different location, a search for better employment opportunities in a different city, the avoidance of long commutes, the pursuit of a better educational opportunity, and reunion with a family that could provide additional emotional and financial support. As long as the move was not motivated by an intent to keep the other parent from seeing his or her child and the noncustodial parent could still have frequent and continuing visitation, what was the problem?

Noncustodial parents—usually fathers—were permitted to move whenever they wanted, wherever they wanted, for as long as they wanted, and they could do so without seeking permission from the court or risking the loss of their visitation rights. They didn't even have a legal duty to visit a child, and many did not.

Why was it that fathers could move without risking the loss of their visitation rights, but when custodial parents (usually mothers) moved, they risked losing custody? We filed a petition with the California Supreme Court, which agreed to hear the case in 1996. The court not only agreed with us that Wendy Burgess should be allowed to move, but it further declared that a custodial parent no longer had to prove in court that such a move was necessary, once she or he established that the move was in good faith (defined as not motivated to deprive the father of his visitation rights). This decision severed the legal chain that bound divorced custodial parents to the whims of their ex-spouses. We had won a precedent-setting victory for Wendy and millions of other mothers—and their children.

It certainly helped pave the way for Californian Gina Ocon, who also wanted to move to better her life and that of her ten-month old daughter. Gina wanted to move to Cambridge, Massachusetts, to complete her degree at Harvard University, but the father of her child went to court in California to seek a change of custody if Gina relocated. His legal action essentially forced Gina to choose between the best education available and the custody of her daughter. To please her daughter's dad, Gina considered quitting school, but she concluded that dropping out would set the wrong example for her baby girl.

She came to me for representation. We argued in court that no mother should have to make such a choice. The judge agreed that Gina could be trusted to decide what was in the best interest of her baby and that she could move with her child. It was another victory for us and for Gina, who ultimately earned her degree from Harvard.

Empowerment Lesson

In today's mobile society, parents who separate often feel it is best that they relocate. They should never have to face the horrendous consequences of losing custody of their children because they choose to make a move that they, in good faith, believe is in their children's best interest. As long as custodial parents can find ways for the noncustodial parents to have frequent and continuing contact with their children, parents with primary custody should be able to move.

"Move-away" laws vary from state to state. Consult a family law attorney in your state about your "move-away rights" before you move with your children.

THE CRUELEST KIND OF CUSTODY

In 1998, I became involved in a case that was and still is one of the most emotionally challenging of my career.

It all began when Teri Martinez asked me to assist her after her twin sister, Toni Dykstra, was killed in mysterious circumstances in the presence of Carlo Ventre, the father of Toni's child. Carlo and Toni had met in a restaurant in 1994. Carlo Alberto Ventre was an Italian citizen (born in Libya), who said he owned a plumbing supply business in Los Angeles. Toni Dykstra was a pretty woman with blond hair who was raised in Riverside and loved to barrel race horses with her twin sister, Teri. When she met Ventre, she was struggling to raise two daughters from a prior marriage. Toni fell in love with Ventre, who was twenty-two years her senior, and months later moved in with him. Their daughter, Santina, was born on November 15, 1995.

After Santina's birth, their relationship steadily deteriorated. Police were summoned to the house several times to quell domestic disputes. Toni is no longer with us to explain what she experienced with Carlo Ventre when Santina was an infant, but her voice can be heard in sworn declarations that she filed with the court. In these, she claimed that Ventre did not allow her to breast-feed Santina or even give the infant a bath. She claimed that Ventre would not allow her to leave the house; that he kept all the keys to the house they shared, and that he had the phones turned off. She alleged that Ventre told her that the neighbors were watching her. According to Toni's declarations, there were times when Ventre would not allow Toni's other two young daughters to see their sister Santina. Finally they separated. Then an intense and heart-breaking battle for custody of Santina began.

Toni claimed in court declarations that Ventre was constantly threatening to take Santina to Italy so that Toni would never see her daughter again. Worse, she alleged that he was threatening to kill her, as well as her two older daughters. Ventre drew up custody papers awarding custody of Santina to him. He allegedly told Toni that if she didn't sign the custody agreement, he would throw acid in her face so that she would never be attractive to anybody again.

Finally, in August 1996, when Santina was nine months old, Toni sought refuge with her two other daughters in a shelter for abused women. She was unable to take Santina when she left in the middle of the night because Ventre had locked himself in the room with the baby. According to Toni's declarations, Ventre refused to allow her to take Santina when she returned the next day.

The ensuing court struggle for custody of Santina was ugly. During a mediation with the couple, Ventre, according to Toni's testimony, became so aggressive on the issue of custody that the mediator told Ventre he'd have to behave or leave the room. On September 25, 1996, a Los Angeles Superior Court judge issued a temporary order granting joint custody to the couple and ordered Ventre not to take Santina to Italy without three days' written notice to Toni.

Before permanent custody could be resolved, Toni alleged that on March 11, 1997, Ventre called her to tell her that he was in Ostia, Italy, with Santina and was going to Rome—and that he was never coming back to America. Toni said Ventre told her he was going to look for a new mother for Santina. Toni called the police and filed a report. Ventre did return to California with Santina a month later, but in October 1997, he allegedly again threatened to take his daughter to Italy.

Toni, a paralegal, worked with lawyers in her office to help her regain custody of Santina. She felt that her chances were looking good for the next hearing, which was scheduled in the spring of 1998. As Toni's spirits rose in anticipation of the hearing, in January 1998, Ventre kidnapped Santina and took her to Italy. Toni alleged that he again called her from Italy and told her they were never coming back.

Toni was frantic. She filed another report with the police and asked for a court hearing regarding Ventre's alleged violation of the court's order. Throughout this period, Toni alleged that Ventre called her repeatedly and told her to cancel the hearing, or else she would never see Santina again. According to Toni's declarations, he said that if he had to return to the United States for the hearing, he would kill Toni and her two other daughters.

At her custody hearing in March 1998, which Ventre did not attend, the judge granted her sole legal and physical custody of her daughter. The judge also stated in his order that Ventre had "wrongfully caused the residence of the minor child Santina Ventre . . . to be changed to the country of Italy in direct violation of prior orders of this court." The court referred the case to the Los Angeles County District Attorney's office for assistance in obtaining Santina's return.

Although Toni Dykstra sought help from the DA's office under that court order, none was forthcoming under the reign of Los Angeles County DA Gil Garcetti. Toni came to the painful conclusion that if she ever wanted to get her daughter back, she would have to go to Italy herself to get her. She realized that she was risking her life but she felt that she had no alternative.

In April 1998, Toni asked for assistance from the U.S. State Department under the Hague Convention on Child Abduction. Armed with the Los Angeles Superior Court judge's order and a court date in Rome, Toni, using her life savings, went to Italy in July 1998, to try to bring back Santina. U.S. State Department officials arranged for her to stay at a convent near the Vatican.

At her Italian court hearing on July 20, 1998, the Italian Hague court found that Ventre had wrongfully taken Santina from the United States, and ordered that she be returned to her mother. When authorities went to pick up her daughter, however, Santina was said to be sick with pneumonia and was taken to the hospital.

As she waited for her baby to recover, Toni visited Santina every day at the hospital. She also called home every day. On July 28, 1998, the day before she was to return to the United States with Santina, she told her twin sister Teri that she feared for her life. Her premonition proved tragically accurate. Later that day, Toni was found dead on the floor of Ventre's Italian apartment. Newspaper accounts say neighbors heard a woman screaming "Help! No!" earlier that day.

Ventre told the Italian authorities who took him into custody that Toni came at him with an axe and when he pushed her away, she fell and hit her head on the fireplace. It was an accident, he said.

He was released just days later. In the meantime, two-year-old Santina was sent to an Italian orphanage and then to a series of foster homes in Italy. Toni's nightmare had now become her daughter's as well.

Toni's sister Teri came to me for help after Toni's tragic death because she couldn't get her sister's body back and didn't know where Santina was being held. In addition, she wanted to know the truth about her sister's last moments and she wanted justice if Carlo was criminally responsible for her sister's death. She told me that Toni had just become a paralegal but that her goal had been to go to law school "and become the next Gloria Allred." That is why Teri called me. For once I was speechless. Sitting in front of me was a young woman who was clearly devastated by the death of her sister, who had been both her identical twin and her best friend. Teri described the circumstances surrounding Toni's death, which struck me as highly suspicious. I decided that I would do what I could to help her. At that time, I had no idea that my battle for justice for Toni would last for more than seven years.

We began by protesting Ventre's release from custody by picketing outside of the Italian Consulate in Los Angeles. Given the mysterious circumstances of this case and the fact that Santina was still in Italy, we believed that Ventre should be kept in jail until a trial was held, or until the case was resolved. If the authorities refused to put him in jail, we didn't want him to be allowed to visit Santina.

I went to Italy to expedite the return of Toni's body for burial by her loved ones, and to find out where Santina was, win her return to the United States, and explore whether the Italian legal system would provide justice for Toni. I put together a team of U.S. lawyers who agreed to work for free. Now I needed to find Italian lawyers in Italy who would also agree to work pro bono (for free). It wasn't easy.

When I met with the first attorney recommended to me in Italy, I told him about Toni's allegations of emotional abuse by Carlo Ventre that were contained in court documents. I said that I had become aware that Carlo had been accused of violence by other women. The attorney shrugged, asking, "Why does that matter in this case?"

It was one of those moments when I felt that my whole life was passing before me. In the United States, we are very aware that prior allegations of domestic violence can be relevant in an appropriate criminal case involving the death of an intimate partner. I was shocked that someone would even raise the question of whether it mattered. I looked for another lawyer.

I wondered if there was a women's rights group in Italy who could help, and got a referral to one. I don't speak Italian, but I made the telephone call hoping that someone on the other end would speak English. I said, "I'm Gloria Allred, an attorney from the United States and I need to make an appointment to come in and talk about a case."

There was silence on the other end of the line. Suddenly the woman shouted, "Gloria Allred! O. J. Simpson! Come right over!" It was hilarious. I ended up meeting a wonderful group of women lawyers who helped women who were victims of violence in Rome. They helped for a while, but because the case was extremely time intensive, they were unable to continue.

I met with a prosecutor in the Italian judicial system about whether Ventre would be prosecuted for Toni's death. He replied, "But it's his word against hers—and she's dead." Again, I was stunned. The victim is always dead in homicide cases—that's why they call it a homicide. If that were the criterion for deciding whether to pursue a case, who would ever be prosecuted?

I mentioned prior allegations by other women who'd had relationships with Ventre. One woman alleged that he'd thrown her against a radiator in the presence of her child. The official hadn't seen the report of the incident. Apparently he hadn't even bothered to look into whether Ventre had prior allegations of violence against him.

Nobody seemed to want to conduct a comprehensive investigation into the circumstances of Toni's death. I was concerned, but I was determined to win justice for Toni. Ultimately, we found a dynamic young woman lawyer in Rome, Alessandra Neri, who worked with us on the custody case in Italy. Still, Ventre fought us every step of the way. As an Italian citizen and the only surviving parent who was fighting in an Italian court for a child that the court considered to be an Italian citizen, he appeared to have the home court advantage.

Even getting visitation while Santina was in foster care in Italy was a struggle. However, the Court of Minors in Rome finally allowed Milt Dykstra, Santina's maternal grandfather, to visit her. I also represented Milt and he had come with me to Italy to fight for his granddaughter. When I called the group home where Santina was staying, I told the woman who answered that it was extremely important that Carlo Ventre not be there when Milt and I arrived—since Milt believed that Carlo had killed his daughter. The representative of the home assured me that Ventre would not be permitted to come at the time of our visit with Santina.

Inside Edition had come with us and was interviewing Milt outside the home when Milt suddenly said, "Carlo!" Ventre was there, despite the home's assurance that he would not be there at that time of day.

Milt started shouting, "You killed my daughter! Why did you kill my daughter?"

Ventre replied, "I didn't kill her! I loved her! I loved her! I loved her!"

And I asked, "Did you love her to death, Carlo? Is that how much you loved her?"

It was a very emotional moment. Finally, Ventre got into a car and left.

We did get in to see Santina and it was wonderful for Milt to be reunited with her. At this point, she was about two years old and only speaking Italian, but Milt was great with her, very loving.

The battle to get Santina back to the United States was particularly difficult because the issue we raised before the Italian court had no precedent at all. Using the Hague Convention on Child Abduction, Toni had won a court order stating that Carlo Ventre wrongfully removed Santina from the United States and that the child had to be returned to her mother in the United States. Before Toni could take her daughter home, however, she was killed.

Now Ventre and Milt both wanted custody of Santina. The court's natural inclination would have been to grant custody to a parent as opposed to a grandparent. Here, it was complicated by the fact that we were alleging that Ventre might have killed Toni—yet Italy was not prosecuting him for that. Further, since the Italian "Hague" Court had awarded custody to Toni, after Toni's death we had to return to the California court to obtain a California court order awarding custody of Santina to Milt in place of Toni.

The Italian court wondered what it should do under this circumstance, when the father has no criminal history and is not being prosecuted for the death of the mother. The Italian system is very different from ours. We considered Santina a U.S. citizen because she was born in the United States, whereas the Italians considered her an Italian citizen because her father was an Italian. The odds were against us, and there was no legal precedent under the Hague Convention to determine what should happen in these circumstances.

As tough as this battle was, it was not one I was willing to lose. No matter what happened, I did not think that under the circumstances Carlo Ventre should have custody of his daughter. I didn't think that would be best for Santina, and I was confident that it wasn't what Toni would have wanted, either. In addition, if Ventre were responsible in any way for Toni's death, I didn't think he should be rewarded for it by being awarded custody of the child.

Although the State Department, particularly Consul Jill Byrnes at the U.S. Embassy in Rome, was very helpful, our government couldn't give that much assistance in the Italian Court for Minors, which would decide whether Ventre should get custody or whether Santina should be returned to the United States to her maternal grandfather. I got the sense that neither the United States nor Italy wanted to see this case become a public issue given the embarrassing fact that an American mother had met a tragic end in Italy after going there to recover her kidnapped child—and that no hearing was even being held to determine whether or not an Italian citizen was telling the truth about the circumstances of her death. The general view of both governments appeared to be, *Why provoke an international incident over Toni Dykstra, a nobody?*

To me, Toni's father, and Toni's sister, however, Toni was somebody. I knew that our only hope of winning Santina's return to the United States was if I could attract media attention to this case. I went to CNN, which sent a reporter to the courthouse. The Italian newspapers also took an interest in the case, but they generally appeared to side with Carlo Ventre, the Italian father.

I also engaged in some informal diplomacy by attending a meeting with certain high-level Italian diplomats to present my arguments as to why Santina, "The Littlest American Citizen," should be able to go home to her country of birth. I have never argued as hard in my life as I did in that meeting. At the beginning, it did not appear that we would prevail, but ultimately we did. I went into great detail about Ventre's relationship with Toni and others. We were informed at the meeting that the judge on the case had not been aware of Ventre's history and that the judge wanted information about Santina's future if the Italian court returned her to Milt. I pointed out that her future situation in the United States was not a factor that should be considered under the Hague Convention. The court should only be considering whether the child had been wrongfully removed from her home state of California. The court had already decided that she had been removed in violation of a court order and that therefore she should be returned.

I explained that Milt had been substituted in place of Toni in the court order by a California court, and now the court was legally required to return the child to the United States. Legally, the court should not be deciding whether or not Milt was an appropriate caretaker of the child. I argued that the California court was the appropriate forum for that decision. I also explained that if the child were returned to California, Ventre would have a fair hearing in his custody battle there.

Concern was also expressed at the meeting about a different child abduction case involving an Italian child allegedly abducted from Italy to Los Angeles, how it was being handled in California, and whether appropriate respect and sensitivity were being shown toward Italian diplomats who were attempting to assist in that matter. I volunteered to look into that issue upon my return to the United States and assist in any way which we agreed was mutually acceptable and appropriate. I fulfilled that promise upon my return.

As a result of that meeting, we were permitted to file a legal brief with the court making our arguments. Our small team of attorneys—which included Alan Skidmore, Merritt McKeon, Alessandra Neri, and me—worked nearly all night on that brief, using the hotel lobby as our office.

In November 1999, the State Department called with the news for which we'd been working and praying. The Rome Court of Minors rejected Ventre's arguments and ordered Santina returned to California and her grandparents, Milt and Betty Dykstra. It was a precedent-setting decision. I flew to Italy to pick her up, accompanied by an exceptional FBI Special Agent named April

Brooks, who had been working very hard investigating the potential kidnapping case against Ventre. No family member could go because of their fear of Carlo. On the long flight home, I taught Santina the words to the song "California, Here I Come." When we landed at LAX the press was waiting. When I walked off the plane with Santina, Milt and Betty Dykstra were waiting to meet her. It filled me with joy to place her in their arms. They loved her so much and were so happy to see her.

Ventre wasn't far behind. He filed a request to return to the United States and regain custody of Santina. I predicted that, if he set foot on U.S. soil, he would be arrested by the FBI for kidnapping, since there was an outstanding warrant for his arrest. I planned to fight his efforts to win custody of Santina in the U.S. and go eye-to-eye, toe-to-toe with him, every step of the way. He was never going to get this baby.

Ventre arrived six weeks later, in December, and was immediately handcuffed and taken away by FBI Special Agent Brooks, who had obtained the arrest warrant for International Parental Kidnapping against Ventre. Agent Brooks, a true law enforcement professional, proved to be a godsend in this case.

Ventre was released on $100,000 bail posted by his brother, Gianfranco, who lived in Las Vegas, but Ventre's freedom didn't last long. He was taken back into federal custody in May 2001, for violating the terms of his home detention. Meanwhile, Carlo and Gianfranco Ventre sued the Dykstras for custody of Santina.

The new custody/guardianship case took place in Los Angeles in the courtroom of Commissioner Victor I. Reichman. He appointed a neutral expert, prominent child psychologist Kay Bathurst, who was very experienced in custody cases, to evaluate the parties and make recommendations to the court. In addition, I retained an expert who also was prepared to provide his recommendations for custody. Ultimately, the court-appointed psychologist, Dr. Bathurst, testified that it was important for Santina to stay with her grandparents, Milt and Betty, because she needed stability and a home, given what she had suffered during the past two years. Our expert agreed. No expert testified that Santina should be sent to live with her uncle, but Commissioner Reichman went against Dr. Bathurst's recommendations and ruled that Carlo's brother be given joint legal custody of Santina with Milt. Further, he ordered that Carlo's brother have physical custody of Santina, although Milt and Betty could have time share of custody.

While Milt Dykstra had made several visits to Italy to see Santina, and retained attorneys in the United States and Italy to fight to bring her back, Ventre's brother admitted under oath that he never visited Santina while she was in Italy. We believed that the decision was as wrong as the one made in the O. J. Simpson custody/guardianship battle—when Sydney and Justin Simpson were taken away from their maternal grandparents, who had cared for them since the death of their mother, Nicole Brown Simpson, and were returned to the man who killed their mother. Ultimately that decision was reversed on appeal. I felt that the decision in this case would be reversed on appeal as well, but the Dykstras, for personal reasons, decided not to appeal and let it stand. The good news, however, was that we prevented Carlo Ventre from winning custody of Santina.

On July 12, 2001, on the eve of his criminal trial in Los Angeles, Carlo Ventre pled guilty in U.S. District Court to the international parental kidnapping charge as part of a plea bargain. His behavior in the courtroom was so outrageous that the judge almost took the plea bargain away. Ventre claimed that kidnapping his daughter was justified because she needed to "escape from a pattern of domestic violence." He then asked to be sent to a prison close to his daughter so that he could have visits from his child, since he was her only parent. Judge Stephen Wilson angrily told Ventre's attorney that his client's story was a variation of the old story "where a boy who kills his parents then throws himself at the mercy of the court because he's now an orphan." After Ventre re-stated "I believe I am guilty" to the kidnapping charge, the judge let the bargain stand, which sentenced him to 364 days in prison.

Although Carlo Ventre was finally incarcerated, I wasn't done with him. Shortly before his release in April 2002, I urged the Immigration and Naturalization Service (INS) to take him into custody and hold a deportation hearing to decide if he should be returned to Italy, since he had been convicted of a felony. The INS failed to respond to my letter and phone calls, and Ventre's attorney reportedly indicated that Carlo Ventre would soon be free in Southern California when his prison term was served. I learned later that Carlo's INS caseworker was on vacation at that time, and that is the reason that I had received no response to my request for a deportation hearing.

I called an urgent news conference with Milt and demanded to know why the INS was not going to take Carlo, an Italian citizen who had been convicted of a felony, into custody and hold a deportation hearing. Apparently officials at the INS saw the news conference and agreed that Carlo should be taken into custody and that a deportation hearing should be held. Carlo was sent to an INS detention center pending the outcome of that hearing. He remained there for three years while he fought deportation.

While he was in custody, Carlo appealed his criminal conviction to the U.S. Court of Appeals for the Ninth Circuit. In essence, the basis for his novel appeal was that since his child had been returned to the United States under the Hague Convention, he couldn't be prosecuted on international kidnapping charges. His argument would have serious consequences if it succeeded. It would mean that parents could kidnap their children and take them thousands of miles away without fear of criminal consequences, if their child was ultimately returned to the United States.

I waited anxiously for the news of the decision. On August 11, 2003, the Ninth Circuit Court of Appeals upheld Carlo Ventre's conviction and the International Parental Kidnapping Law. They rejected the argument that if a kidnapped child were returned to the United States, the Hague Convention prevented a criminal prosecution of the abducting parent.

This was an extremely important precedent that nearly moved me to tears. Toni had not died in vain. Not one, but two legal precedents protecting children had been won after her death as a result of the battle with Carlo. The first was in Italy with the Hague court's decision to return Santina to the United States rather than to the parent who had kidnapped her and in whose home her mother was killed under suspicious circumstances. The second precedent was the Ninth Circuit U.S. Court of Appeals decision in the criminal case.

As if this case were not unusual enough, it soon took yet another strange and chilling turn. In November 2002, Immigration Court Judge Rose Peters ordered Carlo Ventre deported. She stated that among the many reasons for her decision was evidence she'd received during a closed hearing that Ventre, while in INS custody, tried to hire someone to murder Santina's grandparents, Milt and Betty Dykstra. The judge stated that Ventre's plot was audiotaped by law enforcement and included details such as the weapon that should be used to kill the Dykstras (a gun), what to do with the bodies (don't remove them), when to do it (only while he is in custody, because if he is out he will be suspected), and the payment for the crime (possibly $100,000).

The judge also stated that Ventre had indicated that Milt and Betty should be killed in their home and that it should be made to look like a botched robbery. He provided the Dykstras' address, suggested finding their photos on the Internet to identify whom to kill, and discussed a code that would be used to communicate to him that the murder had been accomplished. Another possible plan involved kidnapping Santina. According to the judge, Ventre had told all of this to a confidential informant.

On July 28, 2005, coincidentally the seventh anniversary of Toni Dykstra's death, the Los Angeles County District Attorney's office announced that it had filed a criminal complaint against Carlo Ventre charging him with two counts of solicitation of murder (of my clients Milt and Betty Dykstra) and one count of solicitation to commit kidnapping (of Santina). An arrest warrant was issued with bail set at $2 million. The announcement meant that if Ventre ever tried to slip back into the United States, he would be greeted with handcuffs and prosecution. If the Italian Court fails to do justice, he can now be returned here for trial.

Also in July, Ventre was finally deported to Italy and the *Los Angles Times* reported a new development: He faces a hearing in Italy on a charge of "voluntary murder" in the death of Toni Dykstra. Despite this charge, however, Ventre was permitted to remain free in Italy. The first hearing in the homicide case was set for September 30, 2005. I returned to Rome for that hearing. I had made four prior trips to Italy to win custody of Santina and finally to bring her home after we won. CBS's *48 Hours* was also there and planned to produce a one-hour television program about this extraordinary case, tentatively set to air in February 2006.

On that trip to Rome, I once again confronted Ventre, both inside and outside the courtroom. He was sitting in the front row of the court and turned around to see me. At first he smiled, but his grin faded quickly when I suddenly held up a large photo of Toni. A reporter who was there told me that Ventre began to shake and looked shocked. Outside of the court, on the sidewalk, I called out to him, both in Italian and English, "Carlo, tell the truth in the name of God!" He began to shout at me and make wild and totally false accusations about me in front of the press.

One of his attorneys intervened and in essence told me to stop talking to Carlo, accusing me of harassing his client. He asked if I wanted him to call the police. I told him that I thought that the

Italian Constitution guaranteed free speech. I was not about to be intimidated.

Unfortunately the hearing of September 30, 2005, was continued, allegedly because Carlo had obtained a new attorney. The new date was November 7, 2005. I was ready to return for that hearing, but on November 4, 2005, I was told that it was continued again, until December 19, 2005.

The hearing was finally held in December 2005 and I returned to Rome for it. I am now working with two Italian attorneys, Ms. Neri and Luca Ciaglia, who have generously agreed to represent Milt, Teri, and Toni's two other now-motherless daughters in a civil case for damages against Ventre, which will proceed as part of the criminal case. At the hearing the judge ordered Carlo Ventre to stand trial in March 2006 on a charge of voluntary (first degree) murder.

Criminal prosecution to determine who was responsible for Toni Dykstra's death is long overdue. I will never rest until Carlo Ventre is fully accountable for the terrible suffering he inflicted on Toni and her entire family. Toni risked her life for her baby, and she deserves justice.

Empowerment Lesson

Be careful in choosing your life partner. Male chauvinists can be dangerous to your health, your family, and your life. Take your time and find out as much as you can about the person with whom you plan to have a relationship. If possible, learn what you can about his or her prior relationships with others, including ex-spouses, live-in partners, coworkers, and business partners. Remember that information is power, and sometimes that power can actually save your life.

If you are being emotionally and/or physically abused by your partner, tell people who can help you. Abusive partners want to isolate you from family, friends, and coworkers. Don't let them succeed.

Elect district attorneys who will assist parents whose children have been abducted in violation of court orders (former Los Angeles County District Attorney Gil Garcetti failed to assist Toni Dykstra and as a result she had to go to Italy alone. The next Los Angeles County DA, Steve Cooley, in contrast, has been very supportive of victims' rights.)

Use the media carefully to help accomplish your goals, but consult an attorney before you go public.

Work to pass a federal law that would provide funds for attorneys of abducted children. Most innocent parents are not able to afford an attorney to help them to obtain the rescue and return of their kidnapped children. It is essential that these parents receive meaningful assistance from private attorneys.

If persons accused of a crime are entitled to public defenders paid for by taxpayers, shouldn't our youngest, most vulnerable, and innocent American citizens have attorneys paid for by public funds to help them be returned to the United States?

CHAPTER 12

Fight the Boobs
Behind the Tube

THE SCARLET "P"

A ctress Hunter Tylo was no stranger to television in 1995
when she caught the eye of one of Hollywood's most powerful producers, Aaron Spelling. For six years she had appeared as Dr. Taylor Forrester on one of TV's longest running
soaps, *The Bold and the Beautiful*.

However, when she was hired to appear on the prime-time hit,
Melrose Place, Hunter knew she was headed for the big time. In
February 1996, the beautiful actress signed an agreement with
Spelling Television to play a sexy, man-stealing seductress. She
gave notice to the producers of *The Bold and the Beautiful* and
they reduced her role in preparation for her move to *Melrose
Place*, where she would begin filming in June 1996.

Hunter and her husband sold their house in Nevada and
moved to Valencia, California, where *Melrose Place* was produced.
In March, the actress was thrilled to learn that she was pregnant
with her third child. This was becoming a year of wonderful surprises and opportunities. All that came to an abrupt halt a month
later when she received a letter from Spelling Television. It was
about her pregnancy.

"Although we wish you much joy in this event," the Spelling
attorney wrote, "your pregnancy will result in a material change in

your appearance during production of a substantial portion of the 1996/97 season of the series." That appearance, the letter continued, "does not conform with the character you have been engaged to portray. This character is by necessity not pregnant and your material change would not meet the requirements for the portrayal of the character." Her contract was terminated, the letter stated. She was fired. Hunter was stunned.

Her representatives called Spelling Television and pointed out that its actions constituted unlawful employment discrimination, but their protests fell on deaf ears. The termination generated a lot of gossip in Hollywood, which at times seems more like a small-town high school campus than one of the world's biggest industries. Hunter was embarrassed and humiliated. As Hunter saw it, she was faced with losing her dream job unless she terminated her pregnancy. It was a choice no woman should have to make. Hunter bravely decided to stand up for the right to be both a mother and an actor. That's when she contacted me.

Hollywood doesn't like lawsuits from actors, and the bigger the target of the lawsuit, the bigger the consequences. Many who have sued or otherwise challenged Hollywood power brokers have seen their careers evaporate as a result, but Hunter felt she shouldn't have to choose between her baby and her career. Why should she get an abortion to keep a job? Hunter felt she had been branded with the scarlet letter "P" for pregnancy and expelled from her new *Melrose Place* family because she wanted to be a mother.

I agreed. Pregnancy isn't a crime or a communicable disease. A woman shouldn't be punished or treated as a pregnant pariah because she chooses to become a mother. Big business should not be permitted, in essence, to veto a pregnancy by terminating the potential mother from her job because she wants to have a family. We filed suit against Spelling Television in May 1996. Although many actresses had been released from their contracts for being pregnant, apparently it was the first time an actress had ever fought back with a lawsuit that was headed to trial. The case was closely watched by the entertainment industry. In the meantime, Hunter became the proud mother of a new baby girl named Katye.

Spelling Television attorneys grilled her during depositions in the months before the trial began. During one, Hunter was asked bizarrely personal questions, such as "Did your husband have a vasectomy? Did he have a vasectomy reversal?" She was asked to describe the state of her marriage, and when she responded, "Perfect," she was prodded, "Perfect for all of 1994?" Our objections about the intrusive nature of the questions, which invaded the privacy of her marital relations, went all the way to the California Court of Appeals. It ruled that the questions were "unprofessional and inappropriate," and that Hunter's constitutional right to privacy outweighed the Spelling attorneys' "right" to know the answers.

Hunter's trial, which started in November 1997, was a celebrity-studded affair. *Melrose Place* star Heather Locklear took the stand to describe how the show's producers had worked around her pregnancy, which occurred a year after Hunter had been fired. Even her replacement on the series had gotten pregnant with no job repercussions.

At one point, the defense put up a big chart showing how many pounds Hunter had gained each week during her previous pregnancy, as if she were a prize cow. The jury didn't like it.

One of the biggest bombshells dropped during the trial was Hunter's announcement on the stand that she was eight months pregnant with another child. The gasp in the courtroom was so loud, it must have sucked the oxygen right out of the room. She was described in one article written that day as "looking slender and fit in an off-white miniskirt." The revelation was extremely damaging to Spelling's attorneys, who had no idea that Hunter was again pregnant. It sure didn't help their argument that she had become unattractive during her previous pregnancy by gaining fifty-seven pounds.

Shortly before Christmas, the jury reached a decision and it was a whopper. Instead of awarding Hunter the $2.5 million she had asked for, it concluded that Spelling Television had indeed discriminated against Hunter and awarded her almost $5 million in damages for her emotional distress! It was a unanimous verdict. We had won. My partners Nathan Goldberg and Dolores Leal and my associate Margery Somers had done an outstanding job of lawyering in this unusual "David v. Goliath" lawsuit.

Apparently the "pregnancy is unattractive" argument hadn't worked one bit, judging from juror Pete Ortiz's comments to the media: "Even if she gained forty-seven pounds or whatever, she's still a beautiful person. She's still a working mother, she's still an actress, pregnant or not."

Although we had won, Spelling Television stubbornly rejected the verdict. Declaring it to be the result of a "runaway jury," the company appealed in 1998. On April 1, 1998, Judge Fumiko Hachiya Wasserman upheld the verdict and additionally ordered the defendants to pay almost a million dollars to us in attorneys' fees. They hadn't gotten the message when they fired Hunter. They didn't get it when the jury awarded her almost $5 million in damages. Maybe now they would finally get that what they did was wrong. It was wrong then and it was wrong now. A woman should not be fired simply because she is pregnant. The reason they lost this case is because they discriminated against a pregnant woman.

I said that the defendants should pay the damages and start focusing their energy on making sure that in the future they did not discriminate against actresses who become pregnant. Ultimately, the case was settled. We had won an important victory for pregnant working actors. To our knowledge, a similar case hasn't been filed and tried since. Hollywood realized it had to reassess its policies and practices. The entertainment industry pays close attention to the bottom line—and the bottom line is that it may now be too costly to fire actresses who get pregnant.

Hunter stood up for herself and pregnant women everywhere, who are often faced with pregnancy discrimination by many employers throughout this nation, but who are frequently not in a position to assert their rights at a very vulnerable time in their lives.

Legal rights for women are meaningless unless women know that they have a right to be free from discrimination and unless they exercise that right. Some pundits bashed Hunter for asserting her rights under California's law against pregnancy discrimination, but she refused to back down. With our help, she stood up for herself in a court of law, and in the court of public opinion.

The press coverage that celebrity cases attract helps educate the public and potential wrongdoers about women's rights and the ability women have to vindicate them. Few people are taught their rights in school. Most people learn about them through the media—through television shows such as *Law and Order* and televised trials such as O. J. Simpson's. It isn't the way it should be, but that is the way it is. The media often portray women as powerless and in need of men to rescue them. This is another reason why I want the public to see women like Hunter fighting back against injustice. They inspire other women to tap into their own courage.

I ran into Aaron Spelling not long ago outside Spago. He kissed my hand and couldn't have been nicer. His lawyers had fought the lawsuit like it was World War III, but he was gracious in defeat. It is ironic that, as a result of the lawsuit, he ended up contributing a lot more to the entertainment industry than just his enormous talent and creative spark.

Empowerment Lesson

Life can be unfair, especially to women, but when you have the opportunity to fight against injustice, take it. Pregnancy discrimination is still rampant in our nation. If you learn what your rights are and assert them, you may win new rights and protections for yourself and other women as well.

HOOTERS' SECRET REALITY SHOW

As the Hooters restaurant chain's name implies, if you go there, you'll be looking at more than the menu. Obviously, there are a lot of men out there who don't think a meal is a meal without an ample serving of cleavage. I believe that if women want to work there, that's their choice.

However, young women who wanted to work at the Hooters in West Covina, California, were served up a situation that no one should have to tolerate: They were secretly videotaped while changing into Hooters uniforms during the interview process.

Hooters was getting ready to open its West Covina restaurant, and started to interview women in November 2003. Interested job applicants went to a construction trailer set up outside the restaurant to meet with the general manager, Juan Aponte. They were given job applications and told to try on a Hooters uniform consisting of a pair of nylons, shorts, and a tank top. They were also told where to stand in the room while trying on the outfit. Aponte told them it was to prevent them from being spotted by the construction workers who were passing by the trailer. Some young women were told to take off underwear that would show panty lines—evidently a thong or no underwear at all was preferable. Aponte told each applicant he would then photograph them in the outfit and put the picture in her application file. There were plenty of pictures of other women wearing Hooters outfits already pasted on the trailer's wall. After they had changed, the general manager touched some of the women without their consent, making adjustments to the uniform and, in some cases, commenting on their bodies.

The young women who later contacted me were all hired. Before they went to work, however, they learned that they had been secretly videotaped as they changed into and out of their uniforms. They were understandably upset, as were many of their parents. Some of our clients were as young as seventeen years old.

I was furious. My clients, who eventually numbered fifty-seven in all, were stripped of their rights. Hooters had a lot of explaining to do. No one should ever have to endure the invasion of personal privacy that these young women were forced to suffer. They were simply looking for a job. Instead, they were embarrassed, humiliated, and emotionally violated.

Juan Aponte was charged in a fifty-seven-count criminal complaint. If convicted, he faced a maximum of nineteen years in prison. Instead, in July 2004, he pled no contest to three counts of eavesdropping and two counts of using a minor for a sex act. He was sentenced to five years in prison, and will have to register as a sex offender when he is released.

The Hooters chain cooperated with the police investigation. It stated that trying on the Hooters uniform was not part of the job application process.

My clients filed a civil case against Hooters in West Covina, alleging invasion of privacy, employment discrimination (sex discrimination and harassment), negligent supervision, and battery. We also alleged a violation of a California law that states, "No employer may cause an audio or video recording to be made of an employee in a restroom, locker room, or room designated by an employer for changing clothes, unless authorized by court order."

We hope through this lawsuit to send a message that women will not tolerate such shameful conduct and that they can and will fight back.

Empowerment Lesson

Although it is illegal to tape employees or prospective employees at their workplaces while they are changing their clothes, it is a widespread practice. Be careful when you're undressing at work. If it doesn't feel right, it probably isn't. Ask questions.

DUDE, YOUR REALITY SHOW SUCKS

Reality TV is the programming phenomenon of the decade. Television audiences can't seem to get enough of real people facing unreal situations. Behind the scenes of all those crazy stunts, however, there are some real victims. I've represented several of them and expect to represent more until Hollywood starts thinking more about people and less about profits.

Two teenagers, whom I will call Jane and Mary, were elated when they became part of the audience invited to attend the taping of a television show, *Dude, This Sucks.* The January 2001 weekend event was sponsored by a television network at Snow Summit, a ski resort in the mountains east of Los Angeles. The girls, both thirteen, were directed by staffers to stand right next to the stage where the performance would take place. They had a VIP view for the "Shower Rangers" act, which they had never seen. Jane and Mary were so excited that they didn't give much thought to the plastic covers placed over the expensive camera equipment nearby.

The two "Shower Rangers" took the stage dressed in scouting-type uniforms and began to act out a campfire scene. Suddenly, the pair turned their backs to the audience and opened flaps on the backs of their shorts, exposing two naked butts.

It got worse, much worse. The Shower Ranger closest to the girls spread his buttocks cheeks and sprayed them with fecal matter. The girls were hemmed in by the crowd and had nowhere to run.

"All of a sudden I was smelling something disgusting and I started to gag," one of the girls said later. "I looked around at my friends. They were covered in something. As I looked down at myself, I realized I was, too."

As the girls stood, dripping and humiliated, the host announced, "The water was brown," and congratulated the [Shower Rangers] on a job "well done." Staff then came out and hosed off the stage, and the girls were again sprayed with the act's leftover feces.

Finally, the two teenagers and several other girls who'd been victimized were taken to a small backstage room where they were given a few towels and some bottled water with which to clean themselves.

When the two went to school the next day, some of their classmates had heard about the incident and "wouldn't come near us because . . . they said we smelled," one of the girls told the *Los Angeles Daily News*. "No one can say or do anything to make the memory of that day ever go away," the other girl added.

It is revolting to subject children—or anyone—to such an outrageous and indecent act without their knowledge or consent, or that of their parents, which of course never would have been given. No television or cable network should ever allow anything like this to happen in the future.

When we announced that we were filing a lawsuit on behalf of the girls for intentional infliction of emotional distress, negligence, and battery, the television network's president of programming apologized for the incident. He said the show, a pilot for the series, would never be aired. He promised to take steps to ensure that "an incident of this nature never happens again." He never explained who thought something as disgusting as this would be funny in the first place.

The case was ultimately resolved. "Humilitainment" for public consumption continues on other networks, presenting many more battles to be fought and won.

Empowerment Lesson

Reality bites, but you can bite back. When teenaged girls show courage, they can win changes, even from major corporations. If you find yourself in a similar situation, discuss it with your parents and with an attorney.

Television networks are not above the law, but producers will often cross the line in order to increase ratings.

You have rights, even against powerful broadcast media, but you need to assert them in order to win change.

THE INTERVIEW FROM HELL

In September 2002, Thea Robinson went to a large and reputable temporary services agency in Los Angeles to find a job. After filling out all the paperwork and passing assorted proficiency tests, she was sent out on a job interview later that month. The agency told Thea about the job and the potential salary, and then sent her to meet with the prospective employer at a Woodland Hills, California, restaurant.

As the interview began in the crowded restaurant, the prospective employer began to argue with a noisy patron at a nearby table. When a third person became involved in the noisy exchange, Thea became uncomfortable and went off to find the restaurant manager to request a table in a different room. Instead, the manager returned her to the same table where, this time, an actual fight broke out between her prospective employer and another patron. Tables were overturned and dishes flew.

Frightened, Thea exited the room and wanted to leave the premises, but was told by the manager that she could not leave because she would need to identify the fight participants. She tried to explain that she didn't know either of them, that she was just there on a job interview. However, the floor manager, who was standing next to a uniformed guard, told her again that she couldn't leave.

Thea went back to retrieve her resume from the prospective employer and, as she once again began to leave, the room burst into applause and laughter. Some people shouted, "You've been Xed!" She was told that she'd been part of *The Jamie Kennedy Ex-*

periment. Her "prospective employer" had, in fact, been the host, Jamie Kennedy.

Thea was in a state of shock. She was led to an area in the back of the restaurant where she was provided with a chair and something to drink. Soon she went outside and telephoned her husband. As she explained what she had been through, she broke down crying. Thea had preexisting health problems that made her particularly susceptible to injury from this type of victimization.

These sneak attacks on innocent people couldn't go unchallenged. We filed suit against *The Jamie Kennedy Experiment* and its producer, Warner Bros. Television Productions, alleging fraud, unfair business practices, intentional infliction of emotional distress, false imprisonment, and more.

This case was important because many people are particularly vulnerable when they are looking for a job in an economy where unemployment is high and good jobs are hard to find. Everyone has some vulnerability, either physical or emotional, or both. Such an "ambush attack" places people in a highly stressful situation and may seriously impact the innocent victim—especially if the victim happens to have a heart condition or other medical problems that puts him or her at greater risk.

Reality shows, in my opinion, have no right to play this kind of game with people's lives. The only purpose for such "humilitainment" is to increase ratings, in order to make a profit by charging more to advertisers. Choosing its targets at random, such shows may assume that most people will laugh it off, and that those who are upset won't do anything about it. However, stunts like this can hurt people, and it is time that such shows stop this business practice of using members of the public as guinea pigs for their so-called "experiments."

Unemployed people who are desperately looking for jobs are no laughing matter—they are looking for work in order to support themselves and their families. They want a job, not a practical joke. They are not seeking to be placed in a dangerous situation in which they may be hurt, deceived, and traumatized by a cruel hoax for other people's entertainment.

Ultimately Thea's lawsuit was resolved. Thea stood up for others so that they will not be forced to suffer as she did.

Empowerment Lesson

Fight back against companies and television shows who video and audiotape you without your knowledge and consent. Your actions can help protect others from becoming victims of those who wish to profit at the public's expense.

CHAPTER 13

Fight for the Children

CHEERLEADING BUSTED

Should the size of a teenager's breasts prevent her from participating in a school activity? Vicki Ann Guest got a startling answer in April 1986, when the seventeen-year-old tried out for the cheerleading squad at her high school in Huntington Beach, California.

When she wasn't chosen, she decided to visit her cheerleading coach to find out why. The answer shocked her. The coach allegedly told Vicki that her cheerleading skills were much better than those of the girls who were selected. Her 3.4 grade point average was certainly acceptable as well.

Vicki's problem, her coach said, were her breasts. They were too big. She should have breast reduction surgery and she should have it done soon. The teacher allegedly suggested that Vicki not try out for *any* other school activity until she had the surgery.

These kinds of comments, especially by a school official, can be extremely hurtful to teenaged girls for whom self-image and self-esteem are such important issues. Even more troubling: What is a nonphysician doing giving advice about *any* kind of surgery? Shouldn't such a suggestion come from a physician rather than from a high school coach, if he or she believes it is necessary and appropriate?

Vicki was devastated. She went home and was barely able to communicate with anyone for three days. She had pursued her dream of becoming a professional dancer since she was six. She had been a cheerleader in elementary school and junior high school. She'd been a four-year member of the school's Advanced Dance Team and studied jazz ballet and tap dancing six days a week. In the wake of the coach's remarks, Vicki's self-confidence evaporated and she stopped all of her extracurricular activities.

It got worse. Word of the coach's comments spread through Vicki's high school like wildfire, causing Vicki further humiliation. She began to wear baggy shirts and sweatshirts in dance class. At one point, she stopped going to school altogether.

Vicki and her parents complained about the situation, but the school brushed off their complaints over a five-month period. Finally, the Guests came to see me about filing a lawsuit. Having had a teenage daughter myself, I know that young women are very insecure about their bodies. Comments about the size and shape of their breasts could leave emotional scars for a lifetime.

The size and shape of a girl's breasts should be totally irrelevant to her right to participate in any school activity, especially if she is otherwise qualified for it. The school's policy needed to be changed. Vicki didn't want any other young woman to be subjected to the kind of severe emotional distress, embarrassment, and humiliation that she had suffered as a result of her teacher's remarks and her exclusion from cheerleading.

The school's refusal to let Vicki be a cheerleader because of the size of her breasts was a violation of the state's sex discrimination laws, as well as Vicki's constitutional rights. We filed suit in October 1986 against the Huntington Beach Union High School District for violating Vicki's right to equal protection under the law, violation of her right to equal privileges and immunities, and right to due process of law.

We wanted the court to declare that the school district's policy of considering breast size as a prerequisite to participation in school activities was unconstitutional We also sought a court declaration that permitting a teacher to recommend plastic surgery to a student violated the student's constitutional rights. In addition, we asked for a permanent injunction to prevent the school district from advising students to get cosmetic surgery as a condition of participating in any school event, and we wanted damages.

The news conference about Vicki's case generated an unusually large media turnout. There seemed to be more men than women, and one reporter told me afterward that there had been battles in the newsroom about who would be sent to cover the press conference. I wasn't surprised by the reaction, which is why I made sure that Vicki would not be wearing a form-fitting sweater.

After I explained our case, I asked if there were any questions. There was silence. Finally one of the reporters said, "I really don't want to ask this question, but if I don't ask it, and I go back to my newsroom, my boss is going to be very upset with me and ask why I didn't ask it, so I have to."

There was another pause.

I said, "Yes?"

I knew very well what the question was going to be.

"Well, um, er . . . how big are they?" the reporter stammered.

The room fell totally silent.

I paused. Then I said, "We didn't think her breast size was relevant to whether she could be a cheerleader and we also don't think it is relevant to our lawsuit, so we are not going to answer that question."

It took a lot of courage for Vicki to bring the lawsuit, and to have her body and the school's policy become the subject of public debate. Vicki conducted herself with dignity and I was very proud of her.

It took a year, but the school district finally acknowledged the harm it had inflicted on one of its students. As part of the settlement, the school district issued a formal apology to Vicki for the "damages and hardship" she suffered from "the unfortunate and inappropriate situation of a teacher suggesting breast reduction surgery."

It also adopted a formal written policy that would forever prohibit selecting students for school activities based on the shape or size of their breasts. Students' participation would be based only on criteria related to the activity, and no teacher would ever again be permitted to suggest breast surgery to a student.

That was a policy to cheer about.

Empowerment Lesson

Fight for your right to be judged on your merits, not your looks. If you believe that an educational institution has excluded you from a school activity based on a factor over which you have no control—like breast size—discuss it with your parents and then take appropriate action to assert your right to be treated equally.

A DIFFERENT KIND OF CHILD

My fight for victims' rights and family rights has sometimes led me to some very unusual cases. One that I will never forget involved a California couple and their struggle with the West Covina city government over the custody of their "child," a chimpanzee.

For more than thirty years, Moe the chimpanzee had lived with LaDonna and St. James Davis in their Southern California home. During a visit to Africa in 1967, St. James had rescued Moe from poachers, fallen in love with him, and brought him back to his childhood sweetheart, LaDonna. Moe had even stood up with the couple at their wedding.

The Davises raised him as their only "child," since a hysterectomy at an early age prevented LaDonna from having her own. He slept with them until he got too big, ate at the table, and watched television with them.

When Moe was three years old, a complaint was filed against Moe's "parents" for keeping him at their home, but it was later dismissed and Moe was permitted to stay with his human family. The judge in the case stated, "From what I've observed of Moe inside and outside the courtroom, he doesn't have the traits of a wild animal, and is, in fact, somewhat better behaved than some people."

Over the years, Moe became a well-known celebrity and a good citizen of West Covina. He sold cookies for the Girl Scouts, and was invited and accepted invitations to be the ribbon-cutter at many city functions and fund-raisers. He appeared in several episodes of the TV series, *B.J. and the Bear.* At one point, Moe even became a crime-fighting hero. On April 9, 1998, West Covina police were searching for a car thief. Moe pointed to the place where the thief was hiding and the police arrested the suspect.

However, Moe's idyllic existence was about to take a turn. On August 16, 1999, the chimp was accidentally electrically shocked while a worker attempted to fix something in his backyard enclosure. Frightened, Moe ran through the neighborhood. When animal control and police officers tried to grab him, one of the officers was allegedly bitten.

In September, the Davises were contacted by a West Covina community relations officer who wanted to arrange a visit for someone to see and photograph Moe. Although the woman was allegedly told not to go near the enclosure, she placed her finger inside. Moe was used to eating red licorice. The woman's fingernails had red nail polish on them. Moe took a bite.

The next day, West Covina police, county health officials, and county animal control descended on the Davis household. With no advance notice, no warrant, and no court order, they took Moe away to the Wildlife WayStation, an animal sanctuary. Authorities filed a misdemeanor criminal complaint charging LaDonna and

St. James with thirty-nine counts of keeping a wild and dangerous animal in the City of West Covina—the same charge a judge had thrown out years earlier.

Moe had never been separated from the Davises, who were distraught. LaDonna's mother suggested that she give me a call. I thought the city's decision to criminally prosecute Mr. and Mrs. Davis was unnecessary and cruel to Moe and to the Davises, so I agreed to take the case. I told city officials that if they wanted a "monkey" trial in West Covina, that's what they would get—but they should be careful about what they wished for because I intended to do everything possible to defend my clients.

We vigorously fought the charges as city officials sought in my view to bully our clients and deny them due process. In the end, a judge found that the city had not obtained a signed arrest warrant, as required by law. Instead of proceeding, the city dropped the criminal charges.

From the beginning, we told city officials that a criminal prosecution was not the proper way to achieve their goals. Still, I felt that they wasted thousands of taxpayer dollars on what seemed like a shameless vendetta against the Davises and Moe. When government overreacts, as the city did, it can hurt innocent citizens and their companion animals.

Although we prevailed in the criminal case, the city refused to allow Moe to come home to his family and friends in West Covina. He would have to remain at Wildlife WayStation. The Davises were allowed to visit him once a week for fifteen minutes. LaDonna and St. James faithfully made the drive each week to the refuge.

Some months later Wildlife WayStation officials said that, because they didn't have a state license for exhibiting animals, it would be a violation of the law if they continued to let the Davises visit their beloved chimp. When I learned of this situation, I thought it was important for us to work out a resolution that would allow the Davises to be reunited with Moe without placing the Wildlife WayStation at risk.

We were able to work out the legal issues and the Davises were able to visit Moe in January 2004. Then a new problem developed. Although they were permitted to visit, Wildlife WayStation officials wanted them to pay several hundred dollars per visit to reimburse the WayStation for the cost of a fire safety officer whom the county required to be present during a visit. The Davises' small income made such an arrangement prohibitive.

They needed to find another home for Moe, where they could be with him whenever they wished and for as long as they wished, without payment. They found Animal Haven Ranch near Caliente, California, and Moe moved there on September 28, 2004. On October 16, 2004, for the first time in almost five years, the Davises were able to spend unlimited time with their adored "child."

I wish I could stop the story here, with this happy ending, but I cannot because the Davises' happy reunion was followed by a shocking and horrible turn of events.

On March 3, 2005, St. James and LaDonna arrived at Animal Haven laden with surprises for a very special occasion. They had come to celebrate Moe's thirty-ninth birthday. As Moe watched with delight from his enclosure, the couple set up the food and party favors that they had brought. St. James poured Moe some chocolate milk, which Moe loved and drank in his enclosed habitat. LaDonna cut the birthday cake and gave Moe his piece. She then cut one for St. James. As she was cutting her own slice, she caught some movement out of the corner of her eye

She turned, but before she even had time to react, she was hit from behind by 130 pounds of black fury. It was a teenaged male chimpanzee who had escaped from his enclosure elsewhere on the property. He was loose, he was vicious, and he wasn't alone.

Four chimps had escaped from their cages. Two of them were now bearing down on the Davises. LaDonna was knocked into her husband, and one of the chimpanzees bit her thumb off. St. James pushed his wife aside to safety. He took the brunt of the attack in order to save his wife. LaDonna watched in horror as the two chimps tore into her husband.

"It looked as if they were eating him alive," she told reporters later.

The chimps bit off most of the fingers and thumb on St. James's right hand. They tore back the skin on the bottom of his left foot and gnawed on his heel. His left eye and eye socket were ripped out to the sinuses and the skin on that side of his face was peeled back. One chimp bit deeply into his skull and into his back, and dragged him through the dusty yard.

A ranch hand heard LaDonna's screams and came running with a gun. He shot and killed both chimps, then ran to the house to call for an ambulance. The two female chimpanzees had not been involved in the attack. They had run for nearby mountains and were later caught and returned to their cages. LaDonna knelt by her husband's side, whispering to him not to die. Moe cowered in his cage, in shock at what he had just seen the other chimpanzees do to his loved ones.

St. James was airlifted to Loma Linda University Hospital, where he spent months in an induced coma so that doctors could work to save his life. For the next six months, he underwent more than a dozen surgeries, with many more necessary to reconstruct his face, hand, and foot. St. James had also inhaled a great deal of bacteria into his lungs and bloodstream from the ground and from the chimps, which caused breathing problems. No one was sure whether he would live.

The Kern County Sheriff stated in his report on the investigation that "Virginia Brauer [the owner of Animal Haven] left the bunkhouse in a hurry to greet the Davises . . . when she exited the bunkhouse she did not secure the interior and exterior doors . . . the chimpanzees were still in the open caged area and the trapdoor was closed. As Virginia assisted the Davises, the four chimpanzees escaped from the cage compound. They accomplished this by exiting all three doors." The Sheriff's report concluded, "On the day of the incident, a chimp or chimps probably manipulated the locking mechanism on the trapdoor allowing their access to the bunkhouse . . . [and] were able to exit the cage compound through the interior and exterior doors which were left unsecured."

On April 18, 2005, the Kern County District Attorney's Office announced that it would file no charges against Virginia Brauer or Animal Haven. It believed that Brauer had no criminal intent to let the chimps escape from their cages.

Even though there was a decision not to prosecute, it was obvious to us that there must have been negligence in order for the escape to have occurred. Clearly, a locking device that could be pulled out by a chimpanzee was not sufficient to protect the public. It certainly had not been adequate in preventing the catastrophic consequences suffered by St. James Davis.

The Davises have already incurred hundreds of thousands of dollars in medical bills, and there is no end in sight. In addition, Animal Haven Ranch informed them that it did not have adequate insurance to cover all of these bills. Today, the Davises face financial ruin.

St. James was finally released from his three-month induced coma and is slowly, slowly recovering. On August 16, 2005, he was released from Loma Linda Medical Center to go home, but he will have to undergo more surgeries. Moe remains at Animal Haven, although Brauer recently announced that she wants him moved. The Davises still love Moe and are making plans for his future. LaDonna demonstrated how much she loves her husband by visiting him daily in the hospital and emotionally supporting him throughout his recovery. At home she is now his primary caregiver, even though she was a victim herself. Her devotion to her husband has been an inspiration to everyone who knows her, and I firmly believe that the power of her love has been the major reason that St. James has survived.

LaDonna is also determined to see that some good comes from this devastating tragedy. She and I are working to convince the California State Legislature to pass a law mandating that, in the future, any animal sanctuary in the state must carry liability insurance as a condition of being licensed.

Empowerment Lesson

Many people love their animal companions as they do their children.

When government insists that they be separated from their animal it can cause devastating results. Do what you can to support and help keep family units together, even if they include animals, as long as there is no proven and substantial risk of harm to others.

THE MYSTERY OF MICHAEL JACKSON

In December 2002, Michael Jackson, hobbling on crutches (reportedly from a tarantula bite), made his way through the press crowd outside a Santa Maria, California, courthouse for an appearance in a $38 million civil case—a contractual dispute filed against him by a concert promoter.

"Michael! What do you think of Gloria Allred?" called out Jane Velez-Mitchell from TV's *Celebrity Justice*.

From underneath a black umbrella held by his security guard to shield him from the sun's glare came the response, delivered in his trademark breathy baby's voice.

"Who's Gloria Allred?"

The question drew chuckles from some of the press corps. How could Michael Jackson not know who I was? I had briefly represented a young boy in 1993 who accused him of child molestation. More recently, on November 26, 2002, I had filed a complaint with authorities in Santa Barbara, California (the jurisdiction that includes his Neverland estate) after seeing him dangle his nine-month-old baby, Prince Michael II, over the side of a fourth floor hotel balcony in Berlin, Germany.

Mitchell replied, "She's the attorney who's filed a complaint against you with Child Protective Services."

Again, the voice came from under the umbrella: "Ahh . . . tell her to go to hell."

Some reporters told me later that they were stunned by the response—not by the words, but by the tone in which they were delivered. The baby voice was replaced by a deep, angry adult male voice no one had ever heard before in public. I suspect that the real Michael Jackson temporarily peeked through the crack in his carefully maintained facade.

His "tell her to go to hell" comment played over and over on the evening news and reporters called me for a response.

I said, "While Michael Jackson wants me to go to hell, I want him to go to parenting class to learn how to protect rather than endanger his baby. My hope is that, upon reflection, he will realize that this is not about me, but about his behavior."

Michael Jackson needed a wake-up call. He appeared to live a sheltered life surrounded by people who might only tell him what he wanted to hear. He seemed to think that what he did was okay. Well, I wasn't a member of his entourage. I didn't think that he deserved special treatment or that he should be allowed to take advantage of his fame to engage in actions that endangered a child—actions which, if engaged in by a noncelebrity, would have been condemned and investigated.

Dangling his baby over the side of the fourth floor balcony was reckless and irresponsible conduct. It demonstrated a complete lack of parental awareness of the substantial risk of great bodily harm or death that could have resulted had he dropped the baby. I told reporters that if Michael Jackson was truly sorry, he should demonstrate that in deeds not words by voluntarily submitting himself to a Child Protective Services investigation into whether he had endangered the baby and whether the child should be removed from his care. I said that children of celebrities deserve no more and no less protection than any other child. Rather than attacking me, Michael Jackson needed to address the problem. I felt that he needed to recognize that his baby was not a toy and that he had a duty to keep the child safe. I said that he should attend parenting class as soon as possible to learn how to become a responsible parent.

That he was able to avoid many of the consequences of his questionable treatment of children is disturbing to me. Acting as a private citizen following the child-dangling incident, I wrote to Child Protective Services and the district attorney of Santa Barbara County, Tom Sneddon, asking that they investigate Jackson's behavior toward children. This was not the first scandal involving Michael Jackson and children, but it made me wonder why the system seemed to give the one-gloved wonder the kid-glove treatment. The mystery behind this apparent special treatment for Jackson dates back to a 1993 incident in which a young boy accused him of sexual abuse.

Law enforcement has publicly confirmed that the child made serious allegations against Jackson and cooperated with police and the district attorney's office by providing statements. In fact, I took that child to the district attorney's office in Los Angeles myself when I briefly represented him, and the child gave extensive and detailed answers to those who questioned him. At least one law enforcement officer involved in that investigation said publicly that he found the child to be credible.

At the time, I noted that children everywhere were watching to see how this child, who had bravely come forward with allegations against a celebrity, would be treated. Other children might fear what could happen to them if they accused a celebrity or other powerful person of child sexual abuse. Many people loved and trusted Michael Jackson. This thirteen-year-old boy loved and trusted him as well. Unfortunately, that trust was destroyed. At the time, I waited to see if Jackson would be held to the same standards of conduct as any other person. I wondered if he thought that he was above the law.

The outcome was disturbing. In 1994, while the criminal investigation was being conducted, a settlement was reached in a civil lawsuit brought by the boy against Jackson. Another attorney represented him at that time. Although the amount was confidential, reports put the possible settlement at between $15 and $20 million.

After that settlement, Los Angeles County District Attorney Gil Garcetti and Santa Barbara District Attorney Tom Sneddon announced that there would be no criminal prosecution of Jackson. They said that the child in question now refused to testify, and without his cooperation, the case could not be proven. Was there a connection between Jackson's civil settlement payment and the sudden implosion of the criminal case? That mystery would take almost a decade to unravel.

In the ensuing years, Jackson married twice and became the father of three children. His 1994 marriage to Lisa Marie Presley ended after twenty months. During his three-year marriage to Debbie Rowe, from 1996 to 1999, she gave birth to a son and daughter, Prince Michael I and Paris. The mother of the third child, Prince Michael II, is unknown.

Just months after the baby-dangling incident, in January 2003, ABC aired a British documentary about Jackson that was taped with interviewer Martin Bashir. Its contents were shocking and ultimately set off Jackson's latest legal battle. Jackson said that he had slept in his bed with young children unrelated to him and admitted to sleeping on the floor while a child named Gavin slept in his bed.

Bashir asked Gavin, "When you stay here, do you stay in the house? Does Michael let you enjoy the whole premises?"

Gavin replied, "There was one night, I asked him if I could stay in his bedroom. He let me stay in the bedroom. And I was like, 'Michael, you can sleep in the bed,' and he was like 'No, no, you sleep on the bed,' and I was like 'No, no, no, you sleep on the bed,' and then he said, 'Look if you love me you'll sleep in the bed.' I was like 'Oh man. . .' so I finally slept on the bed. But it was fun that night."

Jackson then interjected, "I slept on the floor."

Later in the interview, Jackson said, "I have slept in a bed with many children. I slept in a bed with all of them when Macaulay Culkin was little. Kieran Culkin would sleep on this side, Macaulay was on this side, his sisters in there—we all would just jam in the bed . . ."

My concern deepened when Jackson said during the same interview that he would allow—and even condone—his own children sleeping with unrelated adult males.

Bashir said, "But Michael, I wouldn't like my children to sleep in anybody else's bed."

Jackson responded, "Well, I wouldn't mind if I know the person and, well, I am very close to Barry Gibb. Paris and Prince can stay with him anytime. My children sleep with other people all the time."

I was extremely upset by these new revelations and by Jackson's seeming total lack of understanding of the true significance of his behavior. I believe it is highly inappropriate for a young child to sleep in the same bedroom with Jackson, in light of the prior accusations of child sexual abuse made against him. A vast number of child psychologists would recommend against such behavior.

Jackson's apparent condoning of it flew in the face of what many would approve and of common sense.

Jackson's conduct once again demonstrated a lack of good judgment and a failure to appreciate appropriate adult/child boundaries. Once again, I filed a complaint with the Santa Barbara County Department of Child Welfare Services and forwarded a transcript of the interview. I also sent a complaint to Child Protective authorities in Los Angeles. I urged them to "interview the child named Gavin and any other child who has been in Mr. Jackson's home and/or bedroom without the presence of their parents."

Although I received a letter from the Santa Barbara authorities acknowledging receipt of my letter, I had no idea if they acted on it because that information is kept confidential. During Jackson's 2005 criminal trial, however, a social worker from Los Angeles testified that my name was on her referral—and that this was the reason she went to interview Gavin.

There was another part of the Bashir interview that I believe offered new insight into the sudden implosion of the 1993 child sexual abuse criminal case.

Bashir asked Jackson: "The reason that has been given for why you didn't go to jail [in 1994] is because you reached a financial settlement with the family?"

Jackson responded, "Yeah, I didn't want to do a long drawn-out thing on TV like O. J. and all that stupid stuff, you know, it wouldn't look right. I said, 'Look, let's get this thing over with. I want to go on with my life. This is ridiculous, I've had enough. Go.'"

To me, Jackson's comments answered the question that had been hanging in the air since 1994: *Was there, at a minimum, a connection in Mr. Jackson's mind between payment to the child to settle a civil suit and his being spared from a criminal prosecution which might have resulted in his going to jail?*

The answer, if one listened to Jackson's own words in the Bashir-Jackson exchange, seemed to be yes. The "long drawn-out thing on TV like O. J." to which Jackson was apparently referring was the criminal trial of Mr. Simpson, since the civil case was never televised. Arguably, in this context, the only way that Jackson could go on with his life when he'd "had enough" was for the criminal case to "go" or disappear. That is exactly what happened after the settlement.

I took my concerns to Los Angeles County District Attorney Steve Cooley in March 2003. I asked him if the payment of the civil settlement might be viewed as an effort on Michael Jackson's part to obstruct justice in the criminal case. California law makes it a felony to bribe a witness not to attend trial or withhold testimony. The purpose of these laws is to assure that the justice system can operate fully and fairly, without improper interference. It must not be corruptible. While civil settlements may be reached in cases that may also allege acts that could be criminally prosecuted, those agreements may not include promises not to testify in a criminal case. If they do, the settlement itself would be void and parties to it might be subjected to obstruction of justice criminal charges. I felt that a grand jury should have been impaneled years ago by former DA Gil Garcetti to determine whether or not there was an obstruction of justice or an attempt by Michael Jackson to obstruct justice.

DA Steve Cooley and I agreed that victims of child sexual abuse should know that civil settlements can't preclude a victim or witness from talking to law enforcement about a crime. A person cannot enter into a legally enforceable contract to conceal illegal activity, such as child abuse. In other words, a person accused of such a crime can't buy a child's silence.

Unfortunately, even if a crime had been committed, it was now too late to prosecute—the six-year statute of limitations on the case had expired. I was concerned that Jackson had left the impression that the rich and powerful can buy their way out of the criminal justice system. The public might have been left with the impression that the system allowed poor defendants to be prosecuted for child sexual abuse, while it spared the rich, who could afford multimillion-dollar civil settlements.

I appreciated the opportunity to meet with District Attorney Cooley to discuss these important issues with him and I vowed to continue to be alert to both public and private reports about Michael Jackson and his behavior with children.

In November 2003, those reports became very public indeed. Jackson was arrested on seven counts of lewd and lascivious acts with a child under the age of fourteen, and two counts of using an intoxicating agent to commit those acts. An article in *Vanity Fair* suggested there might be evidence that Jackson placed alcohol in the soda pop cans of the minor and showed pornography to him.

I again filed a formal complaint asking the Santa Barbara Department of Child Welfare Services to open an investigation into whether Michael Jackson's children should be removed from his care and custody and whether the Juvenile Court should immediately assume jurisdiction over the children for their protection.

California law provided that the Juvenile Court could step in when "there is a substantial risk that a child will be sexually abused by his or her parent or by a member or his or her household."

In light of the criminal charges against Jackson, coupled with the 1993 sexual abuse complaint and his own admission that he has slept with young children in his bed, I felt there were more than sufficient grounds for such an action. Authorities have the right and responsibility to protect children who are at substantial risk or harm, even before a conviction or acquittal in a criminal case. Protection of children is always paramount. Many people feel that if Jackson were not a celebrity, but had the same history with children, his own children would have been temporarily removed from his care long ago.

On January 14, 2004, after Michael Jackson moved his legal residence from Neverland in Santa Barbara County to Beverly Hills, in Los Angeles County, I filed a similar complaint with the Los Angeles County Department of Child and Family Services asking that it temporarily remove the children from his care. The next month I filed a formal application with department director David Sanders, asking that Juvenile Court proceedings be started.

In March I was notified that the department would not be taking any court action. Based on that decision, I felt it was absolutely necessary for me to file directly with the Juvenile Court, which I did on March 17, 2004. The Court now had to review the decision of the social worker who had decided not to remove the children, and it could either affirm his or her decision or order the social worker to commence Juvenile Court proceedings. The response of the Court was that that matter was still being investigated. It remains a mystery to me why Jackson's children have not yet been temporarily removed from his care, in light of the known facts.

I was happy to hear in April 2004 that Jackson would go to trial. All of the facts could now come out in a court of law, where Michael Jackson would not be able to hide behind his fame, money, or power. The public would finally be able to see the face behind the mask and the life behind Neverland's closed doors. "Mr. Jackson, the gloves are off!" I said at the time.

Michael Jackson went on trial in March 2005. As it unfolded, we saw and heard a great deal of new and deeply troubling evidence in regard to his behavior around children. The alleged victim, first seen in the Martin Bashir TV interview, claimed under oath that Jackson molested him on a minimum of two occasions when he was thirteen years old. According to the child, the two were alone in the master bedroom suite of Neverland when Michael Jackson offered to teach him how to masturbate. The child testified that he hesitated, but Jackson explained to him that men who did not masturbate could become unstable and rape women. He said that Jackson told him "It was okay—it was natural . . . that's when he put his hand down my pants." The child went on to relate in some detail his allegation that Jackson molested him that night, and again on the following night.

The child's younger brother testified under oath that he personally witnessed Michael Jackson masturbating his brother on two occasions, in Jackson's bed. "I saw Michael's left hand in my brother's underwear and saw his right hand in his [own] underwear," he testified. "He was masturbating. He was rubbing himself." The younger brother also testified that Jackson had provided him, his brother, and other boys with wine, adult-oriented magazines, and access to sexually explicit Internet sites.

Both brothers testified that on one occasion Jackson appeared in front of them naked, with an erection. The alleged victim testified that [the brothers'] response was, "Eeuuww! . . . [because] we never really saw a grown man, like, naked before."

They also testified that Michael Jackson provided them with wine and hard liquor on multiple occasions. The alleged child victim said that Jackson routinely gave him wine in soda cans, encouraging him to drink it and referring to it as "Jesus Juice." He described his feelings when he drank vodka that he testified Jackson supplied: ". . . it smelled like rubbing alcohol . . . I chucked it back really quick . . . it really burned. And then like two or three seconds later my head started . . . like it looked like the room was spinning, so I put my head inside the couch."

The alleged child victim testified that he'd had concerns about all the liquor he was drinking with Jackson, because it might show up on routine urine tests he underwent as part of his treatment for cancer. The child said he asked Jackson what to do about it and Jackson replied, "Doo-doo, just don't take the test."

A former Neverland housekeeper and former Neverland house manager testified that they had seen children intoxicated on the estate on multiple occasions. The former house manager testified that he once saw three boys whom Mr. Jackson had taken on a tour of the wine cellar come out "drunk."

A twenty-four-year-old man gave emotional testimony that Jackson had molested him multiple times when he was a young boy staying at Neverland while his mother worked as Jackson's personal maid. After the first incident, which the man testified began as a "tickle session" but escalated into unwanted sexual touching by Jackson, the pop singer allegedly slipped the boy a $100 bill and said, "Don't tell your mom." Similar incidents of tickling-into-sexual-touching by Jackson continued for approximately three years, until the child was ten-and-a-half years old, according to the witness.

The same man's mother, the former personal maid, testified that she had seen multiple boys spend the night in Michael Jackson's bedroom. She had seen one young boy she could identify taking a shower with Jackson, as their underwear lay together on the floor. She had also once seen Jackson in bed, nude from the waist up, watching TV with a boy. She also testified that child actor Macaulay Culkin had spent nights in Jackson's bed with him during her employment there.

A man testified that he was once called to bring French fries to Jackson and Macaulay Culkin at around 3:00 A.M. When he arrived with the snack, he testified, he saw Jackson fondling the child: "[Jackson']s left hand was inside the pants of the kid . . . down in the pants . . . in the crotch area. I was shocked. I nearly dropped the French fries."

Macaulay Culkin denied that Michael molested him, but a former security supervisor at Neverland testified that he witnessed a late-night Jacuzzi session with Michael Jackson and Culkin, after which the two disappeared behind a locked restroom door, then emerged wearing only towels, with Jackson carrying the child "piggy-back" style into the house and locking the door behind them. The security supervisor noted that in the past he'd "never recalled Mr. Jackson locking the house." He later observed two pairs of swimming trunks about two feet from each other on the stone floor of the restroom. A former Jackson security guard also allegedly witnessed this incident; he testified that, out of curiosity, he peeked into the restroom containing Jackson and Culkin and observed Jackson kneeling down to perform oral sex on the boy.

Still, Michael Jackson was acquitted on all charges on June 13, 2005.

Several of the jurors said later that they believe molestation had occurred. Juror Raymond Hultman said on the *Today* show that he believed Michael Jackson has a pattern of molesting young boys, although he was not persuaded of guilt beyond a reasonable doubt in this case.

Given the serious and substantial new evidence provided under oath during the criminal trial, I again sent a complaint to Santa Barbara Department of Child Welfare Services requesting that they initiate a much-needed investigation into Michael Jackson's activities with children at Neverland. I urged that the Jackson children be immediately removed on a temporary basis from his custody during the investigation.

Although in a criminal case the prosecution is required to prove guilt beyond a reasonable doubt in order to obtain a conviction, the burden of proof for removal of children by Child Protective or Child Welfare Services is much less. There must be clear and convincing evidence of a substantial danger to the physical health, safety, protection, or physical or emotional well-being of the minor if left in parental custody, and there must be no reasonable means of protecting the minor's physical health without removing the child from parental physical custody.

Therefore, whether or not Michael Jackson was convicted is irrelevant to the issue of whether or not his children should be temporarily removed from his care and declared dependent children

of the court. Given the testimony at trial by the alleged child victim in the criminal case, his brother, and other witnesses, I believe
that the Department of Child Welfare Services of Santa Barbara
County should have immediately intervened in order to protect
the health and welfare of Jackson's three minor children. I am
convinced that they would have done so if that parent had not
been a celebrity.

Children of celebrities should not receive less protection than
children of noncelebrities.

Empowerment Lesson

Any citizen can contact authorities if he or she has reason to believe that a child is being abused, neglected, or abandoned, or is
the victim of an act of cruelty. You do not need to be a relative or
even know the child, and you do not have to be a lawyer, in order
to lodge the complaint. Even if the system doesn't do what you
think it should, keep putting pressure on it to do the right thing.

Do what you can to expose any double standard of justice (for
celebrities versus average citizens), particularly when children
might be at risk.

For information about how to contact child protective services
in your county, check your telephone book or the Internet.

Conclusion

What I Have Learned in the Past Thirty Years Can Help You

In the past thirty years our law firm has won hundreds of millions of dollars in verdicts and settlements on behalf of victims of injustice. We have sued their employers, government, husbands, businesses, and others who have inflicted pain and suffering upon them. This book contains only a few examples of how we have challenged the establishment.

Throughout my career, many individuals have asked me, "What are the secrets of your success? How can I fight back and win in my own life?" I have given these questions much thought and, based on the battles I have won in both my personal and professional life, I have come to some powerful truths.

When you are victimized and you fight back, you are empowering yourself and other victims. You cease to be alone. On a very basic level, it feels good to take action.

Even if you are not famous or wealthy, and even if you do not have the best education, you still have the power to win change at home, at your workplace, in your school, and in your community. Most of my clients are individuals with claims against large companies or government agencies, and they almost always feel powerless when they first come to see me. I feel for them. The row house that I grew up in is never that far from my thoughts or my heart.

To win change however, you must be committed to making a change. Nothing gets done without sacrifice, discipline, resources, struggle, and courage. You must understand that fear is a weapon that bullies use to keep women and minorities paralyzed and "kept in their place." You must overcome that fear.

I truly believe that the power that resides within me resides within everyone. Find it, use it, and learn how to tap into your own strength.

Do not let adversity break you. Think of it as a learning experience that will make you stronger in the future.

Always stay on the path that you know is right, no matter how difficult that path may be. Even at the lowest moments, when you are afraid and feeling completely alone, remember that there are people out there who will assist you if your fight is righteous.

Choose your battles wisely. Not every battle is worth fighting. Determine whether you actually have a situation that needs to be addressed, or whether you have simply misunderstood it.

Timing is also important. Assess whether or not it is the right time to fight your battle. Balance the cost of fighting for change versus the cost of not fighting for change. Can you afford not to fight your battle? What will it cost you if you do? Remember that the costs may not only be financial. They may include taking time away from work and family, sacrificing privacy, and reliving emotionally painful moments. Are you willing to pay the price?

Next, in facing a problem, be sure to gather all the facts. Assess your financial situation, and learn your legal rights. Remember, ignorance strips you of your power and may invite others to take advantage of you. Knowledge is power. Learn all that you can.

Form a support network to assist you in your efforts. In my life, I would never have been able to succeed in the practice of law without the support of my law partners Nathan Goldberg and Michael Maroko, as well as my other partners and associates. However, don't be lulled into believing that someone or something in your support system—such as a family member, a friend, an employer, or the government—will take care of all your needs. Be prepared for a crisis in which you must rely upon your own strength and resources.

If you have a legal problem, seek an attorney who is committed to the justice of your cause and has experience in solving the type of problem that you have. There are lawyers in your state who, like me, will take on the struggles of women and minorities against the large corporations, government, spouses, and other wrongdoers.

Some may take your case on a contingency—that is, they won't make you pay any legal fees in advance, but will take an agreed upon amount as a fee only if they recover money for you through a settlement or judgment. Other attorneys may charge you on an hourly basis, and still others may require some combination of the two.

Put money away for a rainy day because lawyers and lawsuits can be expensive. There is a saying that most people will get as much justice as they can afford. This implies that most people won't get any justice at all—because they don't have the economic wherewithal to wage a legal battle. If you have no resources, contact your county bar association to see if they can suggest lawyers who can help you.

In all legal matters in every area of law, the courts are far from perfect, but if you have the right attorney, a meritorious case, and are forceful and determined about the righteousness of your claim, you can prevail.

Remember that the denial of civil rights is not a small thing. It is an extremely important issue because it is about human dignity, which is everyone's birthright. When that dignity is not respected and when individuals are treated differently, subordinated, or excluded on account of factors over which they have no control—such as their gender, race, age, sexual orientation, or national origin—they and society are irreparably harmed. Freedom, liberty, and equality are fundamental values that every human being should have a right to enjoy.

Rosa Parks refused to sit in the back of a bus. Susan B. Anthony was arrested for trying to vote. The holocaust began when the Jewish people in Germany were initially deprived of their civil liberties. It escalated into them being deprived of their lives. We must take a stand wherever and whenever someone is denied a basic civil right.

To those who suffer the daily indignity of discrimination and are treated as second-class citizens or as sexual objects, I say, *Enough!* Don't tolerate it for a single day or even a single minute. You have the power to stop it. You have more power than you believe you have. All you need to do is exercise your power and fight for your right to enjoy equal opportunity under the law.

To those women out there who are suffering from sexual harassment on the job, I say, *Don't put up with it!* Ignoring the problem won't make it go away. Even transferring to a new job won't guarantee that you will find a workplace free from harassment.

Change does not come overnight. However, in the three decades that I have been practicing law, I have witnessed dramatic changes that have been substantial in the area of women's rights and minorities' rights, especially in employment law. I believe a glass ceiling still exists where women and minorities can see through to the top but still can't get there. There is a lot more work to be done. There are cracks in that ceiling, and I believe that some of the cases I've handled have been directly responsible for them. You can help to win more breakthroughs at your workplace in your town and your state.

Today there are more women than ever in the legal profession. When I attended law school, only a small percentage of the student body was female. Now at least half of the graduating lawyers in many law schools are women. There are also more women judges and elected officials. The legal and political landscape is changing. These changes are primarily the result of individuals who felt that they had been shut out of the system because of their gender or race, and who had the courage to seek change. Unless there is change, the status quo continues, which is generally *not* favorable to the rights of women, minorities, and other victimized groups.

You can take part in positive, important change. Consider going to law school. Contact the National Women's Political Caucus (www.nwpc.org) for ideas about how you can run for political office, be appointed to a board, commission, or agency, and support other candidates who are committed to improving the rights of women and minorities.

Based on the thousands of family law matters that we have been involved with in our thirty years of practice, I also have firm beliefs about what is necessary for a strong marriage. Equality, fairness, and honest communication are essential for a marriage to last and be successful. It is important that spouses be best friends and equal partners. Generally, dictatorships do not work in marriage—or, for that matter, in any other relationship.

Isolation from family, friends, and coworkers can be dangerous. If your spouse or intimate partner tries to isolate you, consider this a warning that you may be living with an abusive or potentially abusive partner. If you are living with an abusive partner, get counseling and consider getting out. There is no excuse for abuse, and over time battering usually escalates in frequency and severity. Batterers and male chauvinists are dangerous to your physical and emotional health. To victims of domestic violence, I say, think of yourself as strong, not weak. Remember the words of Eleanor Roosevelt, "Women are like tea bags—they never know how strong they are until they get into hot water."

If you are a mother who has had a child outside of marriage, be sure to legally establish paternity as soon as possible. Mothers who do not get their child support on time or in the correct amount should not sit back and wait for the father of their children to do the right thing while their families suffer in silence. Get angry, but use that anger constructively to accomplish your goal. Contact a private attorney or your county district attorney to help you establish paternity and collect the child support that is owed your children. District attorneys are mandated by law to help you establish and enforce child support orders and they are not permitted to charge you any attorney's fees for this service.

Sometimes the ultimate outcome of a case is not as important as the struggle for justice. If you fight for what you believe is right and speak out publicly about it, raising that issue and generating public discussion might cause change even if the lawmakers at that time are not ready to enact that change. Creating a climate of opinion that's supportive of change is an important step toward winning it. However, be careful what you say and seek counsel before you make public statements or leap into the unknown.

Throughout my entire career, people in corporate America—my adversaries and even other lawyers—have tried to intimidate me. It has not always been easy, but I have learned that if you have a firm and burning commitment to right the wrong, and you are prepared for the battle, then you can overcome intimidation. Remember, if you are generating a strong reaction, you are probably saying something important.

I have won many battles in my career by applying certain basic concepts and principles to my life. I start every day with the knowledge that helping people and fighting for justice is my duty, and that nothing worthwhile comes without sacrifice, self-discipline, and courage.

I am a lawyer but you don't have to be one to help win change. At Rosa Parks's funeral on November 2, 2005, U.S. Senator Barack Obama reminded us that Ms. Parks had "held no public office, she wasn't a wealthy woman, didn't appear in the society pages. And yet, when the history of this country is written, it is this small, quiet woman whose name will be remembered long after the names of senators and presidents have been forgotten."

That is because she was, as Michigan Governor Jennifer Granholm called her, "a heroic warrior for equality." You, too, can be "a heroic warrior for equality," even if you are not rich or famous. You, too, can make the choice to make a difference. U.S. Senator Hillary Clinton reminded us that we, too, can have a "Rosa Parks moment." I would urge you to have a "Rosa Parks moment" every day. Challenge yourself and challenge others to stand up for what is right.

More than anything, in the face of adversity and injustice, I want you to overcome your fear and be fearless, find your voice and not be voiceless, exert your power and not be powerless. I want you to be able to fight back and win justice for yourself, your children, your family, and your community. When you are feeling pessimistic or even hopeless, remember the words of Susan B. Anthony: "Failure is impossible." There is no defeat in standing up for what is right and fighting injustice. As suffragist Carrie Chapman Catt once said, "Whenever a just cause reaches its flood tide . . . whatever stands in the way must fall before its overwhelming power."

Speak up, fight back, and seek positive change. Others will follow your lead and, ultimately, you'll come out a winner.

Acknowledgments

T his book would not have been possible without:
My publisher, Judith Regan, who believed in me and felt that I had an important story to tell. Thank you for giving me my voice.

Deborah Caulfield Rybak, who struggled with me to tell this story in a way that would be meaningful to the greatest number of readers. Thank you for your insights, your humor, and your skill.

Anna Bliss, my editor, thank you for seeing me through this process and helping me to get it right.

My law partners, Nathan Goldberg and Michael Maroko, who for thirty years have been the kind of human beings and partners that every woman dreams of and would be fortunate to have in her life. You are what I always knew you would be—great lawyers and real mensches.

Nina Sheffield, my assistant, who assisted me with research and the countless changes that were necessary. I could not have done the book without you.

My daughter, Lisa Bloom, who wrote the Foreword to this book with the intelligence, wit, and heart that only she has.

My grandchildren, Sarah and Sam. Your loving presence in my life has helped me to have the strength to dare to do that which often seems impossible.

Everyone else at Allred, Maroko & Goldberg—my partners, Dolores Leal, Tomás Olmos, John West, my associates, María

Díaz, Renee Mochkatel, Margery Somers, and our staff, Bill Beazley, Esther Fleischmann, Jocelyn Gan, Mary Guluzza, Helen Norwood, Lee Olitt, Alma Olivera, Angie Paz, Josie Peña, Tanisha Preer, Rozalia Rybakova, and Jennifer Scobey. You are an important part of the team effort that makes our successes possible. Thank you for all that you do to support our clients in their battles.

The suffragists: Susan B. Anthony, Elizabeth Cady Stanton, Sojourner Truth, and the Pankhursts—Christabel, Emmeline, and Sylvia. Your courage and accomplishments have changed *herstory* and serve as constant inspiration to me in my battle for women's rights.

My parents, Morris and Stella—Thank you for believing in me. You were and are "the wind beneath my wings."

All of my clients over the past thirty years. You are the real heroes. My thanks to all of you for bravely seeking justice. You are exceptional individuals. It has been an honor to represent you.

Index